GREAT
COMMANDERS
OF THE
ANCIENT WORLD

GREAT COMMANDERS OF THE ANCIENT WORLD

Edited by

Andrew Roberts

Quercus

Dedicated to Johnnie Heffer and Matthew Sadler

First published in Great Britain in 2008 by Quercus

This paperback edition published in 2011 by

Quercus
55 Baker Street
7th Floor, South Block
London
W1U 8EW

CONTENTS

INTRODUCTION TO THE HISTORY OF
ANCIENT MILITARY COMMAND

'How can one hundred people be led by a single person?' That was one of the essay questions in my Cambridge University entrance paper in 1981, and although it has long fascinated me, it is only thirty years later – and with the help of some of the most distinguished military historians of our age – that I have tried comprehensively to answer it, here in the four volumes of the *Great Commanders*, of which this is the first. When one asks 'What is leadership?', I believe the answer is to be found in these pages, as the top experts in their field examine the careers of the greatest soldiers in the history of mankind, and explain concisely how it was that not merely one hundred people, but sometimes one thousand, one hundred thousand, or even millions could be led by a single person, to both victory and defeat.

This first volume covers the whole story of the ancient world, up to the fall of the Roman Empire, a natural place to stop. The commanders of the great Egyptian, Judean, Assyrian, Greek, Macedonian, Roman and finally Hun empires not only provide examples of terrifying and inspiring leadership in themselves, but also supplied the template for all great commanders who came after them. It is impossible to consider the military and political career of Napoleon Bonaparte, for example, without reference to the fact that he consciously saw himself as the only worthy modern successor to Alexander the Great and Julius Caesar, and said as much during his exile on St Helena.

Leadership in the ancient world was often a visceral, deeply personal attribute. Commanders had no microphones to relay their stirring pre-battle harangues; they had to rely on bellowing their messages to their troops. They could not command from chateaux miles behind the front line as in the First World War; they had to be physically present, and often visible to their men. Nor were the military and the political separate as they became in the early-modern and modern periods covered in volumes 3 and 4; the duties of statesmanship seamlessly overlapped with those of generalship. Success in one implied and produced expectations of success in the other, with the same true of failure.

Several of the military leaders in this volume were born to command. Men like Alexander the Great, Ramesses II, Julius Caesar, Arminius and Trajan were the heirs of kings, princes and senators, and so were trained from birth to lead men into battle. Of course that does not guarantee genius – history is littered with the abject failures of golden-boy heirs apparent – but they had an automatic advantage over many of the others. How impressive, therefore, are those leaders who rose purely by their own efforts – such as King David, Cyrus, Judah Maccabeus and Aetius – who commanded the loyalty of nations in a time of exaggerated deference to inherited rank. Several of the leaders in this volume wound up as heads of state, often as a result of their prowess on the field of battle. Timing was as essential as ever, as when Alcibiades neatly swapped sides at the key turning point of the Peloponnesian War, and Caesar crossed the Rubicon river when he saw, intuitively, that the use of the Triumvirate was past.

One of many fascinating aspects of this volume is how little the technology of weaponry changed during the course of the nearly two thousand years that it covers. Thutmose and Ramesses would have instantly recognized the combination of horse, sword, arrow and spear that dominated the battlefields of Zhuge Liang and Alaric. It was the social composition of the societies that produced the armies that changed over that vast period, rather than the actual implements used by men to slaughter one another. This is in stark contrast to later volumes, especially from the Age of Gunpowder onwards, where the invention of key new weapons could radically affect the outcome of campaigns.

The ability to inspire as well as to threaten is also an integral part of leadership; what King Leonidas of the Spartans proposed at Thermopylae was nothing less than mass suicide, yet his men stood by him; Hannibal not only crossed the greatest mountain range in Europe, but did so with vast pachyderms in terrain more suited to mountain chamois; Alexander somehow marched his army across the inhospitable, pitiless terrain of the Makran desert in baking heat. Feats such as these could not have been achieved without motivational power rarely seen in ordinary life.

As with any such collection of individuals, subjective judgement has to be exercised about who is selected. No two historians' lists will be identical. The overwhelming criterion for inclusion in this volume has not been the numbers of troops commanded, or nations subdued, or territories conquered, or even battles won, but who has shown that special spark that in music makes a Mozart, or in physics a Newton, or in cosmology a Hawking. Few will agree with every single selection; everyone will be able to argue for people who have been omitted and against those who have been included, but that is part of the delight of a subjective collection of this nature. Who were the greatest commanders of the ancient world? This is my personal selection; let the great debate begin.

Andrew Roberts, May 2011
www.andrew-roberts.net

CONTRIBUTORS

MARTIN VAN CREVELD

Martin van Creveld, formerly of the Hebrew University, Jerusalem, is a leading expert on military history and strategy, with a special interest in the future of war. He is the author of twenty books, including *The Culture of War* (Presidio Press, 2008); *The Changing Face of War: Lessons of Combat from the Marne to Iraq* (Presidio Press, 2007); *The Transformation of War* (The Free Press, 1991); *Command in War* (Harvard University Press, 1985) and *Supplying War* (Cambridge University Press, 1978). Between them, these books have been translated into seventeen languages.

He has acted as consultant to defence establishments in several countries, and has taught or lectured at practically every institute of strategic studies from Canada to New Zealand and from Norway to South Africa. He has also appeared on numerous television and radio programmes as well as writing for, and being interviewed by, hundreds of newspapers and magazines around the world. He is married to Dvora Lewy, a painter, and lives in Mevasseret Zion near Jerusalem.

JAMES DOYNE DAWSON

Doyne Dawson received his Ph.D. in ancient and medieval history from Princeton. He is the author of *The First Armies* (Cassell, 2001), a history of warfare to 539 BC; *Origins of Western Warfare: Militarism and Morality in the Ancient World* (Westview Press, 1996) and *Cities of the Gods: Communist Utopias in Greek Thought* (Oxford University Press, 1992). He is a visiting professor in the Asian Studies Program at Sejong University, Seoul, South Korea.

BEN DUPRÉ

Ben Dupré read Classics at Exeter College, Oxford. He taught English in Germany before pursuing a career in reference book publishing. He was Children's Reference Publisher at Oxford University Press from 1992 until 2004 and, all told, has more than twenty years' experience of editing and writing information books for a general audience. He is the author of *Where History Was Made* (Quercus, 2008). A gifted performer on both harpsichord and viola da gamba, he lives in North Oxford with his family.

JONATHAN FENBY

Jonathan Fenby has written five books on Chinese history, including *The Dragon Throne: Dynasties of Imperial China 1600 BC–AD 1912* (Quercus, 2007) and *The Penguin History of Modern China* (Allen Lane, 2008). He is also the author of

On the Brink: The Trouble with France (Little, Brown, 1998) and *Alliance: The Inside Story of How Roosevelt, Stalin and Churchill Won One War and Began Another* (Simon & Schuster, 2007). A former editor of the *Observer* and the *South China Morning Post*, he has held senior editorial posts at the *Economist*, the *Guardian*, the *Independent* and Reuters news agency. He was made a Commander of the British Empire in 2000 for services to journalism.

ADRIAN GOLDSWORTHY

Adrian Goldsworthy read Ancient and Modern History at St John's College Oxford, and remained there to complete his D.Phil. in Ancient History. His thesis was subsequently published as *The Roman Army at War, 100 BC–AD 200* (Oxford University Press, 1996). After holding a series of research and teaching posts in universities he now writes full time. His books include *Roman Warfare* (Cassell, 2000); *The Punic Wars* (Weidenfeld & Nicolson, 2000; published in paperback as *The Fall of Carthage*, 2003); *Cannae* (Cassell, 2001); *The Complete Roman Army* (Thames & Hudson, 2003); *In the Name of Rome: The Men Who Won the Roman Empire* (Weidenfeld & Nicolson, 2003) and *Caesar: The Life of a Colossus* (Weidenfeld & Nicolson and Yale University Press, 2006). He has acted as consultant on several television series and appears periodically as a talking head in documentaries on aspects of the ancient world.

JOHN HAYWOOD

John Haywood studied medieval history at the universities of Lancaster, Cambridge and Copenhagen. His doctoral research was on early medieval naval warfare. He is now a full-time historical writer with more than a dozen titles to his credit, including *The Penguin Historical Atlas of the Vikings* (1995) and *The Penguin Atlas of British and Irish History* (2001). His most recent books are *The Dark Ages: Building Europe* (Thalamus, 2008) and *The Great Migrations* (Quercus, 2008).

TOM HOLLAND

Tom Holland is the author of *Rubicon: The Triumph and Tragedy of the Roman Republic* (Little, Brown, 2003), which won the Hessell-Tiltman Prize for History and was shortlisted for the Samuel Johnson Prize. His book on the Graeco-Persian wars, *Persian Fire: The First World Empire and the Battle for the West* (Little, Brown, 2005), won the Anglo-Hellenic League's Runciman Award in 2006. He has adapted Homer, Herodotus, Thucydides and Virgil for the BBC. He won the 2007 Classical Association prize awarded to 'the individual who has done most to promote the study of the language, literature and civilisation of Ancient Greece and Rome'.

ROBIN LANE FOX

Robin Lane Fox has been a Fellow and Tutor in Ancient History at New College, Oxford since 1977 and the University Reader in Ancient History since 1990. His books include *Alexander the Great* (Penguin Books, 1973); *Pagans and Christians* (Penguin Books, 1986) and *The Classical World* (Penguin Books, 2006), all of which are in print in many languages. In 2003–2004 he was the historical consultant to Oliver Stone for his film *Alexander*, in which he led the Macedonian cavalry in their battle charges.

ADRIAN MURDOCH

Adrian Murdoch is a historian and journalist. Educated in Scotland and at The Queen's College Oxford, he has lived in London, Glasgow, Berlin and Singapore. He currently works for Thomson Reuters. He is the author of *Rome's Greatest Defeat: Massacre in the Teutoburg Forest* (Sutton Publishing, 2006), which was named one of the books of 2006 by the *Daily Telegraph*; *The Last Roman* (Sutton Publishing, 2006), a biography of Romulus Augustulus, the last Roman emperor in the west, and *The Last Pagan* (Inner Traditions, 2008), a biography of Julian the Apostate. He is also the co-translator of a book of Latin and Greek erotic literature, *Emperors of Debauchery: The Dedalus Book of Roman Decadence* (Dedalus, 1994). He is a Fellow of the Royal Historical Society.

ANDREW ROBERTS

Andrew Roberts took a first in modern history from Gonville & Caius College, Cambridge, from where he is an honorary senior scholar and PhD. His biography of Winston Churchill's foreign secretary Lord Halifax, entitled *The Holy Fox*, was published by Weidenfeld & Nicolson in 1991, followed by *Eminent Churchillians* (Weidenfeld & Nicolson, 1994); *Salisbury: Victorian Titan*, which won the Wolfson Prize and the James Stern Silver Pen Award (Weidenfeld & Nicolson, 1999); *Napoleon and Wellington* (Weidenfeld & Nicolson, 2002); *Hitler and Churchill: Secrets of Leadership* (Weidenfeld & Nicolson, 2003) and *Waterloo: Napoleon's Last Gamble* (HarperCollins, 2005).

He has also edited a collection of twelve counterfactual essays by historians entitled *What Might Have Been* (Weidenfeld & Nicolson, 2004) as well as *The Correspondence of Benjamin Disraeli and Mrs Sarah Brydges Willyams* (2006). His *A History of the English-Speaking Peoples Since 1900* (Weidenfeld & Nicolson, 2006) won the US Intercollegiate Studies Institute Book Award for 2007. Dr Roberts is a Fellow of the Royal Society of Literature, an honorary Doctor of Humane Letters, and reviews history books for more than a dozen newspapers and periodicals. His *Masters and Commanders: How Churchill, Roosevelt, Alanbrooke and Marshall Won the War in the West, 1941–45* (Allen Lane 2009) won the International Churchill Society Award, and his *The Storm of*

War: A New History of the Second World War (Allen Lane, 2010) won the British Army Military Book of the Year Award. His website can be found at www.andrew-roberts.net.

JOYCE TYLDESLEY

Dr Joyce Tyldesley has a degree in the archaeology of the eastern Mediterranean from Liverpool University and a doctorate from Oxford University. She is currently Lecturer in Egyptology in the KNH Centre for Biomedical Egyptology at the University of Manchester, a Fellow of the Manchester Museum, and an Honorary Research Fellow at Liverpool University. Her main area of interest is the Egyptian New Kingdom. She has worked on many excavations in Britain, Europe and Egypt.

Her many published works on Ancient Egypt include *Cleopatra: Last Queen of Egypt* (Profile Books, 2008); *Egypt: How a Lost Civilization was Rediscovered* (BBC Publications, 2005); *Ramesses: Egypt's Greatest Pharaoh* (Viking, 2005); *Egypt's Golden Empire: The Age of the New Kingdom* (Headline, 2001); *Judgement of the Pharaoh: Crime and Punishment in Ancient Egypt* (Weidenfeld & Nicholson, 2000); *Nefertiti: Egypt's Sun Queen* (Viking, 1998) and *Daughters of Isis: Women of Ancient Egypt* (Viking, 1994).

ROBIN WATERFIELD

Robin Waterfield is an internationally acclaimed scholar

and author, whose publications range from abstruse academic articles to children's fiction. He has been an employed or incidental lecturer at a number of universities, mainly in Britain, but now scrapes a living as a writer and small-scale olive farmer in the far south of Greece. He has had about forty books published, most of which, these days, are scholarly works aimed at undergraduates or intelligent lay readers, rather than fellow academics. His most recent books are *Xenophon's Retreat: Greece, Persia and the End of the Golden Age* (Faber and Faber/Harvard University Press, 2006) a translation of Plato's *Timaeus and Critias* (Oxford University Press) and *Why Socrates Died* (Faber and Faber/Norton/McLelland & Stewart), the definitive book on Socrates' trial and death. His most recent publication has been *Dividing the Spoils: The War for Alexander the Great's Empire* (Oxford University Press, 2011).

THUTMOSE III

r.c. 1479–1425 bc

JOYCE TYLDESLEY

HAVING INHERITED HIS THRONE AS AN INFANT, Thutmose III ruled Egypt for fifty-three years, ten months and twenty-six days during the New Kingdom 18th Dynasty. Widely recognized as Egypt's greatest warrior king, Thutmose developed and ruled an empire that extended from Gebel Barkal, below the Third Nile Cataract in Nubia, to the banks of the River Euphrates in Syria; its sphere of influence, however, spread much further.

The first two decades of Thutmose's reign were spent in the shadow of his aunt, stepmother and co-regent, the formidable female pharaoh Hatshepsut. Hatshepsut's foreign policy is generally considered to have been one of peaceful trade rather than aggression, but there is evidence of at least six campaigns by her armies to quash local uprisings in both Nubia and the Levant. Towards the end of the joint reign there was a clear shift in the balance of power as the elderly Hatshepsut allowed the adult Thutmose to assume a more prominent role in matters of state. Thutmose now stood beside, rather than behind, his co-regent, and as commander-in-chief of the army he assumed responsibility for defending Egypt's borders. Egypt was already being troubled by sporadic unrest amongst its client states to the east and Thutmose was forced to commit his troops to the first of a series of military campaigns in order to reimpose firm control of the Levant.

The death of a strong king was traditionally a time of rebellion amongst Egypt's vassal states. Hatshepsut's death in *c.* 1458 BC was no different. Thutmose was compelled to act, both to protect Egypt's interests and, perhaps, to develop his own reputation as a warrior king. The long-established religious duty to defend Egypt against her traditional enemies can be traced back to the Narmer votive palette, carved over one thousand five hundred years earlier, at the dawn of the dynastic age.

The Annals

The vast majority of Thutmose's military activities were conducted to the northeast of Egypt. The minutiae of these campaigns were preserved by a band of military scribes who recorded events in an official 'day book'. Later in his reign, details of the eastern triumphs were inscribed on the walls of two newly built halls situated behind Pylon (gateway) VI in the Karnak temple of Amen-Re at Thebes (modern Luxor): 'His majesty commanded the workmen to record the victories his father Amen had given him by an inscription in the temple which his majesty had made for [his father Amen so as to record] each campaign, together with the booty which [his majesty] had brought ...' (from the Annals of Thutmose III).

Today known as the 'Annals', this account forms Egypt's longest surviving monumental inscription. The Annals cover the events of Regnal Years 22–42, concentrating on the earliest campaign. They give details both of military victories and of the impressive amounts of booty, tribute and tax collected from Egypt's eastern vassals. Although they can hardly be classed as unbiased histories in the modern sense (being clearly designed to show Egypt, Egypt's king and Egypt's gods as superior to all others, and containing obvious errors, omissions and exaggerations), the Annals allow us an unprecedented insight into Thutmose's military exploits. Further details of Thutmose's campaigns can be gleaned from a series of stelae (inscribed monumental stones) erected by the king, and from a number of private inscriptions (Theban tombs, statues and stelae).

The Growing Threat of Mitanni

New Kingdom Egypt recognized three traditional enemies: the Libyans, the Nubians and the Asiatics or easterners. At the time of Thutmose's succession the various Libyan tribes who occupied the western desert were temporarily quiet and posed little threat to the status quo. To the south, Nubia too was relatively peaceful, a series of campaigns by the earlier 18th-Dynasty kings Ahmose, Amenhotep I and Thutmose I having ensured that it had effectively become an Egyptian province. Nubia was now governed by an Egyptian viceroy and, although there remained a chain of impressively large mud-brick forts built during the more aggressive Middle Kingdom occupation, the main instrument for Egyptian control was a series of fortified towns populated by expatriate Egyptians.

To the northeast, however, there was a growing danger. The political map was undergoing rapid change, and the city-states of Syria and Palestine were growing restive. The coastal city of Byblos retained a long-standing loyalty to the Egyptian kings. But to the north, in the lands today occupied by modern Turkey, the Indo-European Hittites had become a well-established nation whose natural expansion routes, to the southeast and southwest, would eventually bring them into conflict with Egyptian interests in north Syria. Also interested in this region were the Hurrians, an ethnic group originally from northern Zagros (modern Iran) but now based in the nation-state of Mitanni. Over thirty years earlier, Thutmose I, grandfather of Thutmose III, had raided Mitanni, and on reaching the Euphrates river had erected a boundary stela to commemorate his achievement. The elderly Thutmose had, however, died before he could complete his plans for an eastern empire. The Mitannians had rejected the Egyptians and recovered from their humiliation, spending the intervening years consolidating their hold on north Syria and Mesopotamia. Now, with the important, independent city-states of Kadesh and Tunip as friends, the Mitannian alliance posed a threat to Egypt. More specifically, the king of Kadesh, backed by the king of Mitanni, was rumoured to be preparing for war with Egypt.

Thutmose could not afford to lose his eastern territories. Control of the Levantine seaports would allow Egypt to dominate the eastern Mediterranean trade routes that underpinned the Bronze Age economy and provided Egypt with much-needed timber, while a controlling interest in Syria and the Levantine states would block the expansion of potential enemies. He therefore prepared, in his own words, to 'overthrow that vile enemy [the king of Kadesh] and to extend the boundaries of Egypt in accordance with the command of his father [the god] Amen-Re'. Thutmose was to invest seventeen years in this mission. His army – the professional and semi-professional troops of the royal household, supplemented by large numbers of non-professional soldiers summoned to national service – soon developed a time-consuming yet ultimately effective technique. The soldiers fed themselves with provisions gathered as they marched; it was therefore important to march at times when food was easily available. Major, set-piece battles – two opposing armies assembled to fight – were rare. Instead, the Egyptians followed a seasonal campaign trail that led them from one fortified city-state to the next. Many city-states found it prudent to concede without fighting, effectively paying Thutmose and his army to go away and then, all too often, reverting to their previous allegiances once the Egyptians had left. Those who resisted soon found themselves under siege. Lacking any sophisticated equipment – he had no battering rams or towers – Thutmose would simply surround the city and wait for the enemy to run out of supplies. He would then sack the city and appoint a local ruler to govern on his behalf.

Thutmose soon developed the long-term policy of sending the children of the local chiefs to be educated in Egypt. Following his sixth campaign, thirty-six sons of the chiefs were sent to be taught in the palace schools alongside the sons of the Egyptian elite. After many years of indoctrination they returned home, fully Egyptianized, to govern on the pharaoh's behalf. Meanwhile the daughters of the chiefs became permanent hostages in the royal harem. The Annals tell us that Thutmose married the daughter of a chief from Retenu, who arrived in Egypt with a valuable dowry plus an assortment of attendants, while an undecorated tomb in the remote Wadi Gabbanat el-Qurud (the Valley of the Ape) on the Theban west bank has yielded the robbed burials of three foreign wives named Manuwai, Manhata and Maruta, whose names suggest that all three came from the Syrio-Palestine region.

The Victorious Campaigns

In his Regnal Year 22 (his first year of sole rule following the death of Hatshepsut) the Annals tell us that 'His Majesty passed the fortress of Sile on his first victorious campaign to crush the people who were assaulting Egypt's borders in valour, strength, might and right.' Thutmose crossed the north of the Sinai Peninsula using the military road known as the 'Ways of Horus', and headed for Gaza, a city loyal to Egypt since the beginning of the New Kingdom. From there he attacked and occupied Yehem, a fortified city occupied by a consortium of enemies headed by the king of Kadesh. It was at Yehem that he planned his next move: an advance eastwards across the Carmel mountain range to the fortified city of Megiddo, where he was to face a daunting coalition of enemies, again led by the king of Kadesh. Meanwhile Thutmose's general, Djehuty, was left to besiege the city of Joppa (modern Jaffa). Papyrus Harris 500, a Ramesside papyrus today housed in the British

Museum, tells us that the enterprising Egyptians were smuggled into Joppa hidden inside large baskets.

This campaign allowed Thutmose to demonstrate his tactical ability and his personal bravery, which contrasted with the cowardice of his generals. As the king himself tells us, there were three possible ways of approaching the city. In a council of war, his generals made it clear which routes they preferred:

> What will it be like to go on this path which keeps getting narrower? We have received reports that the enemy is waiting on the other side and that their numbers are constantly increasing. Will not our horses have to go in single file and our army and people likewise? Will not our vanguard have to fight while our rearguard is still standing here in Aruna unable to fight? But there are two other roads here. One of them is to our east – it comes out at Taanach. The other goes north of Djefti – and would lead us to the north of Megiddo. Our lord should go on whichever of these seems best, but do not make us march along that difficult path.

Ignoring this advice, Thutmose decided to avoid the two long, relatively easy but very obvious roads to Megiddo. Instead he personally led his troops – an estimated ten thousand men – on a three-day march in single file along a winding mountain pass, which daring move allowed him to creep up on the enemy camped outside the city walls.

As dawn broke, the rising sun illuminated the high ground which, it was plain to see, was occupied by a massive Egyptian army. At the head of his troops stood Thutmose himself: 'The southern wing of his majesty's army was at the southern hill of Kina and the northern wing was north-west of Megiddo. And his majesty was in the middle. [The god] Amen was protecting his body, the blood-lust and strength of [the god] Seth were flowing through his limbs.'

The Battle of Megiddo was easily won when, briefly, Thutmose lost control of his men. As the defeated enemy ran back towards the city walls, the Egyptian soldiers defied orders and paused to loot the abandoned camps. The city gates were slammed shut. Enemies trapped outside the gates had to abandon their chariots and flee, and the Egyptians watched in amazement as the kings of Megiddo and Kadesh were hauled up the walls by their clothing, and 'sheets were lowered down to lift them [the enemy] into the town'. Cursing his ill-disciplined soldiers, Thutmose built a thick wall around the city and, lacking any form of siege-breaking equipment, simply waited. Seven months later, the starving citizens of Megiddo surrendered.

Thutmose instantly reaped a reward of chariots, armour and weaponry (which he used to equip his troops), gold, livestock and prisoners of war, who were sent to Egypt to work. While the king of Kadesh escaped, many of his allies were captured and forced to swear an oath of loyalty to Egypt. The defeat of Megiddo was to linger in folk memory for centuries. Over a thousand years later, when the writer of the biblical Book of Revelation described the last battle of doomsday, he set it at Megiddo: 'And he gathered them together in a place called in the Hebrew tongue Armageddon.' (Revelation 16:16)

Following a gap in the military records, we next see Thutmose, in his Regnal Year 29, capturing the Tunip-controlled coastal towns of Ullaza and Ardata before, in Year 30, attacking Kadesh itself. Once again the king of Kadesh experienced humiliation at Egyptian hands, but the fortified city, protected by the curve of the River Orontes, survived substantially intact.

Finally Thutmose turned his attention towards his arch-rival, Mitanni. There was to be a direct confrontation. Year 33 saw the Egyptian army sailing to the port of Byblos. Here they made camp and waited, as the carpenters of Byblos – making good use of the plentiful Lebanese timber – built a fleet of specially designed boats. These were to be loaded in pieces on to carts, and transported with the army as the troops made their way over the mountains, along the Orontes valley and past the subdued Kadesh and Tunip. Their target was Aleppo, occupied by the king of Mitanni.

Here Thutmose enjoyed three fierce, satisfactory confrontations. The enemy retreated in disarray, and Thutmose found himself standing on the west bank of the Euphrates at Carchemish, facing the Mitannian army now occupying the east bank.

The Mitannians had commandeered or scuppered all the available boats, so it should have been impossible for the Egyptians to chase them across the river. Believing themselves to be totally safe, the Mitannians relaxed. Thutmose, however, knew differently. Assembling his prefabricated boats, he crossed the Euphrates and continued his rout, advancing deep into Mitannian lands, seizing property and burning towns as he went. The Mitannian high command, fleeing before the Egyptians, was forced to hide ignominiously in caves. As had his grandfather before him, Thutmose was able to erect a celebratory boundary stela on the east bank of the Euphrates. He then paused on the long march home to enjoy a relaxing elephant hunt in Syria. He was not, however, able to retain his hold on the newly captured lands. Two years after the glorious victory the Egyptian army again faced the troops of Mitanni, and this time the enemy gained the advantage.

The final entry in the Annals shows Thutmose campaigning in the north in Year 42. Tunip was captured, and it is possible that Kadesh was also attacked. This was followed, in Year 50, by a brief and unremarkable Nubian campaign.

The Egyptian Napoleon

Although by no means vanquished, and soon to re-emerge as an important regional power, Mitanni was temporarily subdued and had learned to be wary of Egypt. With his empire secure, Thutmose found himself inundated by gifts from 'brother kings', the monarchs of Babylon, Assyria and Hatti (the Hittite kingdom), who prudently wished to become his friends. Meanwhile tribute and taxes were donated by the lesser states that wished to earn his protection. The funds now pouring into the royal coffers were used to finance an impressive temple-building programme. There was a new phase of building at the Karnak temple complex, while all the major Egyptian towns from Kom Ombo to Heliopolis benefited, as did several sites in the Nile Delta and Nubia.

Egypt's monumental inscriptions, the Annals included, were royal propaganda. They invariably depicted Egypt's kings as fit, brave and intelligent, and frequently distorted details of ancient wars to allow the Egyptians unearned victories. This makes it difficult for modern historians to develop a true assessment of a king's military prowess. Thutmose's accounts, taken from contemporaneous records and supported by archaeological evidence from Syria and Palestine, appear to be more accurate than most. They show us a man of great energy and tactical ability. Not only was Thutmose Egypt's greatest warrior king, he was also a skilled horseman, a superb athlete and a scholar whose interests ranged from botany to reading, history, religion and even interior design.

After fifty-four years of rule, Amenhotep II buried his father Thutmose III in a rock-cut tomb (KV 34) in the Valley of the Kings. More than three thousand years after the funeral, the mummy of Thutmose III, superficially intact and lying in its original inner coffin, was recovered as part of a cache of New Kingdom royal mummies that had been hidden in a private tomb in the Deir el-Bahri bay at Thebes. The mummy was taken to Cairo Museum and unwrapped, and it became clear that the king's body had been badly damaged in antiquity by tomb robbers. The head, feet and all four limbs had become detached and the mummy was held together by wooden paddles hidden beneath the linen bandages. His short stature (the king would have stood just over 1.5 metres or 5 feet tall, although it is not clear whether the detached feet were included in this measurement) and his unparalleled military achievements prompted historians to dub Thutmose III 'the Egyptian Napoleon'.

RAMESSES II

r. c. 1290–1224 BC

JOYCE TYLDESLEY

RAMESSES II, THIRD KING of the 19th Dynasty, ruled New Kingdom Egypt for sixty-six years. The first decades of his lengthy reign were dedicated to establishing himself as a great military leader, following the glorious precedent set by Thutmose III. His proudest achievement, a tale that he told repeatedly in epic poetry, prose and a series of temple-wall illustrations, was his 'victory' against the Hittites at the Battle of Kadesh in 1275 BC. Modern historians are generally agreed, however, that Ramesses' propaganda was greater than his actual military prowess, and that his famous 'victory' may well have been nothing of the kind.

All of Egypt's kings had a religious duty to impose order (*maat*) on chaos (*isfet*). The exterior walls of Egypt's stone temples are decorated with carved images of kings fulfilling this duty by fighting – and, of course, defeating – the traditional chaotic enemies of Egypt. Some of these scenes depict purely symbolic encounters, but many, including those carved by Ramesses, are based on real battles that have been exaggerated to enhance the king's reputation. The same three enemies – Nubians from the south, Libyans from the west and Asiatics from the east – appear time and time again in these scenes. Ramesses cannot have considered the southerners to be a serious threat, as throughout his reign Nubia was effectively an Egyptian province; yet he included dark-skinned Nubians amongst his official foes. The tribes that were grouped together as 'Libyans', distinguished by their fair skins and goatee beards, were enemies of long standing who posed a constant threat to Egypt's western border. The Asiatics appear with red-brown skin and non-Egyptian profiles and beards, but although earlier periods had witnessed the occasional Syrian campaign, it was only during the New Kingdom that the Asiatics came to be seen as official enemies.

The Warrior Prince

Ramesses was trained in warfare by his father, Seti I, a former professional soldier, who reigned from *c.* 1306 to 1290. Seti had been determined to restore Egypt's eastern empire, created by Thutmose III and maintained by his immediate descendants, which had been lost during the atypical reign of Akhenaten, the so-called 'heretic king'.

The summer of Seti's Regnal Year 1 saw a brief campaign to reassert Egyptian control over the Sinai land bridge that connected Egypt to the province of Canaan (modern Israel). Later in the same year, Seti travelled further north to suppress disturbances in the Jordan valley. Over the next few years, he returned to Canaan and the northern province of Upi (inner southern Syria), advancing inland as far as Damascus and securing the Phoenician ports of Tyre, Sidon and Byblos. Control of the ports was important, as it allowed treeless Egypt to import much-needed timber from Lebanon.

The stabilized Egyptian empire now shared a common border with the Hittite empire. It was perhaps inevitable that the two would come to blows but, before he could commit to a full campaign, Seti's attention was diverted by trouble in the western Nile Delta. Libyan tribes were moving eastwards and attempting to settle on Egypt's fertile land. The army marched home to repel the tribes in a brief clash which allowed the 14-year-old Ramesses, 'Commander-in-Chief of the Army', to experience his first taste of battle.

With his western border secure, Seti was free to resume his eastern mission. Ramesses accompanied his father on a campaign to subdue the province of Amurru (coastal Syria) and capture the city-state of Kadesh (modern Tell Nebi Mend) which, strategically situated at the tip of the

Lebanese mountain range, was protected by the north-ward-flowing Orontes and an eastward-flowing tributary. A channel cut between the two rivers made the fortified city into an island. Although there was a brief moment of glory (which enabled Seti to erect a triumphal stela in Kadesh), there was no decisive confrontation with the Hittites. Instead, an agreement was reached and Kadesh and Amurru reverted to Hittite control while Egypt retained her hold on the valuable seaports.

In Year 13 a minor revolt in Lower Nubia gave Ramesses his first opportunity to take sole command of the army. This was the briefest of battles – it seems that the rebels simply lost courage and fled before the Egyptians – and there was so little danger that Ramesses even allowed his eldest sons, aged 4 and 5, to participate in the chariot charge. Nevertheless, Ramesses felt it appropriate to mark his victory by building a small rock-cut temple at Beit el-Wali. Here, alongside images of the old Syrian and Libyan campaigns, he displayed scenes of Nubians offering tribute.

Defending the Delta

The Bronze Age eastern Mediterranean swarmed with merchant boats – owned by the state, the temple and privately – sailing in an anti-clockwise trade route that linked Egypt to Cyprus, Greece, Crete and the Levantine ports. Now, at a time of general unrest and population movement in the Near East, these ships were being menaced by pirates – known as the Sherden people – who had the temerity to land and wreak havoc amongst the many towns dotted along Egypt's northern coast. Ramesses, now co-regent with his father, was entrusted with their elimination. Posting troops and ships at strategic points along the coast, he waited. When the Sherden people next appeared, they were captured and persuaded to serve as mercenaries in the Egyptian army.

The Nile Delta was still vulnerable to Libyan invasion and so, early in his solo reign, Ramesses established a defensive line of mud-brick forts along Egypt's northwestern border. The ruins of three of his forts have been discovered along the coast to the west of Alexandria (at Gharbaniyat, el-Alamein and Zawiyet Umm el-Rakham) and two more are known to have been situated in the western Delta (at Tell Abqa'in and Kom el-Hisn), the remains of what was probably an impressive chain of forts stretching from Memphis to Umm el-Rakham. The forts would have dominated the coastline, offering protection and provisions for ships sailing from Crete to Egypt, although their primary purpose was almost certainly to offer a defence against overland invasion from the west.

The Battle of Kadesh

Ramesses now looked to the east. Remembering his father's

earliest campaigns, he was determined to challenge the Hittites and recapture the province of Amurru and the city-state of Kadesh. The summer of his Regnal Year 4 saw the 'Campaign of Victory'. Ramesses marched along the coast to confirm his hold over Canaan and the all-important ports before turning inland. Benteshina, prince of Amurru, was easily persuaded to switch his allegiance from Hatti to Egypt (the sight of Ramesses' impressive army presumably helped to convince him), and Ramesses returned home, leaving a division of elite soldiers garrisoned in Amurru.

Unwilling to be thought a traitor, Benteshina immediately wrote to his former master explaining that his province was now, against his will, under Egyptian control. Angered by this news, the Hittite king Muwatallis swore a sacred vow to regain his lost territories. Calling on friends and allies from sixteen different provinces, he assembled a magnificent army. Egyptian records, which may be expected to contain some exaggeration, tell us that he commanded 2,500 chariots and 37,000 foot-soldiers including infantrymen, mercenaries and pirates.

In the spring of Regnal Year 5, Ramesses rode eastwards at the head of an army of 20,000 men sub-divided into four divisions of 5,000, each a mixture of infantry and chariotry and each marching under the standard of a local protective god: Amen Division (soldiers recruited from the Theban region, home of the warrior god Amen), Re Division (from the region of Heliopolis, home of the sun god Re), Ptah Division (from the region of Memphis, home of the creator god Ptah) and Seth or Sutekh Division (from the northeast Delta region, home of the mischievous god Seth). The army, and its accompanying pack animals and carts laden with provisions and equipment, took a month to pass along the coastal road through Canaan and south Syria to approach Kadesh from the south via the Bekaa valley. Meanwhile the elite force garrisoned in Amurru had also started towards Kadesh.

There has been much debate about how the battle unfolded, in particular Ramesses' involvement in it. According to the Egyptians Ramesses had camped with his army in the Wood of Labwi, some 10 miles to the south of Kadesh. Here, he had a stroke of luck. Two Shosu Bedouin joined the camp, offering the allegiance of their tribes to the Egyptians. The Bedouin were able to confirm that the Hittites were cowering near Aleppo, some 120 miles to the north of Kadesh, and that they were reluctant to fight. On the strength of this dubious information (the Bedouin were, it was later realized, Hittite spies), Ramesses decided to head straight for Kadesh, hoping to take the city before the enemy arrived. The army divided and Ramesses, riding at the head of Amen Division, forded the Orontes and marched to make camp to the northwest of Kadesh. Re Division followed close behind, while Ptah and Seth Divisions were left on the far bank of the river.

Then two further spies – spies so obvious that even Ramesses recognized them – were captured. Their confessions, encouraged by a sound thrashing, made the true situation horribly clear. The Hittites were just 2 miles to the east of Kadesh, and were preparing an ambush. Ramesses summoned his officers to an urgent council of war. Messengers were dispatched to summon the missing divisions, and the vulnerable royal family was led westwards to a position of safety.

Suddenly the Hittites launched a chariot attack on Re Division as they marched towards the Amen Division camp. The Egyptian soldiers, isolated and taken completely by surprise, scattered and fled north, running straight to Ramesses. Now it was Amen Division's turn to be taken by surprise. The Egyptians took one look at the approaching chariots, and ran. Ramesses found himself surrounded by the enemy. Only the great god Amen of Thebes – and the loyal shield-bearer Menna – could help him now. Ramesses prayed desperately to his god, and a miracle happened:

> Although I prayed in a distant land my prayer was heard in Thebes. Amen came when I called to him; he gave me his hand and I rejoiced ... My heart grew stout and my breast swelled with joy ... I

found the enemy chariots scattering before my horses. Not one of them could fight me. Their hearts quaked with fear when they saw me and their arms went limp so they could not shoot. They did not have the heart to hold their spears. I made them plunge into the water like crocodiles. They fell on their faces, one on top of another ...

Single-handed, Ramesses subdued the Hittites. Those who were not killed by the king turned and fled in panic; many drowned attempting to cross the Orontes. The next day Ramesses prepared to fight again, but the enemy begged for peace.

Realizing, perhaps, that this story might not be totally credible even to his uncritical Egyptian audience, Ramesses added an oath to his account: 'As I live, as Re loves me, as my father Atum favours me, everything that my majesty has told I did in truth.'

What really happened at Kadesh? The story of the ambush is almost certainly true. But Muwatallis did not commit his full infantry to the attack on Re Division. Instead, it seems that the bulk of the Hittite army waited with the over-confident Muwatallis on the east bank of the Orontes. The totally unexpected arrival of the Egyptian force from Amurru came as a demoralizing shock. Reinforced, Ramesses was able to push back the Hittite chariots, whose occupants, perhaps wondering how many more troops were about to arrive, turned and fled, swimming across the Orontes. As the Hittites struggled and drowned in the water, Ptah Division arrived and the deserters of Re and Amen Divisions slowly returned to stand by their king. Seth Division arrived even later, and, with order restored, the reunited Egyptian army settled down for the night.

The following morning, Egyptian accounts tell us, there was more bloodshed. It is not, however, obvious what happened, as the texts are ambiguous. Was there a battle? Or did Ramesses, as perhaps seems more likely, punish his own troops for their desertion? The two greatest armies that Syria had ever seen stood on opposite banks of the Orontes, each reluctant to make a move, in what had become a stalemate. Neither side would have welcomed an open battle: the Hittites preferred to ambush their enemies; the Egyptians, accustomed to siege warfare, had never before met such a large, well-disciplined army. Eventually, or so Ramesses tells us, the Hittite king seized the initiative and sent a letter to the Egyptian camp. Negotiators were summoned and a truce was agreed, although Ramesses refused to sign a formal treaty.

So much for the Egyptian version of events. Hittite records recovered from Bogazkoy in modern Turkey (the ancient Hittite capital Hattusas) tell of a very different battle, ending with a humiliated Ramesses forced into retreat.

Events after the battle do tend to support this Hittite version. Ramesses' departure without a signed treaty allowed the Hittites to reinforce their hold on Kadesh and regain control of Amurru; the unhappy Benteshina was deposed and sent to work as a servant in Hattusas. The Hittites were then able to push south through the Bekaa valley, taking Damascus and the province of Upi, which was placed under the personal control of the king's brother Hattusilis.

The Kadesh debacle and the subsequent unchallenged loss of Upi inspired several local rulers to neglect to pay their annual tribute, forcing Ramesses to reassert his authority over his vassals. With order restored, he started to think again of extending his borders. A series of Syrian campaigns are recorded on the walls of the Karnak temple, although an unfortunate lack of dates makes their precise order difficult to determine. It seems that Years 8 and 9 saw Ramesses campaigning in Galilee before marching eastwards to occupy the Hittite-held cities of Dapur and Tunip, which had been lost to Egypt for over a century. A further campaign in Phoenicia occurred in Year 10, while Syria was targeted intermittently between Years 10 and 18.

The siege of Dapur is recorded in detail both at Luxor and at Ramesses' Theban mortuary temple, the Ramesseum. Illustrations confirm that Dapur, a heavily fortified city, was situated on a hill and protected by an inner and an outer wall with towers, forcing the Egyptian soldiers to attack from below. The defenders stood on the walls and used bows and arrows to shoot down at the Egyptians, who were equipped with ladders and battering rams. The Egyptians rarely lost this sort of campaign, but ultimately these sieges were an expensive and time-consuming waste of resources. A town like Dapur would submit easily to Ramesses, only to revert back to Hittite control as soon as the Egyptian army marched away.

Peace with the Hittites

The Assyrians, a new and highly aggressive enemy, were starting to threaten the Hittite territories in north Syria, and it was not long before the Hittite and Assyrian empires shared a common border. Hattusilis, who, after a brief period of misrule, had succeeded his brother Muwatallis, realized that peace with Egypt would free him to concentrate on the Assyrian danger. Having already concluded a peace treaty with the king of Babylon, he focused his consider-able diplomatic skills on Ramesses. In Regnal Year 21 – sixteen years after the Battle of Kadesh – negotiations commenced and terms were eventually agreed. An agree-ment was inscribed on two matching silver tablets and witnessed, the tablet tells us, by the gods of both lands. The Egyptians and the Hittites were now pledged to respect each other's territories and to defend each other against enemy attack, an agreement intended to last beyond the death of both kings. The two courts were suddenly the best of friends. As Hattusilis started to write to Ramesses, his queen, Pudukhepa, started a correspondence with the Egyptian queen, Nefertari. Eventually Hattusilis sent Ramesses his eldest daughter as a bride.

The treaty brought to an end Ramesses' eastern campaigns. Amurru and Kadesh were now irretrievably lost, but the Syrian territories remained Egyptian and there was free access to the port of Ugarit. Ramesses never relaxed his firm control over his eastern vassals and his reign saw the start of a deliberate policy of remodelling which was to continue long after his death. Canaanite cities deemed to be of little or no commercial use were abandoned; cities considered to be of economic or strategic importance were strengthened to serve as Egyptian outposts.

Sixty-six years on the throne allowed Ramesses ample opportunity for self-promotion. By the time of his death, he was known and respected throughout the ancient world. Within Egypt he was regarded as a living legend and a great military leader; in Nubia he was already a god. Ramesses was brave, enthusiastic and ambitious, even if he was perhaps too impatient and naive. The time-honoured convention of portraying the king of Egypt as superior to all other mortals makes it difficult to understand how Ramesses himself evaluated his military career. Did he really believe his own propaganda? Or were his accounts of the Kadesh triumph merely his means of fulfilling the trad-itional role of the king as the vanquisher of foreigners and upholder of *maat*?

JOSHUA BIN NUN

1354–1244 bc

MARTIN VAN CREVELD

THROUGHOUT HISTORY, few commanders have received as much divine assistance as Joshua is said to have done. The little historical evidence that exists, however, suggests that he was a very effective warlord. Not only did Joshua lead his people in conquering most of the land of Israel, but he also managed to hold together their twelve quarrelsome tribes. Considering what took place under his successors, the Judges, this may have been the hardest task of all. Given the nature of the task, the fact that he also engaged in systematic acts of cruelty was perhaps inevitable.

From King David onwards, biblical heroes are frequently the subjects of books, paintings and sculptures, and have music composed in their honour. Very little of this applies to Joshua, however. Although he has an entire book in the Bible named after him, he seems rarely to have appealed to people's imaginations. His prosaic, perhaps even pedestrian, nature was reflected in the fact that, when he died, many of the Israelites he had led so successfully were too busy with their own affairs to take much notice. By the summer of 2007, he failed even to merit an entry in Wikipedia – in our digital world, surely the worst insult of all.

Taking Over

Joshua ('Divine Saviour') was the son of Nun, born into the Tribe of Ephraim. If he had a private life, any secret designs, inclinations or idiosyncrasies, we know practically nothing about them. He appears for the first time in the Book of Exodus when Moses put him in command of the Israelites in their fight against their arch-enemy, the Amalekites. A little later, he was one of the two men Moses chose to accompany him to Mount Sinai and to wait while Moses, we are told, spoke to God and received the Ten Commandments.

He is mentioned again in the Book of Numbers at the time the Israelites were camping east of the River Jordan. Moses is said to have appointed Joshua as one of the twelve spies whom he sent across the river to explore the land of Israel. Returning after forty days, the spies reported that the country was 'flowing with milk and honey'. To verify their report, they displayed a giant bunch of grapes they had brought back with them. However, ten of the twelve also pointed out that the land of Israel was very well forti-fied, populated by 'giants' (they stood to ordinary people as ordinary people to grasshoppers) and that any attempt to conquer it would surely fail. Only two of them, Joshua and Caleb Ben Yepuneh, thought that such a campaign could succeed.

Judging by these brief references to Joshua, Moses clearly considered him able, God-fearing, and trustworthy. Clearly, too, he had three other qualities that every commander needs: namely, hands-on operational experi-ence, an understanding of intelligence work, and, above all, faith in the star of his people as well as his own. When the time came for Moses to choose a successor, it was believed that the Lord told him to pick Joshua as 'a man in whom is the spirit'. A public ceremony was organized, and Joshua was duly anointed by the priest Elazar, son of the late Aron, in front of the entire people. It was shortly after this that Moses died.

The First Victory

Almost immediately after Moses' death, Joshua claimed to have had a long interview with God. 'Arise,' the Lord told him.

'Go over this Jordan, thou and all this people, unto
the land which I do give to them ... There shall
not be a man able to stand before thee all the days
of their life ... [Therefore] be strong and of a good
courage; be not afraid, neither be thou dismayed;
for the Lord they God is with thee whithersoever
thou goest.'

Joshua's first step was to draw up a marching order and
appoint sub-commanders who would oversee it. Next, he
in turn sent out spies to reconnoitre the city of Jericho.
Although they were almost caught, they were able to save
themselves at the last minute, thanks to the efforts of Rahab,
a prostitute with whom they had taken shelter. By way of
gratitude, the men told Rahab to mark the window of her
house with a red thread so that the invading Israelites, once
they had taken the city, would know whom to spare. A
much later Jewish tradition has it that Joshua ended up
marrying her.

Leaving their wives, their children and their cattle
behind, the men of Israel crossed the Jordan in full battle
array. Their first objective was Jericho, just north of the
Dead Sea. However, there was a problem. Jericho was
heavily fortified with walls, the remain of which can be
seen to the present day. Though the Bible has nothing to
say on the subject, it is likely that the Israelites, like all

desert people throughout history, had no experience of siege warfare nor possessed the technology, such as heavy rams, to wage it. Accustomed to raiding and skirmishes, they also tended to be easily discouraged by sustained warfare.

Not for the last time, according to the Bible, God chose to help by a miraculous intervention. Appearing to Joshua, he ordered that the entire Israelite army be summoned in procession, together with all its religious paraphernalia such as the Ark of the Covenant and the trumpets made of rams' horns. His instructions were very detailed. The Israelites were to circle the city six times during six successive days. On the seventh day they were to do so not once but seven times. Next, as they blew their trumpets and raised a great shout, the walls would fall flat in front of them.

These directives were followed to the letter and events took place as promised; as the trumpets emitted their shrill sound (said, by later Jewish tradition, to be capable of piercing the heavens themselves), the walls collapsed. All that remained for the Israelites was to sack the city. This they did, 'utterly [destroying] all that was in the city, both man and woman, young and old, and ox, and sheep, and ass, with the edge of the sword'. Only vessels made out of gold, silver, brass and iron were spared, not for private use but so that they could be consecrated to the Lord.

A possible explanation for the miraculous elements in the Jericho story can be found in geological evidence. The Jordan valley lies on a major geological rift, subject to frequent earthquakes. At around the same time that the city walls fell, the Jordan supposedly parted to enable the Israelites to cross on dry land, a 'miracle' also witnessed in modern times when mudslips induced by quakes have been known to dam the river, most recently in 1927. It seems reasonable that earthquake activity dammed the Jordan and destroyed Jericho's walls (the miracle thus being one of its timing rather than the event itself).

Conquering the land of Israel

Jericho having fallen (from whatever cause), Joshua turned his efforts to a small city further up the Judean hills by the name of Ai.

The capture of Ai was Joshua's only military failure, but one which later he succeeded in turning into his tactical masterpiece. In doing so, he displayed the qualities of a great commander, including determination, leadership (he knew how to rally his discouraged army), guile and the ability to snatch victory from the jaws of defeat. And, of course, he displayed his usual cruelty.

Unlike Jericho, Ai appears to have been a small city of no very great importance. It was, however, located east of Bethel, thus commanding one of the few routes that led west from the Jordan valley into the mountainous interior of the country.

As at Jericho, Joshua started by sending out spies. They reported that the city was weak and suggested that three thousand men should suffice to capture it. Things did not work as planned, and Joshua's men fled in front of those of Ai. They were chased downhill, and thirty-six of them were killed. 'Wherefore,' the Bible tells us, 'the hearts of the people melted, and became like water.'

Clearly there was something very wrong with an army whose troops first underestimate the enemy, then run, and then lose heart because a few of them are killed. Joshua did what was necessary, given the circumstances. He started by making a big show of consulting with the Lord. He then told the people what God had allegedly told him: namely, that the defeat was due to one of their number violating the Lord's orders and taking booty from Jericho. Lots were cast, and the name of one Achan came up. A search was made, and the stolen goods were found. Achan and his entire family were executed with great ceremony, being stoned to death and their bodies then burnt.

With the Lord thus appeased, the rest was straight-forward. 'Thirty thousand mighty men of valour' were chosen and took up concealed positions. If a true figure, this force alone outnumbered the men of Ai many times over. With Joshua himself in command, the bulk of the Israelite army attacked from another direction, pretended to be defeated and fled, drawing the enemy after them. Joshua then gave the signal for the ambush to leave its concealed positions, enter the city from the rear and set it on fire. Twelve thousand men, women and children perished, 'for Joshua drew not his hand back ... until he had utterly destroyed all the inhabitants of Ai'.

Perhaps the most interesting detail in this entire story, however, is one that reveals key information. In order to spring the trap, Joshua waved a spear. Even by men whose eyesight is keen, there are limits to the distance at which a spear can be seen, a fact which tells us how small the battlefield really was, and how few warriors it can have contained.

The extreme cruelty with which he treated the hapless inhabitants of Ai had two very different results. On the one hand, we are told, the inhabitants of at least one city, Gibeon, a few miles northwest of Jerusalem, were so terrified that they decided that they would rather make peace than war. They sent envoys, pretending to come 'from a very far country', to approach Joshua in order to draw up a treaty with them, which was duly signed. When he discovered the deception, Joshua, although very angry, would not go back on his word. He decided to honour the treaty, but subjugated the Gibeonites and made them into 'hewers of wood and drawers of water ... even unto the present day'.

Not all of the country's inhabitants reacted in this way. 'All the kings which were on this side of the Jordan, in the hills, and in the valleys, and in all the coasts of the great sea over against Lebanon ... gathered themselves together, to fight with Joshua and with Israel, with one accord.' Joshua's strategy of terror here caused growing resistance.

This resistance enabled Joshua to fight his first pitched battle. No fewer than five kings gathered 'all their hosts' near Gibeon, and it was the Gibeonites who first sounded the alarm and demanded that their new masters come and rescue them. At the time, Joshua and his army were based at Gilgal, further east in the Jordan valley. Having duly consulted the Lord, Joshua led his force up the mountains in what must have been an extremely strenuous night march, taking the enemy by surprise. While the Bible tells us that there was 'great slaughter', it offers no details. All we know is that the enemy ran west by way of the Valley of Beth Horon, which in turn leads down the mountain to the coastal plain below.

This was not the end of the matter. To add to the fleeing enemy's discomfiture, the biblical account has God intervening in person, raining down 'great stones from heaven' upon them. At Joshua's special request, God even stopped the sun and the moon from moving, adding some hours to the usual twenty-four so that the Israelites could complete the carnage. The five unfortunate kings hid in a cave, but were captured and brought in front of Joshua. First he humiliated them by forcing them to lie down while the Israelite troops put their feet upon their necks; next, he had them hanged.

Completing the Conquest

Joshua's victory over the five kings meant that he was now in control of the centre of the country (although the fact that he did not conquer Jerusalem, which remained in the hands of the Jebusites until the days of King David, casts some doubt as to how firm that control really was). We do not know the location of all the remaining cities he went on to capture. Moreover, our understanding of his strategy is hampered by the fact that geography does not seem to have been the strong point of those who edited the Bible and gave it the form it has today.

All this makes his next moves, and their timing, rather difficult to follow. None the less, Joshua ended up in control of the southern Judean Hills as well as the southwestern coastal plain 'even unto Gaza' and Goshen; considering that the latter is supposed to be located in Egypt, one cannot help but raise an eyebrow. In 'all the country of the hills, and of the south, and of the vale, and of the springs, and all their kings, he left none remaining, but utterly destroyed all that breathed as the Lord God of Israel commanded'.

While Joshua was busy in the south, a second coalition, made up of a larger number of kings, was formed against him in the north, its prime mover being Yabin, king of Hazor. Some of Yabin's allies came from the hills of Samaria; others were gathered from the Plain of Esdraelon and what is today Lower Galilee, all the way to the foothills of Mount Hermon. Quantitatively and qualitatively, these forces were far stronger than any previous enemy the Israelites had encountered. 'Even as the sand that is upon the sea shore in multitude,' the Bible says, 'with horses and chariots very many.'

Once again, Joshua turned to God, who told him that victory was guaranteed. And again, Joshua was able to take the enemy by surprise, though how it was done is unknown. The battle took place at the Waters of Marom, in the Valley of Esdraelon, and was decisive. Whether this took a few months or years, we do not know.

Joshua took all that land, the hills, and all the south country, and all the land of Goshen, and the valley, and the plain, and the mountain of Israel and the valley of the same ... there was not a city that made peace with the children of Israel, save the Hivites, the inhabitants of Gibeon; all others they took in battle. For it was of the Lord to harden their hearts, that they should come against Israel in battle, that He might destroy them utterly.

The victory was not quite complete, for the Philistines, referred to as anakim (giants) were not subdued. Yet it was sufficient to enable Joshua to distribute the conquered land among the twelve tribes. In doing so, the Bible says, he followed the detailed instructions left by Moses. Feeling his death to be imminent, Joshua delivered a final speech in which he reminded the people that their triumphs had all been due to the Lord and that, should they forsake Him, they could expect Him to forsake them in return. At the age of 110 years, he died. He had ruled Israel for twenty-eight years.

The Legend

Given his enormous achievement, perhaps the most surprising thing about Joshua is that there are no legends about him personally. Although he was believed to have had more than his share of divine aid, he did not have any miraculous escapes. He neither persecuted nor betrayed anybody in particular. He did not satisfy whatever lusts he may have had at the expense of others. He did not even try to argue with God, as Moses had often done. In his final message to the people, all he had to say was, 'Fear the Lord, and serve him in sincerity and in truth,' advice which, however useful, must seem somewhat prosaic in comparison to the utterances of Moses, his predecessor.

Seen from a modern vantage point, he was a sort of miniature Genghis Khan, using sword and fire to invade and subdue a country whose inhabitants had done him no wrong. Wherever he went, he committed vast slaughter, only rarely sparing women and children. In his favour, all that can be said is that he was acting on the express command of God (or so he, and those whom he led, believed or affected to believe).

Subsequent generations made a few half-hearted attempts to enhance his stature. We are told that, at the time Joshua was waiting for Moses to return from his encounter with God at Mount Sinai, the Lord, showing His special consideration, made sure that he would get his portion of manna like anybody else. Another story has it that his wife Rahab – if, indeed, she did become his wife – was not a simple prostitute but 'a great soul' (whatever that may mean). A third says that his coins carried an ox on one side and a *re'em* (oryx), an animal with majestic horns, on the other. But that, more or less, is all.

KING DAVID

c. 1037–967 BC

MARTIN VAN CREVELD

KING DAVID OF ISRAEL IS OFTEN SEEN AS one of history's greatest commanders, known also for being an even greater poet and a talented musician who excelled at playing the harp. Above all, he was a man of God; almost everything we know about him comes from the Bible, where he is reported to have been able to talk to God face to face.

At the time that David started his ascent to power, the kingdom of Israel had just suffered its worst defeat at the hands of the Philistines, who had left their homeland in what is today southwestern Israel and the Gaza Strip. Marching north, they advanced to Mount Gilboa, not far south of the Sea of Galilee, where a battle was fought in which King Saul and his son Jonathan lost their lives, their bodies being nailed to the wall of the town of Beth Shean by the Philistines. It fell to David to restore his people's fortunes. By the time of his death, after incessant war, he had not only restored the kingdom but also expanded it, creating a mini-empire in the Middle East.

Youth and Apprenticeship

David was born into the tribe of Judah in around 1030 BC. He was the youngest son of Jesse, the son of Obed, son of Boaz and Ruth the Moabite (Ruth's story is told in the Book of Ruth). He spent his youth as a shepherd near Beth Lehem. Shepherds, then as well as later, were considered to be outside civil society, always ready to fight and to engage in occasional acts of robbery and blackmail; whether David was true to type we do not know. The Bible does tell us, however, that on one occasion he killed a lion that had attacked his flock, and he himself referred to other similar events. It was at this time that the Prophet Samuel, apparently acting on God's express command, anointed David king over Israel, although the reason for his selection is unexplained.

As to what happened next, the Bible is somewhat confused. One version is that King Saul felt depressed and had the young, good-looking shepherd play the harp for him to ease his mood. According to another version, the two of them met when the Israelites were waging one of their frequent wars against the Philistines. The young David, who had come to the Israelite camp to visit his brothers, took up the challenge issued by the Philistine giant Goliath, an encounter that ended when David slew him.

David Against Goliath

The battle between David and Goliath would have appeared as one in which there was simply no contest. On the one side there stood a giant – six cubits and a span tall, the Bible says – fully armed and covered by a shield so big that, until the actual moment of battle, it had to be carried for him by a special assistant; opposing him, an adolescent armed with nothing but a sling. Yet in fact it was Goliath who never stood a chance.

The Philistines were originally an Aegean people. Having left their homeland for unknown reasons, they tried to settle in Egypt but were repulsed; they ended by carving themselves a territory out of what, today, is southwestern Israel and the Gaza Strip. Joshua had fought them, but had not succeeded in subduing them. They used bronze weapons broadly similar to those described in Homer's *Iliad*. Had Goliath ridden a chariot and carried two spears instead of one, then the parallel would have been absolute. By contrast, all over the ancient Middle East the sling was considered a poor man's weapon, only fit for those who could not afford anything better.

When David volunteered to act as Israel's champion and engage Goliath in a duel, King Saul offered him his own heavy armour and weapons to use. David tried them on but found them cumbersome; wearing them, he could barely move. To approach an opponent much stronger than himself and fight him while carrying such arms was to court certain death.

Instead he chose what, today, would be called 'asymmetrical warfare'. Having spent his youth as a shepherd, he had honed his skill with the sling during endless idle hours when he had nothing better to do. An expert with the weapon could fire one pebble every fifteen or so seconds to a distance of 100 yards, hitting his target every time. The heavily armed Goliath could not move very quickly. Hence David had plenty of time to reload his sling and hurl another pebble if, by any chance, the first one missed. If the worst came to the worst, he could always run circles around his enemy.

Before the fight there was a slanging match that angered Goliath and distracted him. Next, breaking into a run, David approached him. While still at a safe distance, he stopped, used his sling – and missed his target. Almost certainly he was aiming at Goliath's forehead, which remained exposed under the helmet. Instead he hit him in the eye, causing a wound that, though very bad, may not have been mortal.

Thereupon Goliath crashed to the ground, his armour and weapons ringing. David went up to the fallen giant and, using the latter's own sword, cut off his head.

From Shepherd to King

From this point, David was a national hero. He continued to play the harp for King Saul, and to form a close bond with Saul's son Jonathan, a relationship that has been the subject of speculation throughout Western culture. Saul gave him his daughter Michal to marry 'that she may be a snare to him'. By way of bride-wealth the king demanded the foreskins of a hundred dead Philistines; the number he actually received was double that. Whether because of the king's temperament or because he suspected David of plotting against him, they fell out. At first Saul himself tried to kill David by throwing a spear at him, but when that failed, he sent men to carry out the assassination. David was saved by his wife, who let him down from the window of their house by rope. In another account, Jonathan warned him of his father's plan.

Initially David sought shelter with the Philistines, but then, fearing for his life, he left, spending most of the following years in what is today the northern part of the Negev Desert. He gathered around him some four hundred tough outlaws: 'every one that was in distress, and every one that was in debt, and every one that was discontented'.

The most important of these were his three nephews, Joab, Avishai and Asael, the sons of his sister Zeruyah. With their help he skirmished with the Philistines, being careful to consult with God, who always promised him victory.

He made a living by blackmailing local landowners, killing at least one of them and marrying his widow. Twice Saul took an army and went out to hunt for him, but David proved a master of evasive tactics and an elusive commander. At one point he even caught Saul unawares and could have killed him, but he preferred reconciliation. It did not last.

At the time Saul died in battle against the Philistines, David was 23 years old. He and his men were far away, waging war against the Amalekites, traditional enemies of the Israelites. Having received news of the defeat, he went to Hebron, capital of his own Judean tribe. Saul and his heir Jonathan were dead, and his surviving sons were unfit to rule; hence they agreed to make him their king, or so the Bible says. After seven years fighting numerous small skirmishes, David finally defeated Saul's remaining supporters and became king of all the tribes of Israel.

King of Israel
Saul, who was a scion of the tribe of Benjamin, had his capital at Gibeah, north of Jerusalem. David felt he needed

a new capital, one not associated either with his predecessor or with any of the twelve tribes. His choice fell on
Jerusalem, well situated in the centre of the country.
However, at this time the owners of Jerusalem were the
Jebusites. To take the fortified city, David had to mount a
siege, which was a struggle; in the end Jerusalem fell only
after its water supply had been cut off.

The Philistines were still the greatest power in the
region. They attacked repeatedly, getting as far as the Valley
of Rephaim, well within the limits of today's greater
Jerusalem; David, consulting with God, was able to repel
them. In doing so he proved himself a fine tactician, on
one occasion using the noise of the wind in the mulberry
trees to cover the approach of his army, which was about
to take the enemy from the rear. Finally he subjugated
the Philistines, who all but disappeared from the stage of
history.

There were, of course, other enemies: Edom to the
south, Moab to the southeast, Ammon to the east and Aram
to the northeast were all brought to heel. It was during the
siege of the Ammonite capital, Rabat, that David saw the
beautiful Bathsheba washing on the roof of her house and
immediately desired her. He took her, slept with her and
sent her home.

When Bathsheba informed him she was pregnant, he
ordered her husband, Uriah, to be brought back to Jerusalem

so he could sleep with her. Uriah, however, took life seriously: he refused to do so as long as the war was going on. Accordingly David sent him back to the front, secretly ordering Joab to expose Uriah to the enemy so he would be killed in action.

The Holy Bible is not a military handbook. It provides few details about the battles in question; the closest we come to learning about any tactical detail is when we are told that, on one occasion, two of David's nephews, Joab and Avisahi, divided their forces to confront an enemy who was advancing on them from two different directions. David was commander-in-chief, but in later days rarely commanded troops in person.

The field commander was Joab, a tough individual who had joined David early in his career. Besides being good with weapons, he quickly made himself indispensable and proved a fine strategist, able and willing to take on armies stronger than his own. Equally importantly, he could act on his own initiative and carry out necessary but unpleasant tasks of the kind that, today, would be known as targeted assassinations. (Ultimately he was killed by Solomon, David's son and heir, on the latter's express orders.)

Joab was but one of thirty-seven 'mighty men' surrounding David, though we know next to nothing about the way they and the rest of the forces were organized and commanded. The army's core consisted of three units of mercenaries, who, no doubt for reasons of security, were drawn from three different foreign peoples. The rest, probably numbering some tens of thousands, were tribal warriors who could be called upon in an emergency.

The Bible has nothing to say about the way all these forces were armed. We can only assume that, like their enemies, they consisted of both infantry – indispensable for siege warfare as well as open combat – and cavalry. Those who could afford it may have worn some elements of armour. Certainly they used the usual edged weapons, such as spears, swords and short daggers, and bows and arrows and slings. The Bible says that, at the height of David's reign, the scope of his power went as far as Damascus and he received the tribute of various client kings. Clearly his army must have been highly efficient.

Quelling Revolt

In some ways, the greatest military challenge David ever faced was mounted by his son Absalom (the name, paradoxically, means 'The Father of Peace'). The revolt arose out of a family quarrel after Absalom had raped his half-sister Tamar, or so she claimed. Absalom was sent into exile but was reconciled with his father by Joab who, on this occasion, proved himself a fine diplomat. The reconciliation did not last. At one point, Absalom, who is said to have been very handsome and popular, rose up against David.

The revolt came like a bolt out of a blue sky. Jerusalem was threatened; of all the people David ruled, the only ones who remained loyal to him were the members of his own household, together with his foreign mercenaries. With them, he fled eastward, leaving behind ten concubines to guard the palace. Allegedly, Absalom, probably in order to prove that the break with his father was final, promptly had sex with them in front of the assembled people.

Originally David seems to have hoped he could gather his forces in the wilderness west of the River Jordan and the Dead Sea. However, his spies in Jerusalem informed him that the enemy was coming for him, so he decided to cross the river. Meanwhile, inside Jerusalem, Absalom's camp was divided. One adviser in particular, Ahitophel ('Brother of Hell'), proposed that twelve thousand men be quickly called up, put under his own command, and used to hunt David down. Had this plan been carried out, it might well have succeeded.

In the end, however, the counsel of one Hushai, who was secretly loyal to David but managed to gain Absalom's favour, prevailed. Absalom was apparently no strategist. Hushai told him that 'thou knowest thy father and his men, that they be mighty men, and they be chafed in their minds, as a bear robbed of her whelps in the field; and thy father is a man of war, and will not lodge with the city'. He therefore suggested that not twelve thousand men but the entire people be mobilized and fall on David 'as the dew falleth on the ground'.

This plan was adopted. It gave David what he needed most: time. As more and more men joined him, he divided them into units and put commanders of thousands and commanders of hundreds in charge of them. The army thus hastily formed was divided into three parts, one commanded by Joab, one by Avishai, and the third by a loyal mercenary chief, Ittai the Gittite.

Apparently David wanted to command in person, but his men, claiming his life was worth that of ten thousand others, refused to allow him. Thereupon he was obliged to let them do as they wished. A battle was fought, and won, in 'the wood of Ephraim'; where that wood was located we do not know. Fleeing after his defeat, Absalom, whose hair was long and of which he had always been extraordinarily proud, was caught in the branch of a tree. His mule bolted, and he was left hanging in mid-air. When his brother Joab was told, and informed that nobody would touch the king's son, he himself went to the spot and killed him. The revolt was over.

And the king was much moved, and went up to the chamber over the gate, and wept: and as he went, thus he said, O my son Absalom, my son, my son Absalom! would God I had died for thee, O Absalom, my son, my son!

And it was told Joab, Behold, the king weepeth and mourneth for Absalom.

And the victory that day was turned into mourning unto all the people: for the people heard say that day how the king was grieved for his son.

2 SAMUEL 18: 33; 19: 1–2

The Aftermath

Originally David had been God's anointed; clearly he was a man who was able to consult with God and receive answers to his questions. At one point he hoped to build a temple to the Lord. However, God, telling him that he (David) was a warrior with much blood on his hands, refused this offer.

Later, through committing various misdeeds, David's relationship with God began to sour. First came the sordid affair with Bathsheba. Then there was the extermination of some remaining sons of Saul, as well as a misguided attempt to go against the laws of the Pentateuch and conduct a census. All this caused God to withdraw his favour.

Furthermore, if the Bible is to be believed, Absalom had been David's most dearly beloved son, and he never came to terms with Absalom's revolt and subsequent death.

In old age the condition of this once formidable warrior and lover – he had dozens of wives and concubines – deteriorated, so much so that they brought him a young virgin, not to sleep with, but simply so she could provide him with warmth. At the very end of David's life he had to deal with another of his sons, Adoniah, who tried to usurp the throne from the designated heir, Solomon. The revolt was quelled, but not before Joab had deserted David.

In all, he reigned for forty-seven years, of which forty were in Jerusalem. His considerable achievement lasted only during the lifetime of his successor; after Solomon's death, the kingdom split in two. If Jewish tradition is to be believed, David left behind a body of poetic work that includes the entire book of the Psalms as well as the lament he composed for Saul and Jonathan. His descendants included a long line of kings, and ultimately Mary, the mother of Jesus.

TIGLATH-PILESER III

744–727 BC

DOYNE DAWSON

TIGLATH-PILESER III is generally considered the greatest Assyrian king and one of the most successful military commanders of the ancient world. He began the process whereby the loosely organized hegemony built up by earlier Assyrian kings was replaced with history's first centralized imperial state, which became the model for all later empires. At the same time he reorganized the Assyrian army and introduced the use of combined arms, or infantry and cavalry working in cooperation.

These claims require some historical background, for readers with any knowledge of ancient history are probably aware that very large empires had existed in the Middle East for over a thousand years before Tiglath-Pileser III. The first genuine empire based on conquest was that of Sargon of

Akkad, who in the early Bronze Age (late third millennium BC) united nearly all of Mesopotamia into a state known as Sumer and Akkad. In the later Bronze Age (second millennium BC) imperial states of comparable size were assembled by the Egyptians of the New Kingdom, the Hittites of Anatolia, and the Hurrians, whose major state was the kingdom of Mitanni in north Mesopotamia and Syria. But these were not centralized empires like the later Assyrian state. They are best described as hegemonies. They were put together by successful kings who reduced their neighbours, made them pull down their walls, and exacted tribute from them; but the native dynasties of these principalities were not replaced, and as long as they paid tribute and made no attempt to rebuild their fortifications they suffered little interference from the overlord. In the Bronze Age such a state was called a 'Great Kingdom', and any king who ruled other kings could call himself a Great King. The client kings tended to be unreliable, of course, and it was frequently necessary to dispatch punitive expeditions to keep them in line.

Assyria had been a Great Kingdom in this sense for centuries before Tiglath-Pileser III, on and off. In the fourteenth century BC the Middle Assyrian kingdom succeeded in uniting all north Mesopotamia ('Middle Assyrian' is a linguistic term referring to the dialect of Akkadian spoken in Assyria in the late Bronze Age); it enjoyed a last spurt of expansion under Tiglath-Pileser I (1114–1076 BC), who sacked Babylon and raided deep into Anatolia and Iran. After that, Assyria was devastated by the migrations of the Aramaean tribes from the Syrian Desert, who were probably the first people to make full use of the Arabian camel for transport. In the tenth century BC the Assyrian kingdom was pushed back into its original homeland, a 100-mile strip along the upper Tigris river containing the cities of Ashur (the ancient religious capital), Nimrud (the royal capital), Nineveh (the main royal capital after 700 BC), and Arbil. A second burst of expansion came between 883 and 824, when two energetic kings, Ashurnasirpal II and his son Shalmaneser III, subdued the Aramaean principalities, restored Assyrian control over north Mesopotamia, and established a block of client states stretching over northern Syria. This was a loosely organized hegemonial structure like the Middle Assyrian state and the other Great Kingdoms of the Bronze Age, and it did not last long. Between 824 and 744 there came a series of weak kings and the client kings broke away. But even during this period of weakness, the Assyrians kept control of north Mesopotamia, including the entire plain between the Tigris and the Euphrates as far west as the great bend of the Euphrates, with the foothills of the Zagros range to the east.

In 744 BC, the last of these weak kings was over-thrown by a rebellion and the throne was seized by the governor of Nimrud, the Assyrian capital city, who claimed to be descended from an earlier king, but this is doubtful. Assyrian tradition cherished the myth that all their kings had come from the same royal family in an unbroken line since *c.* 1500 BC, and scribes tended to cover up breaks in the succession. The real name of the governor of Nimrud is unknown. Tiglath-Pileser is the biblical rendering of the Akkadian throne name, Tukulti-Apil-Esharra, meaning 'My trust is in the son of Esharra [the god Ninurta].' The choice of this name deliberately proclaimed a programme of expansion; he called himself after the hero king Tiglath-Pileser I, who had carried the arms of Assyria further afield than any other king before him.

Campaigns of Tiglath-Pileser III

The documentation – inscriptions, chronicles, royal corres-pondence, treaties, parts of the Bible – is extraordinarily full for this period, compared to other earlier periods of Assyrian history, and allows a relatively full reconstruction of campaigns of conquest.

Immediately after seizing power in 744 BC, Tiglath-Pileser led an expedition into Babylonia (southern Mesopotamia) to protect his ally, the Babylonian king

Nabonassar (Nabu-nasir) from the rebellious Aramaean and Chaldaean tribes, who were supported by the kingdom of Elam in southwestern Iran. The Assyrians now challenged the Elamites for control of the rich and strategic territory of Babylonia. Nabonassar remained king of Babylon for the next ten years but from this time on was a vassal of Tiglath-Pileser.

However, the main threat to Assyria came from the kingdom of Urartu in the Armenian mountains directly to the north. The ethnic and linguistic affinities of the people of Urartu are uncertain; they may have been Hurrians or Armenians, or possibly an older Hurrian elite ruling an Armenian population that had moved in from western Anatolia. (The main reason for assuming an Armenian stratum in the population is that in the sixth century BC, Urartu was replaced by the kingdom of Armenia.) Early in the eighth century, Urartu became a kingdom as large as Assyria, with a block of allies stretching from northern Syria and southwest Anatolia to western Iran, forming a great crescent that hemmed in Assyria's northern frontiers and controlled the main east–west trade routes. The chronology is uncertain, but it appears that in about 743 BC, the Assyrian king attacked a league of Syrian princes, led by the city of Arpad, who were allies of Urartu. The next year, King Sarduri III of Urartu was defeated by the Assyrians at the Battle of Commagene on the upper Euphrates, and thereafter he abandoned his Levantine allies. In 740, Arpad fell after a three-year siege, following which much of northern Syria was annexed by Assyria, and the kings of Damascus and Israel offered tribute.

In 737–736 BC the Assyrian king turned eastward, occupied the central Zagros range and marched across Media, penetrating more deeply into the Iranian plateau than any Mesopotamian ruler had ever gone before. In 735 he turned north and invaded Urartu itself, crossing the formidable Armenian mountains and besieging the Urartuan capital Tushpa (modern Van) on Lake Van; the siege was unsuccessful, but the role of Urartu in Near Eastern affairs had been sharply curtailed.

A second settlement of the Levant became necessary in 734–732 BC. The Philistine rulers of Ashkelon and Gaza organized a league of Palestinian cities against Assyria and were defeated by Tiglath-Pileser. Amon, Edom, Moab, Judah, and a queen of the Arabs paid tribute. In 732, King Ahaz of Judah was attacked by Israel and Damascus and called on Assyria for help. Tiglath-Pileser annexed Damascus and half of Israel, dividing both into provinces, but leaving Hoshea as puppet king of Israel. Judah and the Philistine cities became Assyrian clients.

Assyrian kings routinely boasted of their victories in sanguinary inscriptions. Here is an example from the palace of Tiglath-Pileser at Nimrud celebrating his triumph over King Rezin of Damascus and King Pekah of Israel:

> Rezin the Damascene ... With the blood of his warriors I dyed with a reddish hue the river ... That one *[Rezin]* in order to save his life fled alone; and he entered the gate of his city like a mongoose. I impaled alive his chief ministers ... I confined him like a bird in a cage. His gardens ... orchards without number I cut down; I did not leave a single one. *[Sixteen]* districts of Bit-Humri *[Israel]* I levelled to the ground.

The Assyrian conquests inspired the prophet Isaiah to a cosmic view of history, which was to have great influence on the Judeo-Christian tradition. All historical events were seen as part of a divine plan. The Assyrian was the scourge of God, an instrument used to punish the people of Israel for their sins:

> The Assyrian! He is the rod that I [*Yahweh*] wield in my anger, and the staff of my wrath is in his hand. I sent him against a godless nation [*Israel*], I bid him march against a people who rouse

my wrath, to spoil and plunder at will and
trample them down like mud in the streets.

ISAIAH 10: 5–6

Then came the final settlement of Babylonia. Nabonassar
had died in 734 BC and in 731 a Chaldaean usurper seized
Babylon. Tiglath-Pileser invaded the south, killed the
usurper, and in 729 or 728 took the title of king of Babylonia
under the throne name Pulu (by which he is sometimes
called in the Bible).

By the end of his reign, all the Fertile Crescent above
Egypt, with a population of several million people, had
been brought within the Assyrian empire. A block of new
provinces had been created extending to the
Mediterranean. Beyond these provinces a series of tightly
controlled client states stretched from south Anatolia to
the border of Egypt. Babylonia was under direct Assyrian
control. The terminal points of the major caravan routes
were in Assyrian hands. It was the largest state and the
most complex political structure that the human race had
so far produced.

A striking feature of the new Assyrian imperialism
was the massive deportation of tens of thousands of people
from the conquered populations. This had been done
before in the Middle East, but never on the massive scale
initiated by Tiglath-Pileser. Tens of thousands were relo-

cated by him and the policy was continued by all his successors, so that by the end of the Assyrian empire in 612 BC, if the inscriptions of the kings are to be credited, more than 4 million people had been relocated. The purpose of this policy was, of course, to punish 'rebellion' and to forestall future rebellions by breaking up disloyal populations, but also to provide agricultural labour and other manpower. After the needs of the court had been met, those deported were apportioned among temples, nobles and cities. Most were kept in family groups and settled in small communities. They were treated as Assyrians; the inscriptions often repeat the phrase: 'I carried off [deportees], I settled them, as Assyrians I counted them; the yoke of Ashur [the chief Assyrian god] my lord, like the Assyrians I laid on them; tribute and tax like the Assyrians I laid on them.' It was assumed that they would eventually become loyal subjects of the Assyrian king, and there is evidence that they often did. Most of them came from Aramaic regions, and this helped to further the Aramaicization of Mesopotamia, which was already far advanced.

Administrative Reforms

As his conquests proceeded, the king began to build up a new Assyrian elite to replace the old nobility. The power of the nobles was restricted by reducing the size and multiplying the number of the provinces until there were about eighty, so that the power of any individual governor was reduced. Many eunuchs were appointed governors because they had no families and were totally dependent on the king. Each province was ruled by a governor called either a *shaknu* ('appointed one') or a *bel pihati* ('district chief'). Their duties were to keep order, to collect tribute, to supply the king and his entourage and army when they passed through, and to provide soldiers and labour gangs as needed. The system of conscription was one widely used in the ancient Middle East: individuals received land grants (*ilkum*) on the condition that they supply the king with a certain number of men for military service or labour as needed. Much of the manpower came from those deported, as described above. The empire was crisscrossed by a large road system, its use restricted to those carrying the royal seal. The court kept in contact with governors through the first efficient postal service in history, the model for the famous postal service of the Persians. The king also had at his disposal the *qurbutu*, a small staff of trusted administrators who carried out regular inspections of the provinces and made reports directly to the king. Many client states became provinces; those that remained independent were placed under the supervision of overseers (*qepu*). Failure to render tribute or other signs of disloyalty led to loss of independence and incorporation into the provincial system. The intended result of these reforms, which were continued by all Tiglath-Pileser's successors, was a tremendous strengthening of royal authority.

Military Reforms

The old army, called the *sab sharri*, consisted of *ilkum* holders and peasant conscripts provided by landlords, and was distributed about the empire under the command of the provincial governors. It only campaigned in summer, between the June harvest and the October sowing. The basic unit was the *kisru*, sometimes translated as 'cohort', which was commanded by a *rab kisri*. Under the *rab kisri* were Commanders of Fifty and Commanders of Ten. The absence of any sub-unit larger than fifty may support the assumption that the *kisru* was about the size of a Roman cohort (600 men), in which case the *rab kisri* was about the equivalent of a modern colonel. It was probably Tiglath-Pileser who added a permanent elite force under the direct command of the king, a sort of Praetorian Guard, known as the Royal Cohort (*kisir sharruti*), and a smaller and still more elite force called the Royal Guard (*sha qurbuti*).

All these units used similar equipment, and all included infantry, cavalry and chariotry, recruited from native Assyrians. (It should be mentioned that these native Assyrians were actually a mix of Assyrians and Aramaeans by this time. The Assyrian state had expanded in the ninth century by assimilating the Aramaean peoples of north Mesopotamia, and the widespread displacement of Aramaeans by Tiglath-Pileser continued the process of Aramaicization, so that by the end of the Assyrian empire, Aramaic had replaced Akkadian as the spoken language of Mesopotamia.) Now large numbers of non-Assyrian auxiliaries, chiefly pure tribal Aramaeans, were recruited into the light infantry, some armed as archers and some as spearmen. There were also many allied contingents contributed by the client states on the frontiers, using the equipment of their native traditions. It has been estimated that the total forces available to Tiglath-Pileser numbered half a million men.

A text from Zamua gives us a numerical breakdown of the *sab sharri* troops under the command of a provincial governor in the late eighth century BC: 10 chariots, 97 cavalrymen, 80 Assyrian heavy infantrymen, 440 auxiliary archers, and 360 auxiliary spearmen. There were also 101 Assyrian staff, and grooms and other assistants who accompanied the horse troops. It is interesting that the governor had precisely equal numbers of spearmen and archers, 440 each (counting both the heavy Assyrian and light Aramaean spearmen). These were probably notional figures, but it is still significant that equal numbers of spearmen and archers was the ideal.

The new model army was capable of campaigning all year round. On campaign the Royal Cohort and Royal Guard formed the core of the army, supported by *sab sharri* troops contributed by the governors and by allied contingents as needed. Normally the king commanded in person, but there were also two field marshals (*turtanu*), the marshal of the left wing and the marshal of the right.

Cavalry were the great innovation of this army. Earlier Assyrian armies had relied on chariots, a relic of the Bronze Age. But some time in the tenth century the nomads of the Eurasian steppe had mastered the art of horseback riding. Assyrian cavalry are first mentioned in 853 BC, but for a time they worked in cooperation with chariotry; the art of managing a stirrupless horse had not been mastered, so cavalrymen rode in pairs, one holding the reins of the horses and the other shooting a bow. But by the time of Tiglath-Pileser, Assyrian cavalry consisted of single horsemen, each armed with bow or spear or both, and the chariot had become obsolete except as a prestige vehicle for high-ranking officers.

Finally, the most dreaded service of the new army was its siege train. The Assyrians brought the art of siege warfare to a peak never surpassed until the Greeks invented catapults in the fourth century BC. The main innovation was the battering ram, invented in the ninth century, which made it possible to take cities by assault. Some cities fell to the Assyrians within a day or so, though as we have seen Arpad held out for three years.

Assyrian inscriptions do not contain realistic battle descriptions, and Assyrian art, unlike Egyptian art, never shows troops in formation. No Assyrian battle can be reconstructed in the way that we can attempt to reconstruct the Battle of Kadesh fought between Egyptians and Hittites in 1275 BC. It is clear that Assyrian armies were basically infantry armies: the ratio of foot to horse at Zamua was eight to one. The reliefs showing the battle on the Ulai river, 653 BC, from the palace of Ashurbanipal at Nineveh, the finest battle scenes in Assyrian art, appear to show spearman and archers cooperating, perhaps resembling the cooperation of pikes and muskets in early modern Europe. We may imagine the archers opening the battle under the protection of the heavy infantry, and retreating behind their shields when it came to close contact. Battles were probably won by archery. Cavalry would have operated in support of the infantry, harassing the enemy with arrows and charging in pursuit of the fleeing enemy when they broke.

Though much remains obscure about Assyrian warfare, there seems no doubt that it was the first style of war that could make use of combined arms, a variety of distinct services performing different roles in battle and supporting one another; which is to say it was the first army capable of genuine tactics such as the Greeks and Romans knew.

SUN TZU

c. 544–496 BC

JONATHAN FENBY

SUN WU, *later accorded the honorary title of Tzu (master) in recognition of his status, has been the greatest single influence on the military strategy and tactics of the world's most heavily populated nation. The thirteen-chapter* Art of War, *which is attributed to him (though some parts may have been added later by others), has been studied by Chinese generals and strategists over the centuries. Napoleon may have read a French translation published in 1771. In the twentieth century, the eminent British military theorist Basil Liddell Hart placed Sun above Clausewitz for his 'concentrated essence of wisdom on the conduct of war', and judged that his treatises 'have never been surpassed in comprehensiveness and depth of understanding'.*

Both sides in China's great mid-nineteenth-century revolt by the Taiping rebels applied Sun's teachings. The Japanese, who inflicted a humiliating defeat on imperial China in 1894–5, had studied him. So had at least some of the warlords who ruled China in the 1920s, while the Northern Expedition of the Kuomintang Army under Chiang Kai-shek at the end of that decade put into effect Sun's advocacy of swift movement, deception, spying and political means to achieve victory.

Mao Zedong, too, was a confirmed disciple, coining aphorisms that could come straight from the *Art of War* – when the Red Army reached its haven at Yenan in Shaanxi province at the end of the Long March, Sun's work was published with a commentary for the edification of its officers. More recently, his injunctions have been presented as a guide for business, mentioned in the film *Wall Street* and hailed by an American newspaper as providing tips to rank with books of popular psychology and self-help.

For all this, little is known about the man himself. The classic Han dynasty work, the *Records of the Historian*, written soon after 100 BC and constituting the main guide to early Chinese events and dynasties, describes him as a general who worked for a king of the state of Wu in the sixth century, during an era of Chinese history known as the Spring and Autumn Period.

The story in the *Records of the Historian* has it that the

king of Wu read Sun's injunctions and asked him to conduct an exercise in troop movement using 180 beautiful women. Sun divided them into two companies headed by the king's two favourite concubines. He instructed them in handling halberds, and ordered them to perform drills. The women laughed. So Sun ordered their two commanders to be executed. The king objected to the beheading of his favourite concubines, but Sun insisted. After that, the women did as they were told. The sovereign recognized Sun's prowess as a commander, putting him in charge of a string of campaigns, which he carried out successfully.

Warring States

The timing in the *Records* given by the Han historian appears unlikely for several reasons, including the weapons and the size of the armies he mentions. As the American general and historian Samuel Griffiths has noted, the *Art of War* was written in an era when the earlier knightly code of warfare in China was breaking down. Sun appears to have lived at a time when competing regional states had emerged beneath the nominal rule of emperors who had diminishing real authority. Six major warlords ruled the nation, surrounded by smaller realms that they gradually absorbed. As the scale and intensity of warfare mounted, armies grew larger, led by professional soldiers and consisting of swordsmen, spear carriers, archers and chariots. Soldiers used iron weapons and powerful crossbows. General staffs coordinated tactics. Collective responsibility was often applied, with com-manders being executed for retreating without authorization. By the time of Sun Tzu, therefore, China was well on the way to the formidable forces deployed by the kingdom of Qin, whose ruler would end the period of the Warring States in 221 BC, by claiming the Mandate of Heaven from the gods as the First Emperor, employing lessons laid out in the *Art of War*.

Sun's writings belong squarely in this new and more pragmatic age; the object is not to follow rituals or to practise courtly respect for the enemy, but, quite simply, to win at minimum cost and to maximum effect. Sun, whose teachings received glosses from subsequent military experts, was far from alone in proffering advice on how to fight wars; numerous counsellors moved between the regional courts, where, in historian C. P. Fitzgerald's words, they 'proposed and carried out schemes of the blackest treachery. Frequently they secretly served two princes at once, playing off the policy of one against the other.'

What made Sun different was the breadth of his vision, and his fundamental belief that committing an army to battle was the last resort, while 'to subdue the enemy's army without fighting is the acme of skill'. 'All warfare is based on deception,' he wrote. More than two thousand years before its modern advocates, he championed the indirect approach, avoiding the enemy's strong points and focusing on attacking weaknesses in his line. By out-thinking and outwitting the adversary, a great commander made victory inevitable before the first sword was drawn.

The Importance of the Initiative

'When capable, feign incapacity; when active, inactivity,' he advised at the start of a series of short, sharp injunctions laid out in his first chapter as 'the strategist's keys to victory'.

> When near, make it appear that you are far away; when far away, that you are near. Offer the enemy a bait to lure him; feign disorder and strike him. When he concentrates, prepare against him; where he is strong, avoid him. Anger his generals and confuse him. Pretend inferiority and encourage his arrogance. Keep him under a strain and wear him down. Where he is unprepared, sally out when he does not expect you.

Sun recognized the importance of retaining the initiative by attacking the enemy's strategy. While he laid great store by high morale, solidarity and fighting skills, bravado was not a quality he admired for itself. The lonely, outnumbered army unit fighting valiantly against the odds was not for him. Rather, numbers should be concentrated so as to produce a surrender without the need for combat. Thus, 'when ten times the enemy's one, surround him; when five times his strength, attack him; if double his strength, divide him; if equally matched, you may engage him; if weaker numerically, be capable of withdrawing; and, if in all respects unequal, be capable of eluding him, for a small force is but booty for one more powerful.'

Once war broke out, Sun thought that the aim should be to end it as soon as possible, and to capture enemy troops rather than destroy them. The first army in position was at an advantage, so a proficient general should take up his preferred place and lure the adversary on to the battlefield he had chosen. When he wished to join battle, he drew the foe from behind his fortifications by attacking a position elsewhere which the opponent had to defend; but, when he wanted to avoid fighting, he would ward off an advance by diverting the enemy from his chosen course.

Mobility, initiative and surprise were everything, to be juggled to confuse and outmanoeuvre the adversary until he grew weary and defeatist, unable to pin down the contours of the army he faced. 'The ultimate in disposing one's troops is to be without ascertainable shape,' Sun taught. Like water, war had no constant conditions, and tactics should be changed according to the nature of the battle situation.

Not knowing where he was likely to be assaulted obliged the enemy to disperse his forces to defend many positions. Attacks on cities, which were likely to be lengthy affairs that tied down troops, were to be avoided. 'No country has ever benefited from a protracted war,' Sun wrote. Defeated enemies should be treated humanely to ensure that they did not resume hostilities. Reflecting the growing professionalism of Chinese officers, he warned against interference in campaigns by rulers ignorant of military matters who would only 'hobble the army', causing confusion that would aid the enemy.

The Confucian Code

Sun's approach was deeply rooted in the behaviour code handed down from Confucius (who died in 479 BC), with its belief in reason, which was the foundation for more than two millennia of imperial rule in China – and which still has echoes in today's Communist regime. Knowing yourself and your foe was vital. 'Know the enemy and know yourself; in a hundred battles you will never be in peril,' he wrote. 'When you are ignorant of the enemy but know yourself, your chances of winning or losing are equal. If ignorant of both your enemy and yourself, you are certain to be in peril in every battle.' Invincibility, he

noted elsewhere, depends on one's self, while the vulner-
ability of the enemy depends on him. One has, therefore,
to do all one can to ensure the first by cleverness, reason,
preparation and good organization.

A tale recounts a conversation between Sun and a
disciple of Confucius who asked him which kind of man
he should take with him if he commanded 'the Army of
the Three Hosts'. 'The man who was ready to beard a tiger
or rush a river without caring whether he lived or died –
that sort of man I should not take,' Sun replied. 'But I
should certainly take someone who approached difficulties
with due caution and who preferred to succeed by strategy.'

Sun lays out practical advice, and details the tactics to
adopt in different terrains and on different battlefields. He
devotes twelve points in one chapter to attacks by fire. After
warning of the dangers of camping in low-lying or desolate ground, he tells of the need to cross salt marshes speedily,
and outlines the advantages of taking up position on the
sunny side of mountains. The way birds fly can reveal an
ambush, he notes. Acute observation can tell when the
enemy is tired or desperate. In another practical note, he
advises a commander to treat his men in a civil fashion,
winning their confidence with orders that make sense and
are effective. If he cares for his men as his own sons, they
will march and die with a 'serene and inscrutable, impartial
and self-controlled' leader.

Intelligence and Spies

Sun's great achievement was in taking a broader view of war, tying together the multiple elements and insisting on the need for deep thought and planning, diplomacy, skilful manoeuvres, discipline, intelligence operations and subversion. Close attention to the terrain and the weather is important. So is the ability to avoid traps laid by the enemy – 'Do not gobble up proffered baits,' Sun enjoins.

There is something quasi-mystical about the summary of military expertise which Sun lays out after detailing these multiple ways in which to get the better of an adversary. 'Subtle and insubstantial, the expert leaves no trace; divinely mysterious, he is inaudible. Thus he is the master of his enemy's fate,' Sun wrote. Later, he added that 'One able to gain the victory by modifying his tactics in accordance with the enemy situation may be said to be divine.'

Yet he is also highly realistic in noting that 'what is called "foreknowledge" cannot be elicited from spirits, or from gods, or from analogy with past events, or from calculations – it must be obtained from men who know the enemy situation'. These spies fall into five categories: natives of the enemy territory; people living there with inside knowledge; enemy spies who have been turned; agents sent in with false information who are expected to be caught and to disclose their misleading news; and, finally – the most valuable – agents who cross the lines and return, the best of whom are intelligent but appear stupid, and are able to 'endure hunger, cold, filth and humiliation'. When all five categories are working, they form 'the Divine Skein and the treasure of a sovereign'. Secret operations, Sun concludes in the last sentence of his work, 'are essential in war; upon them the army relies to make its every move'.

It is extraordinary that this complex but immaculately joined-up philosophy of war was evolved at a time when China was divided among warring kingdoms that lived and died by the force of arms. It seems to belong, rather, to a later, more settled period. But whatever the uncertainties about who Sun was, when exactly he lived, and whether he actually wrote the *Art of War* or whether it was a later compilation of texts, there can be no doubting its wisdom and its central role in the Chinese approach to war throughout the centuries.

Sun Tzu's Heritage

Zhuge Liang

In the third century AD, Zhuge Liang (see pp. 296–311) adopted psychological warfare techniques drawn from Sun Tzu, notably in his treatment of the southern rebel leader Meng Huo, whom he released seven times in order eventually to win his loyalty. Zhuge's celebrated use of diversions and trickery was straight out of Sun's book, as was the way he stirred up trouble behind the lines of his stronger foe to weaken its ability to resist the offensives he launched from the kingdom of Shu. But, like Sun, he was also a highly rational commander, and ended several campaigns because of his worries about his supply chain, to avoid being caught without provisions and reinforcements on the far side of the mountains surrounding his base region of Sichuan.

The Taiping

In the mid-nineteenth century, China was rocked by the huge Taiping Revolt, led by a southerner who claimed he was the son of the Christian God. Rebel armies penetrated many parts of China, establishing their capital at Nanjing and even getting within 100 miles of Beijing. Their major commanders applied Sun Tzu's strategy of avoiding imperial strong points and concentrating their attacks on weak areas, using fast marching, espionage and diversions to surprise their adversaries. After fourteen years, they were defeated by armies led by provincial gentry who had also absorbed Sun's teachings, avoiding battle until they enjoyed supremacy, undermining the rebels by winning peasant support and establishing networks of villages protected by local militia, cutting off food and supplies and using a mixture of propaganda and threats to undermine Taiping morale.

Chiang Kai-shek and the Japanese

In the 1920s, several of Sun Tzu's tactics were employed by the Kuomintang army that marched out of Canton in the far south on its Northern Expedition to establish the Nationalist regime that ruled China until 1949. Its leader, Chiang Kai-shek, paid great attention to winning allies among the minor warlords he faced, in order to gain strength against the major militarists who had divided the country among themselves. Bribery and political persuasion were among his weapons, while his Soviet military adviser, Galen, employed flanking tactics to great effect. (Galen was the pseudonym used by Vassili Blücher, a Russian civil war hero who later headed the Red Army in the Far East before being tortured and killed in Stalin's purges.)

In the culmination of the Nationalist offensive against erstwhile allies in northern China, Chiang obtained victory by winning over the wavering Manchurian warlords, forcing his opponents to cave in without a final battle. Chiang used similar tactics against a series of regional rivals, but was at a loss when faced with the full-scale offensive launched in China in 1937 by the Japanese, who had, themselves, absorbed Sun Tzu's teachings from several analyses of his work that appeared in Japan in the seventeenth and eighteenth centuries.

Mao Zedong

China's Communist leader applied Sun's teachings in the different theatres of the war he fought over two decades before the Communist victory of 1949. The evasion of frontal battle against a stronger enemy, the focus on attacking the adversary's weak points, deception, intelligence, swift movement and a readiness to run away in adverse conditions were all central to the guerrilla warfare that Mao advocated and imposed on the Chinese Communists in the 1930s.

His four slogans, coined in his first base in the mountains of Jiangxi, could have been written by Sun:

> When the enemy advances, we retreat.
> When the enemy halts, we harass.
> When the enemy seeks to avoid battle, we attack.
> When the enemy retreats, we pursue.

Or take Mao's eulogy for adaptability, which fits Sun's advocacy of tactical adaptability to perfection: 'Attack may be changed into defence, and defence into attack. Advance may be turned into retreat, and retreat into advance. Containing forces may be turned into assault forces, and assault forces into containing forces.'

In the civil war after 1945, the Communists applied elements of Sun's approach on a massive scale in the great battles with the Nationalists in Manchuria in 1947–8, and in the crucial Huai-Hai battle that won the civil war in the winter of 1948–9. Then, when it entered the Korean War, China deployed two hundred and fifty thousand men in battle positions south of the Yalu river, without the United Nations command being aware of the threat, and unleashed an attack that almost destroyed its adversary, using the precepts laid down by Sun Tzu over two thousand years earlier.

CYRUS THE GREAT

590 or 576–529 BC

TOM HOLLAND

ON A HILL-RIMMED PLAIN in southern Iran there stands a tomb of stone, looking for all the world as though a tent has been perched on a ziggurat. This striking monument was already more than a thousand years old when, in AD 640, the conquering armies of Islam first swept into Persia. Locals, keen to preserve it from the destructive zeal of the Muslims, informed their new masters that the tomb was that of Solomon's mother, and the invaders, respecting the memory of a king who had been hailed in the Koran as a prophet, devoutly preserved it. Whose tomb the monument truly was had long since been forgotten. Not even the Persians themselves had any real conception of their country's ancient past.

Only in the West, among their former enemies, was it still remembered that the Persians had once been the rulers of the most powerful empire in the world. Those who could read the histories of the Greeks knew that in distant times one of their kings had led an immense invasion force from Asia into Europe across a bridge of boats, and had almost succeeded in conquering Greece. Alexander the Great, invading Asia in turn, had claimed to be doing so in revenge. Yet even he, although he had proved himself to be the bane of the Persians' empire, had remained in awe of the achievement of its creator. Like the Muslim conquerors a millenium later, he had visited the tent-shaped tomb in southern Iran. Unlike the Arabs, he had needed no one to tell him whose it was.

'Mortal!', an inscription ran on the tomb. 'I am Cyrus, who founded the dominion of the Persians, and was King of Asia. Do not begrudge me then my monument!' Nor did Alexander begrudge it. Ordering the tomb's lavish refurbishment, he had sedulously paraded his respect for the one conqueror he was prepared to acknowledge as his peer. Indeed, the achievements of Cyrus two centuries previously had been, if anything, even more astounding than those of Alexander. The Persian, unlike the son of Philip, had seemed to emerge to his greatness from nowhere. In 559 BC, when Cyrus came to the throne, the kingdom he ruled was backward and inconsequential. The Persians themselves, originally nomads from the steppes of central Asia, had barely intruded upon the consciousness of the region's great powers; and yet by the time of their king's death thirty years later, they had subdued them all. From the Aegean in the west to the Hindu Kush in the east, Cyrus had made himself the master of an empire without parallel. It was the most spectacular feat of conquest that the world had ever seen.

Cyromania

The man who achieved it had been, self-evidently, a commander of exceptional prowess. Alexander was not alone among the *anairya*, as the Persians termed foreigners, in acknowledging this. Indeed, that we know as much about Cyrus as we do depends to a striking degee upon the admiring testimony of Greeks: for the Persians, with a single exception, did not write anything at all that we can identify as an account of real events. Certainly, there is no equivalent of the campaign records of the Assyrian kings, no loving descriptions of the blood spilled by Cyrus, of the cities he stormed, of the battles he won – only the odd clay tablet or cylinder, redeemed from the rubble of vanished palaces, and inscribed with details that tend to be at best either generalized or elliptical. Compounding the murk is the fact that even the single Persian narrative we do have, an inscription carved at Bisitun, by the side of what today serves as the main Baghdad–Tehran road, is a deliberate and skilful work of disinformation: for the king who commissioned it, Darius I, was almost certainly a usurper, who had murdered one, and conceivably two, sons of Cyrus, and wished to conceal the fact. As a result, for anything that even vaguely approaches a coherent account of Cyrus' life, we have to turn instead to the Greek historian Herodotus: an incomparable source, to be sure, and without whom our understanding of early Persian history would be truly spectral. Yet even so, ever curious and open-minded though Herodotus was, the awkward truth remains that in describing Cyrus' conquests he was often writing about remote and peculiar peoples, whose languages he did not speak, and whose lands, by and large, he had never visited. As a result, he inevitably has to be excused the occasional inaccuracy, the occasional prejudice, the occasional tendency to treat the obscurer reaches of Persian history as fantasy. That a military biography of Cyrus can be written at all owes everything to Herodotus; that it must inevitably be riddled with gaps and uncertainties owes much to him as well.

Iron Fists and Velvet Gloves

Nowhere is Herodotus' inimitable blend of tall stories and telling detail more flamboyantly showcased than in his account of Cyrus' youth. It is the nature of great men, of course, to attract legends, and Cyrus was no exception. Herodotus' biography of his early years frequently verges upon the fantastical: from visions of urinating princesses to grotesque tales of cannibalism, most of the events described in it bear testimony to Cyrus' posthumous status as a figure less of history than of myth. Nevertheless, a few of the details recorded by Herodotus do appear genuine. We are told, for instance, that the young King of Persia was the grandson of another and much greater king, Astyages of Media, a region occupying what is now northwestern Iran; and this may well be true. For Media, during the period of Cyrus' boyhood, was one of the great powers of the Near East; and Astyages, if a Babylonian source is to be trusted, was indeed in the habit of marrying off his daughters to neighbouring vassals. If Cyrus was truly Astyages' grandson, then it meant that he had Median as well as Persian blood in his veins; and, very probably, contacts in the Median aristocracy as well. Astyages certainly came to view him as a potential rival, for in 553 BC, six years into Cyrus' reign, he struck southwards against his vassal, resolved to topple him from his throne. The odds seemed stacked against Cyrus' survival. Not for nothing was the Median cavalry famed as the most devastating strike force in the entire Near East. Sure enough, so desperate did things appear for the Persians at one point that even their women, it is said, had to take to the battlefield. Cyrus, however, refused to submit; and for three years the war raged on. Then, abruptly, it was Astyages who was brought to defeat. So unexpected was this upset that in Babylon, it was reported, the news had been brought to the king by a god. 'The large armies of the Medes were scattered by Cyrus and his outnumbered forces,' reported the divine messenger. 'And Cyrus captured Astyages, the King of the Medes. And he took him to his country as captive.'

Brought to Persia, Astyages was not impaled or flayed or fed to animals, but set up on a country estate. Cyrus' display of mercy towards his grandfather was complemented by a no less gracious refusal to treat the conquered Medes as slaves. Prompted by a naturally magnanimous temperament this may well have been – but it was prompted, too, by a steely measure of calculation. Cyrus, having won the war, had no intention of losing the peace. The Medes were encouraged to feel, if not exactly the equals of their conquerors, then at least associates in the great adventure of their new king's reign. And this was just as well – for his campaigns, as events were to prove, were very far from over. In 547, a bare six years after Astyages had presumed to launch a pre-emptive strike against Cyrus, a second king thought to repeat the gambit. Croesus was the legendarily wealthy ruler of Lydia, a kingdom in the west of what is now Turkey; and he had long nurtured an ambition to extend his empire eastwards. Late that summer, he crossed the Halys, a river that served as the frontier between Lydia and Media – and by doing so effectively declared war on the upstart Persian king. Cyrus, even though winter was coming on, was hardly the man to duck such a challenge. That same autumn, the two kings clashed brutally but indecisively. Croesus, content to have probed Cyrus' defences, then withdraw to his capital, Sardis. Here he intended to hunker down for the winter, in a city that appeared at a perfectly safe remove from his adversary, located as it was only three days' journey from the Aegean. Certainly, it never crossed Croesus' mind that Cyrus might follow him. But follow him Cyrus did – for the Persians and the Medes, with their sheepskin coats and tough mountain horses, were ideally equipped for a winter campaign. Braving the bitter cold, they shadowed Croesus, never alerting him to their presence, allowing him time to dismiss his allies and for his conscripts to melt away. Only once Sardis was denuded did they finally strike. Frantically, Croesus cobbled together what limited forces he could. All to no avail. Riding out from Sardis to confront Cyrus, the Lydian king had made no allowance for the innnovative quality of his opponent's generalship. As his cavalry charged the Persian forces, they were startled to find themselves confronted by a line of baggage-camels. Unfamiliar with the stench, the horses duly swerved and bolted. Croesus' entire army then scattered in disarray, leaving Cyrus free to invest Sardis, storm it, and lay claim to its stupendous treasury. Lydia was duly added to the swelling dominions of the Persian king.

When the Mede Came: the Conquest of Ionia

Even more than the toppling of Astyages had done, Cyrus' victory over Croesus in 547/6 BC burst like a thunderclap across a world that seemed abruptly and spectacularly shrunken by it. On the eastern seaboard of the Aegean, the Greek cities of Ionia found themselves suddenly confronted by conquerors that they called not Persians, but Medes – a linguistic muddle that powerfully conveys just how disorienting had been Cyrus' rise. Terror filled all those who found themselves lying in the Persians' path. One Ionian city, Phocaea, went so far as to evacuate its entire population, 'women, children, moveable property, everything, in fact ... leaving the Persians to take possession of nothing but an empty shell'. Those who opted for resistance were systematically broken to the yoke of the Persian king, amid 'the tearing down of walls, the tumult of cavalry charges, and the overthrow of cities'.

Not once were the Ionians able to confront the invaders successfully in open combat. Indeed, such was the shock of the Persians' coming that it would long serve to darken even the most intimate moments of joy:

In winter, as you lie on a soft couch by the fire,
Full of good food, munching on nuts and drinking
    sweet wine,
Then you must ask questions such as these

'Where do you come from? Tell me, what is your
  age?
How old were you when the Mede came?'

Nor was the sense of fear confined to the limits of Ionia.
A dread of Persian military prowess was instilled in Greeks
everywhere, an inferiority complex that would endure for
decades. Not until 490 BC, and the Battle of Marathon,
would it finally – and even then only to a degree – be
exorcised.

King of Kings

Meanwhile, even as Cyrus was completing his conquest of
the west, trouble had been brewing among the provinces
that extended to the east of Media. Many of these, which
had been tributary to Astyages, had initially proffered a
shadowy submission to his conqueror; 'but then they
revolted, and this defection was the cause and origin of
numerous wars'. As to how and when these wars were
fought, however, we are almost completely in the dark.
Herodotus, whose knowledge of eastern affairs was
inevitably hazy, states only that Cyrus campaigned 'across
the north and the east, and ended up bringing about the
subjugation of every nation, without exception'. The limit
of Persian expansion appears finally to have been set at
the Jaxartes, a broad, island-dotted river that flows through

what is now Kazakhstan, and beyond which the steppelands extended in defiance of the ambitions of even the most prodigious conqueror the world had ever known. Intending to make good the deficiencies of the river as a natural frontier, Cyrus ordered the construction of seven frontier towns, so that the approaches to Persia from central Asia, which had always been open to predatory nomads, could be patrolled effectively. Meanwhile, behind the buffer zone, lands which had once been breeding-grounds of menace and instability – Gandhara, Bactria and Sogdiana – were transformed into bulwarks of the new superpower. Running in a great arc, they stretched from the Hindu Kush to the Aral Sea. Not only had the frontier been stabilized, but yet further reserves of manpower had been added to the armies of the Persian king.

This was just as well – for Cyrus was not done with his conquests yet. By 540, with both the western and eastern limits of his new empire secured, he felt ready for his ultimate test. Incomparable though the scale and range of his victories had been, yet there remained one great power with pretensions still to rival Persia as the mistress of the Near East. Babylon had long been accustomed to regard herself as the very fulcrum of world affairs. Her rulers, with a corresponding display of conceit, thought nothing of laying claim to titles such as 'King of the Four Quarters of the Earth' and 'King of the Universe'. Nor was this entirely braggadocio – for celebrated kings such as Nebuchadnezzar II had indeed cast a lengthy and fearsome shadow. 'Their quiver is like an open tomb,' the biblical prophet Jeremiah had wailed, 'they are all mighty men.' In terms of wealth, size and glamour, Babylon was certainly incomparable. No man could truly consider himself the master of the world until he had subdued her – as Cyrus well knew. Concerned to present himself as a man worthy of such a prize, and skilled as he was at overturning hostile preconceptions, he duly ensured that his assault on the city was accompanied by a masterly propaganda onslaught. Invading Babylonian territory, he claimed to be defending it; leading an army of battle-hardened veterans, he affected to be an avatar of peace. The strategy proved brilliantly successful. Even as he advanced, most enemy strongholds hurried to open their gates.

An unheroic strategy, maybe – but certainly a sensible one. Persian firepower was overwhelming, and Cyrus, who was not averse to staging the odd atrocity where necessary, made sure that the Babylonians knew it. Although his propagandists would later make much play about how Babylon fell 'without a battle', this was not the case. The initial clash, we know from a Babylonian source, took place at Opis, on the banks of the Tigris, in early October 539 BC, and was followed up by much plundering and slaughter. As Nabonidus, the king of Babylon, retreated to his capital,

Cyrus pursued him. There was nothing to block his advance. Even the Tigris was easily forded: for Persian troops were practised in the crossing of rivers while clinging on to horses, camels and inflated animal-skins. One last attempt by Nabonidus to confront his nemesis outside the very walls of Babylon was disdainfully swatted aside, and by the middle of October the great city was acknowledging its conqueror as 'King of the Universe'.

The capture of Babylon marked the climax of Cyrus' military career; but not its end. The sword of such a conqueror did not sleep easily in its scabbard. A decade after his triumphant entry into the capital of the world and Cyrus was still in his saddle, leading his horsemen ever onwards. Various stories are told of his end; but most of them are agreed that he died in central Asia, north of the Jaxartes, far beyond the limits he had once thought to set on his own ambitions. Even though it is evident that his corpse was transported back with full honours to Persia, for burial in his splendid tomb, numerous eerie stories gave a different account. According to Herodotus, for instance, the queen of the tribe which had killed him ordered his corpse to be decapitated, and then dropped the severed head into a blood-filled wineskin, so that Cyrus' thirst for slaughter might be glutted at last. Such a tale powerfully suggests the terror that the great conqueror was capable of instilling in his adversaries: for vampires, demons hungry for human flesh, had long haunted the nightmares of the peoples of the Near East.

Yet a very different tradition also served to keep alive the memory of Cyrus the Great: one that bore witness less to his military prowess, perhaps, than to his aptitude for exploiting the arts of peace. Great commander though he undoubtedly was, his most distinctive achievement was to have launched a novel and far-reaching experiment in geopolitics. Cyrus had not merely conquered his enemies; he had wooed them as well. Brutal though he could certainly be in the cause of securing an enemy's speedy surrender, his preference, by and large, had been to live up to the high-flying claims of his own brilliantly crafted propaganda. Once his regime was established over the corpses of toppled empires, further bloodshed was kept to the barest minimum. His diktats had worn a moderate and gracious tone. To kingdoms far older than his own, venerable with temples and celestial pretensions, Cyrus had presented himself as a model of righteousness, and his rule a payback from the gods. Peoples from across the vast span of his empire had duly scrabbled to hail him as their own. Astonishingly, Cyrus, the man who had, in the awed words of the prophet Isaiah, made 'the world tremble from end to end', would be remembered with an almost unqualified admiration, as the architect of a universal peace. For centuries afterwards, even among its bitterest enemies, the glow of its founder's memory would suffuse the empire of the Persians. 'He eclipsed all other monarchs, either before him, or since.' The verdict, not of a fellow countryman, but of Xenophon – an Athenian.

LEONIDAS

c. 530–480 BC

BEN DUPRÉ

LEONIDAS IS A CURIOSITY in the pantheon of great commanders, for the reputation of the heroic Spartan commander who sought to stem the Persian tide at Thermopylae is built on a single battle – and on a battle, moreover, in which he was manifestly defeated.

In 480 BC, Persia's Great King Xerxes set out at the head of a colossal army, supported by a powerful fleet, to overrun Greece and make it the latest satrapy in what was already the most expansive empire the world had ever seen. The path to central Greece and the Peloponnese lay through the narrow pass at Thermopylae, and it was here that the Spartan king Leonidas and a small band of loyal Greeks attempted to block the Persian advance. Massively outnumbered, the Greeks carried their resistance into the third day.

Then, betrayed by a fellow Greek, they were overwhelmed and annihilated to a man.

Though the Persian juggernaut rumbled on southwards and eventually put Athens to the torch, the almost super-human resistance of Leonidas and his fellows was credited, from antiquity onwards, with providing the spark and in-spiration for the subsequent victories at Salamis and Plataea that finally extinguished the Persian threat. As such, Leonidas has been hailed as the saviour of Greek – and by extension Western – liberty and civilization.

Greece – a Festering Sore

For Xerxes, Greece represented unfinished business. A decade before Thermopylae, his father Darius (the Great) had launched a punitive expedition directed principally at Athens and Eretria, which had supported the Greeks of Asia Minor in the failed Ionian Revolt. Darius' venture, however, came spectacularly unstuck at Marathon in 490, when the Greek (mainly Athenian) forces trounced a far larger Persian army. On Darius' death in 486, Xerxes inher-ited the crown and with it the obligation to avenge his father's humiliation at the hands of the Greeks. Making his preparations meticulously and on a quite unprecedented scale, Xerxes set about launching a second and far greater expedition, mustering tens of thousands of soldiers and hundreds of ships from every part of his kingdom. This time the explicit aim was to subjugate those Greek states that had so far refused to bow to his authority.

The Greek Response

Xerxes made no attempt to conceal his intentions, so the city-states of Greece had several years to coordinate their response. Yet their efforts, for the most part, were fragmented and inadequate. Unable to settle age-old animosities and rivalries, most remained divided and disunited. By the time the Persian threat was almost on top of them, the majority of the Greeks had either 'medized' – gone over to the Persian side – or decided to keep their heads down and stay on the sidelines. Just thirty-one of the mainland Greek states – fewer than one in twenty – agreed to set aside their differences and to resist Xerxes.

Sparta, acknowledged by all as leader of the Greek resistance, was given overall command of both the army and the fleet. As one of Sparta's two kings, Leonidas is likely to have played a leading role in devising the allies' strategy. The plan they agreed upon was to confront Xerxes in northern Greece, blocking his advance simultaneously on land and at sea. After an abortive attempt further north, the Greeks elected to take up a defensive position on the axis running from the Thermopylae pass on the Malian Gulf to Artemisium on the northern coast of the island of Euboea.

The Pass at Thermopylae

Whatever Leonidas' role may have been in determining the broad outlines of the Greek strategy, there can be little doubt that he would have been intimately involved in deciding the minutiae of their response, including the choice of arena and the size and disposition of the forces involved.

An ancient Greek would scarcely recognize Thermopylae today. Over the past two and a half thousand years, the Malian Gulf has silted up to such an extent that the site of the fighting is now several kilometres inland. In 480 BC the Callidromus mountains rose sharply out of the Aegean, forming a narrow pass some 3 to 4 miles (5 to 6 kilometres) long. Along the pass there were three especially narrow constrictions, or 'gates' (*pylai* in Greek; *thermo*, meaning 'hot', comes from the nearby hot sulphur springs). The gates at either end were narrower – Herodotus suggests that there was space only for a single cart to pass – but while the ground at the Middle Gate was wider, at around 65 feet, the cliffs at this point were sheer and steepled up to around 3,300 feet, making them all but impassable. It was here, at the Middle Gate, that Leonidas chose to make his stand. In addition to its natural advantages, running across the pass there was a defensive wall, largely dilapidated by this date, which had been built long before by the Phocians. The Greeks spent the interval before the arrival of the Persians rebuilding it, so gaining an excellent position from which they could make sorties against the enemy.

The Opposing Forces

For all these reasons, Thermopylae, and the Middle Gate in particular, was an excellent choice by Leonidas. In almost every respect this location helped to offset the Greeks' most obvious weaknesses. The Persian cavalry – which could prove devastating in open terrain – was effectively useless here, while Xerxes' archers – another great strength – made little impression on the serried ranks of overlapping Greek shields. Most glaringly, the Greeks were massively outnumbered. It is not certain exactly by how much, but it may have been 20:1 or worse. In any case, fighting on an extremely narrow front, such numerical superiority counted for little.

By contrast, the Greek (and especially Spartan) strength lay almost exclusively in their infantry. The heavily armoured Greek infantryman, or hoplite, was virtually sheathed in metal from head to toe: crested bronze helmet covering all but the eyes, nose and mouth; cuirass or breastplate; and greaves protecting the legs. The secret of the hoplite lay in the disciplined phalanx formation. Each man carried his eponymous shield – the large, round *hoplon* – locked on his left arm, while he thrust over the shield rim with his long (around 8 -feet, or 2.5-metres) spear. In the phalanx, the hoplite's vulnerable right side was covered by the shield of his right-hand neighbour. The only other essential – iron discipline in holding the line at any cost – was the Spartans' speciality.

How big were the opposing forces at Thermopylae? The Greek army is known with some degree of certainty to have numbered around seven thousand. According to the memorial at Thermopylae, which Herodotus saw, there were some four thousand Peloponnesians, including Leonidas' own hand-picked force of 300 Spartan hoplites. As they advanced north, these were joined by contingents from central Greece, whose homes were most immediately at risk: 700 Thespians, 400 Thebans (none too willing, apparently), 1,000 Phocians and the entire army of the Locrians. On the size of the Persian army we can only speculate. Herodotus himself understandably doubts his own estimate of over 5 million (including camp followers), a wildly exaggerated figure that would have been manifestly unsustainable in both food and water. No one since has attempted to defend a figure of this magnitude, and few modern estimates have gone above two hundred thousand.

Whatever the exact figures, it is clear that the Greeks were spectacularly outnumbered. Should Leonidas, as commander-in-chief, be held responsible for the grotesque mismatch? In fact it is quite clear that the Greek army was intended only as an advance force, and Leonidas repeatedly (albeit vainly) requested reinforcements. Through bad luck (or good Persian planning), it happened to be the time of the Olympic festival, during which the Greeks – always scrupulously observant – were required to refrain from fighting. For the hyper-scrupulous Spartans, it was even worse, being the time of their most important annual festival, the Carneia. It is difficult at this distance to distinguish true cause from pretext, but the fact that the Greeks mustered any force at all at such a time may be an indication not of complacency but of the gravity with which they regarded the situation.

A Suicide Mission?

Did Leonidas set off to Thermopylae with the express intention of dying? Various bits of evidence can be pieced together to suggest that he did.

First there is the remark, left unexplained by Herodotus, that Leonidas chose his 300 only from those Spartans who had living sons. A natural interpretation of this is that he knew that none of them were coming back and did not wish to extinguish any Spartan family line. Second, according to Plutarch, there is Leonidas' reply to his wife Gorgo, when she asked before his departure what she could do to help: 'Marry a man that will treat you well and bear him good children.' Then, just before the battle itself, Xerxes is bemused by a spy's report that the Spartans outside the Phocian Wall are combing their long tresses; the explanation given by the exile Demaratus is that such behaviour is customary when Spartans are expecting to die in battle. And on the final morning, Leonidas' gallows humour – 'Eat a good breakfast, for this evening we shall dine together in Hades' – clearly suggests that he did not expect to survive the day.

But none of this need indicate more than that Leonidas and his men were fully aware, before and during the battle, of the grave danger that they faced. This is a far cry from saying that they set out with the *deliberate* intention of dying. One piece of evidence, however, strongly supports the suicide theory. At the very outset of the war, Herodotus tells us, the Spartans received an oracle from Delphi:

> Either your famed, great town must be sacked by
>   Perseus' sons,
> Or, if that be not, the whole land of Lacedaemon
> Shall mourn the death of a king of the house of
>   Heracles ...

While such utterances have always been open to retrospective manipulation, we should not underestimate their reality and significance to ancient Greeks. The Spartans, in particular, were notoriously superstitious and almost obsessively diligent in their observance of religious rituals. Religious scruple was the reason (ostensive, at least) for the small size of the Spartan contingent at Thermopylae, and it is not far-fetched to suppose that Leonidas would have taken a Delphic utterance (perhaps rather more ambiguously stated than in Herodotus' version) very seriously.

Nevertheless, even if we accept that Leonidas was set on sacrificing himself in order to save his city, it is still a big leap to supposing that he would have determined that his 300 fellow Spartans should suffer the same fate. The oracle in no way required it. And while the Spartans were notably scrupulous about making necessary sacrifices, they were just as well known for their unwillingness to make unnecessary ones.

The First and Second Days

Over the first two days of fighting, the excellence of Leonidas' choice of position soon became apparent. On the first day, Xerxes' foot soldiers (including his 10,000 elite 'Immortals') were forced by the terrain into a head-on assault on the Greek phalanx. More accustomed to open skirmishing, with lighter armour and shorter spears, they were no match for the hoplites and rapidly incurred appalling casualties. The Greeks, on the other hand, suffered few losses. The weak point of the phalanx – the extreme right flank – was covered by the sea, while they stayed fresh by fighting in relays emerging from the protection of the Phocian Wall. To add to the discomfiture of Xerxes' soldiers, the Spartans showed off one of their parade-ground manoeuvres, by feigning a retreat and then wheeling around to inflict terrible damage on the overzealous pursuers.

Day two proceeded along similar lines, except now there was an ever-growing pile of corpses building up in front of the Greek line. Even allowing for Herodotean exaggeration (he puts the Persian casualties over three days at twenty thousand), the mountain of bodies – flesh rotting in the searing late-summer heat, the sweet, sickening stench of decay, clouds of flies amid the dust and blood – must have not only presented a major physical barrier but also shattered the morale of the frustrated attackers.

The Position Turned

By the end of the second day, the extreme impenetrability of the Greek line appears to have driven Xerxes to the point of distraction, but then his luck changed. A local man named Ephialtes – a name for ever after held in infamy – agreed, at a price, to guide the Persians along the Anopaea path – a track that snaked through the mountains and led to a point close to the East Gate. The Immortals were promptly dispatched to follow the path overnight with orders to attack Leonidas' position from the rear on the third morning.

We might expect local knowledge to have been a big advantage for the Greeks, so should their intelligence have been better, and should blame attach to Leonidas for allowing his position to be encircled? In fact, the Greek states were, for the most part, fiercely independent, politically divided and often ignorant of what lay beyond their own borders. Herodotus says that the Greek force only found out about the Anopaea path when they arrived at Thermopylae, and that when he learnt of it, Leonidas did what any competent commander would have done – he posted a body of soldiers to guard it.

Was the force, then, inadequate to watch the path – a criticism also levelled at Leonidas? It is true that, in the event, the body of 1,000 Phocians did not cover themselves with glory. They apparently failed to post sentries, were taken completely by surprise, and beat a very hasty retreat beneath a hail of Persian arrows. Yet it is hard to see what better course was open to Leonidas. The size of the guard seems proportionate to his available means, while the reasons for choosing the Phocians appear sound: first, they were familiar with the terrain; and second, they were in effect guarding their own homes and could thus be expected to sell their lives dearly.

The Greeks Split

In the event, the Phocians were simply bypassed by the Immortals, leaving Leonidas' position exposed on two flanks. In the hours after the news of the outflanking reached

Leonidas and before the Immortals arrived, the Greek forces split: the bulk of the army moved southwards to safety, while Leonidas and his Spartans, the Thespians and the Thebans remained, facing almost certain death, to make their famous last stand.

At this point, another major question over Leonidas' leadership arises. Herodotus favours the view that the departure of the main contingent took place in an orderly manner, on the instruction of their commander. On this reading the last stand can be seen as a deliberate attempt to cover the retreat, buying time for the withdrawing soldiers as they moved through the open ground south of the pass, where they would be vulnerable to pursuit by Xerxes' cavalry. But Herodotus also gives an alternative account in which the retreat was basically haphazard – rather a case of the various contingents melting away when it became clear that the game was up. Such a reading does nothing to diminish the merit of those that remained – quite the reverse – but it does cast doubt over Leonidas' own authority and the degree of loyalty that he inspired in those under his command.

The Last Stand

What is not remotely in doubt is the extraordinary bravery of those who remained behind. For Leonidas himself and his fellow Spartans, there clearly can never have been any question of leaving their posts: 'for Sparta, it is not dying but fleeing that is death', as an epigram (inspired by an earlier encounter) put it. Changing their tactics, the Greeks moved forward of the Phocian Wall on to more open ground, determined to inflict the greatest possible damage before the Immortals arrived to complete the encirclement.

It is difficult to assess Leonidas' personal bravery in this context. The essence of Spartan soldiery was collective and disciplined action within the phalanx, based on intensive training since boyhood. 'Fighting singly, Spartans are as good as any,' Herodotus notes, 'but fighting together they are the best soldiers in the world.' Herodotus' account of Leonidas' death is heroic, indeed Homeric – the repeated attempts by his comrades to rescue his body from the enemy and the subsequent desecration of his body by Xerxes are reminiscent of (for instance) Hector's treatment at the hands of Achilles. But this is likely to be conventional and formulaic. There is no reason to doubt that Leonidas fought and died like a model Spartan; but that is precisely what a Spartan was supposed to do.

'Fighting tooth and nail', according to Herodotus, is literally true of the Greeks' final act of defiance. When the Immortals finally appeared, the surviving Greeks closed their ranks and retreated to a small hill, where they fought till their spears were broken, then with their swords, and finally with their hands and teeth. They succumbed at last beneath a torrent of missiles. A Spartan named Dienekes had earlier responded to the news that the arrows of the enemy would be so dense as to blot out the sky with a typically laconic reply: 'All the better: we shall fight in the shade.' In the end, it was in that shade from Persian arrows that Dienekes, Leonidas and all their comrades fought and died.

The Legacy of Thermopylae

If those Greek states set upon resistance had quickly crumbled under the wheels of Xerxes' juggernaut, it is undeniable that the course of history would have been very different. In particular, the magnificent flowering of Athenian democracy and culture in the latter half of the fifth century would not have taken place, and the significance of that for the development of Western civilization is beyond question.

There is an irony in Leonidas – a Spartan – being honoured as the saviour of Western values, for Sparta itself was the oddest and most illiberal of all the Greek states: a culture based on extreme militarism and underpinned by enslavement of fellow Greeks. But the essence of the Greco-Persian War – at least as it was presented by Herodotus and others – is that it was a confrontation between freedom and slavery. As the exiled Spartan king Demaratus (as Herodotus' mouthpiece) explains to Xerxes, the Spartans' only master is the law – an insight that also underlies Simonides' famous epitaph. In effect, the Spartans act freely under their own laws – albeit a very unusual and restrictive set of laws. The fruit of Sparta's self-sacrifice at Thermopylae was a political and cultural efflorescence in other Greek states that was denied – indeed, in many respects was anathema – to Sparta itself. Leonidas' formal defeat was a moral victory. It was also a victory for morale, because it demonstrated to all, not least to the Persians, that when bent on resistance, the Greeks had the determination to defy the odds and struggle through to ultimate victory.

THEMISTOCLES

c. 525–459 BC

ROBIN WATERFIELD

THEMISTOCLES OF ATHENS was the ideal commander, equally at home and effective on the battlefield and in assembly. He was widely recognized as the saviour of Greece in the hour of its darkest peril, during the second Persian invasion of 480–479 BC. Several years before the invasion, he had equipped Athens with a sizeable fleet, the crews of which had sufficient time to master their skills. The victory single-handedly and somewhat deviously engineered by him at the Battle of Salamis in 480 made the final defeat of the Persians in 479 considerably easier, because they no longer dared to face the Greeks at sea.

At the beginning of the fifth century, Athens was a fledgling democracy, where invariably the most important military and political positions still went to members of a tight-knit, intermarrying aristocracy. Themistocles, however, was a 'new man', from a previously unremarkable family, who gained power entirely by his own merits. He was both a clear-sighted democrat and a gifted military tactician. Born around 525 BC, he was therefore old enough to greet the constitutional changes of 508 that laid the foundations for Athenian democracy.

His first major coup, in 493 BC, was to move the centre of Athens' seafaring activities a few miles north, from the old harbour of Phalerum to the Piraeus peninsula, which, with three natural harbours, was better suited to future requirements and easier to fortify. Though briefly eclipsed by rivals, especially Miltiades, Themistocles grew in power and stature during the 480s. Through the process of ostracism, he exiled powerful rivals, particularly those who were pro-Persian or anti-democratic.

In 487 BC Themistocles was instrumental in a far-reaching constitutional reform, whereby the nine most senior political officers of Athens were to be chosen by lot, rather than elected. These offices were therefore side-lined as routes to power, and ambitious Athenians instead sought one of the ten generalships, instituted in around 500, since these were now the only important posts still open to voluntary election, and to which one could be repeatedly re-elected, year after year.

The Development of the Fleet

By 483 BC, Themistocles was the most prominent public figure in Athens, and he used his position to push through a proposal that must have required all his rhetorical powers. A rich new vein of silver had been opened up in the Athenian mines at Laurium, and Themistocles persuaded the Athenians not to share out the surplus among themselves, but instead use it to develop a war fleet, initially of 100 triremes over and above those they had already. The immediate excuse was an ongoing war with the city's trade rival, the island of Aegina, but also the Persians were known to be planning a second invasion following their defeat by Miltiades at Marathon in 490. By the time of the pivotal Battle of Salamis, Athens was able to launch over two hundred ships with experienced crews.

As a democratic politician, Themistocles was undoubtedly also aware of the political repercussions of the development of a fleet. Every single Athenian trireme required a crew of 200, of whom 170 were oarsmen. Even though some of the oarsmen were resident foreigners and hired mercenaries, even slaves, the majority of them were poor Athenian citizens, who until that point had been denied much political power. But the more important they became, first to the defence of Athens, and then to the maintenance of its empire, the more they were able to make their voices heard. Themistocles' development of the navy thus helped to make Athens a true democracy.

A trireme was hugely expensive to maintain; it cost about a talent a year (say, £350,000 in today's terms). Multiplied by two hundred or so, this was not a burden the state could, or chose to endure, and wealthy Athenians were themselves required to pay for the upkeep of one trireme each for a year, the development of the navy again having levelling political repercussions.

A Wall of Wood

Themistocles attracted many apocryphal stories in later antiquity, and even a collection of pseudonymous letters. One such story has a better claim than most to be grounded in truth.

It is certain that, in the face of the imminent Persian invasion, the Delphic oracle consistently counselled despair and surrender. So when the Athenians consulted Delphi about what they should do, they received an unequivocal reply that started: 'Fools, why sit you here? Fly to the ends of the earth ...' But on consulting the oracle a second time, they received a more ambiguous reply which said, among other things, that only a 'wall of wood' would stand intact against the enemy. This provoked considerable debate, with opinions more or less evenly divided between seeing the 'wall of wood' as a reference to a palisade around the Acropolis, so that the god was advising the Athenians to stay in Athens and defend the city, and seeing the 'wall of wood' as a reference to their new navy.

The oracle ended with an equally ambiguous reference to Salamis: 'Blessed Salamis, you will be the death of mothers' sons …' This was regarded as a hint that they should avoid Salamis at all costs, or die there. But Themistocles argued not only that the 'wall of wood' referred to the navy, but that it would be Persians who would die at Salamis, rather than Athenians – otherwise, why call it 'blessed'? Such was his influence in Athens at the time that his view prevailed even over that of the official oracular experts.

The Second Persian Invasion

Still smarting from their defeat by puny Athens at the Battle of Marathon in 490 BC, the Persians had long been planning a second invasion of Greece, a task that Xerxes inherited when he ascended to the Persian throne in 486. When it came, the invasion was massive: modern estimates talk of two hundred thousand land troops and a fleet of over one thousand three hundred warships. The invasion was supported by two extraordinary engineering feats: a double pontoon bridge all the way across the

Hellespont from Abydos to near Sestos (a distance of some 3 miles), and a canal through the neck of the Athos peninsula in northern Greece, to avoid the tricky currents and frequent high winds there. Huge magazines of grain were established on the invasion route in what is now northern Greece, to supply the army as it passed and as it progressed further into the Greek mainland.

Faced with imminent invasion, in 481 BC the Greeks convened a conference in Corinth. It was poorly attended because many Greek states, not unnaturally, preferred to capitulate or to side with the Persians, or to maintain an uneasy neutrality. At the conference, the delegates of thirty-one states – fewer than 5 per cent of those of mainland Greece – agreed to set aside their often long-standing differences, and chose the Spartans, with their military expertise and leadership of a powerful coalition of Peloponnesian states, as the overall commanders of the Greek forces. The following year, they formed two lines of defence: one in the north, directly in the line of the Persian approach, at Thermopylae and Artemisium, and one to fall back on in the south, around the Isthmus to the Peloponnese.

After – or perhaps more or less simultaneously with – the betrayal and glorious defeat of the Spartan king Leonidas and his vastly outnumbered troops at the narrow pass of Thermopylae, it was the turn of the largely

Athenian navy at Artemisium, under the command of Themistocles. Perhaps they could check the inexorable advance south of the Persian forces through Greece. Even though quite a few crack Persian ships were destroyed in a storm, the Greeks were still hugely outnumbered. However, they held their own in an indecisive battle, before falling back south to the island of Salamis, in the Saronic Gulf near Athens.

The Greek army, meanwhile, withdrew to the Isthmus – the neck of land joining mainland Greece and the Peloponnese. There was nothing in the way of the Persian advance, and the Athenian fleet was used, on Themistocles' orders, to evacuate Athens and ferry its inhabitants to safety on Salamis and elsewhere. And the city was indeed soon sacked. The few defenders, those who were too stubborn or too poor to have evacuated, were massacred, and the temples were plundered and burnt to the ground. For many years after the war, the Athenians left the temples as they were, as a reminder of the atrocity – until they replaced them with the magnificent buildings the remains of which can still be seen on the Acropolis and elsewhere.

Many of the Greeks saw their position at Salamis as a dead end, a trap, and regarded the capture of Athens as the end of the war on the mainland. They were now concerned only to retreat to the Peloponnese and make a last stand there. In fact, the Peloponnesians were already in the process of building a defensive wall across the Isthmus near Corinth (close to the site of the modern canal), but this was a futile strategy: even if the wall succeeded in holding up some of the Persian troops, others could be landed beyond it. The Greek fleet could not patrol the whole coastline of the Peloponnese against the seven hundred or so enemy ships that remained after storm and battle losses – and Persia could soon bring up more ships as well.

Themistocles understood that the Greeks had to risk all on a single battle and, with his local knowledge of the waters and the weather, he saw that their position at Salamis could work in their favour, however hopeless it seemed – and maybe he bore the Salamis oracle in mind too.

The Battle of Salamis

The Battle of Salamis in late September 480 bc was the critical battle of the second Persian invasion, involving over two hundred thousand men. After the three-day battles of Thermopylae and Artemisium (where the Greek navy worked together for the first time), the Greek army retreated south to the Isthmus of Corinth, while a revived fleet of 366 ships was beached on the island of Salamis, just west of Athens and about 22 miles from the Isthmus.

The Greek senior command was undecided: the Peloponnesians wanted the fleet to link up with the army for a last-ditch attempt to defend the Peloponnese. Themistocles, however, refused to abandon Athens, or the Athenian refugees on the island of Salamis. When his threat to withdraw the 200-strong Athenian fleet failed to tip the balance, he took matters into his own hands. He sent a secret message to Xerxes, claiming to be pro-Persian (as many Greeks were), and telling him that the Greeks planned to sneak away from the island under cover of darkness.

The Persian king therefore ordered his fleet of some seven hundred warships, recently arrived at Phalerum, to close in on the island by night, and when this was reported to the Greeks, they realized they were trapped. A squadron of two hundred Egyptian ships was detached from the Persian fleet to close off the western exit and four hundred crack infantry troops were quietly landed on Psyttalia (where the next day they were cut off and massacred). The Greeks now listened to Themistocles.

It was critical to Themistocles' plan that the Persians should sail further into the narrows, where their enormous numbers would be a disadvantage, and where the Greeks' heavier ships could not be outmanoeuvred by the enemy vessels. The following morning, then, he arranged for the Greek fleet to launch in seeming disarray, with some ships even breaking off north, as if to make for the Isthmus, satisfying Persian expectations of finding disunity among the Greeks.

The Persians took the bait and sailed into the narrows, with the Greeks backing water with their oars to draw them further in and to keep a tight formation. The tired oarsmen of the Persian ships, which had been maintaining battle stations all night, began to break formation, and the swell that Themistocles had been expecting caused some of the Persian ships to heave and expose their sides. The Greek ships rowed hard into the attack, ramming the Persian triremes or breaking their oars. Many Persian ships chose flight immediately, while the Greeks succeeded in more or less surrounding the remainder. The battle was one-sided: over the course of a long day, the Persians lost over two hundred of their best ships, while the Greeks lost about forty. The victory at Salamis was decisive. Xerxes had set up his throne on a high point on the mainland in order to watch the expected victory. In the wake of the defeat, however, he returned with the bulk of his fleet to Asia Minor, to forestall opportunistic rebellions in other parts of the empire, to secure his line of retreat, and to guarantee provisions for the bulk of the land army, which wintered in northern Greece in order to continue the campaign the following year. Coincidentally, on the same day in 479, Greek forces annihilated the Persians on the mainland at Plataea and on the coast of Asia Minor at Mycale. Many of the Asiatic Greek cities rose up in revolt against their Persian rulers. The Persians withdrew, to recuperate and prepare for the future.

Themistocles after the war

Athens' prominent role in the two Persian invasions made it the equal of Sparta in authority, and it was not slow to grasp the opportunity afforded it by Themistocles. Sparta and Athens promised jointly to continue to keep the Persians at bay, but since this was largely a naval enterprise, the defence of Greece soon devolved on to Athens alone. A league was formed, the members of which contributed ships or, far more usually, money, which was used to help develop and maintain the Athenian fleet.

Themistocles had always seen that Athens would increase in power as a result of its naval expertise, and that this would eventually lead to tension and warfare with Sparta. He therefore pushed for a new defensive wall to be built around the city, and for Piraeus to be fortified. The new wall determined the size of the city of Athens for centuries to come, at about 1½ square miles, but its erection met with strong disapproval from the Spartans, who had become used to regarding themselves as the main power in Greece and wanted to curb upstart Athens. Themistocles arranged that he himself would be sent as ambassador to Sparta to discuss the matter, but delayed his departure for Sparta for a long time, and once there, delayed matters still further, until Athens' new wall was a *fait accompli*.

Themistocles' anti-Spartan stance brought him into conflict with Cimon, the son of Miltiades, who saw the future of Athens lying in cooperation with Sparta. Cimon used his enormous wealth and prestige to gain massive support, and when it came to an ostracism vote between the two men, probably in 470 BC, it was Themistocles who was banished for ten years. It is also likely that Themistocles, newly enriched by the war, was displaying rather too much arrogance: he was, for instance, playing the old aristocratic game of embellishing the city with temples and other buildings designed to aggrandize himself and his achievements.

Ostracism involved exile, but no loss of rights back in Athens, so that an ostracized man could, for instance, still hold property and do business through proxies in the city. However, while Themistocles was in exile in the Peloponnesian town of Argos, he was accused by the Spartans of collaborating with the Persians. We do not know what episode or episodes the Spartans were alluding to, unless they were referring to Themistocles' somewhat underhand dealings with Xerxes at Salamis (see above). At any rate, this charge of treachery made him a criminal exile, not a political one, and he was hounded from place to place until he fetched up – no doubt to his enemies' delight – at the court of the Persian king in Susa.

The new king, Artaxerxes I, received him kindly, and gave him the income from three towns of Asia Minor as a stipend. In return, in due course of time, he demanded Themistocles' help in the ongoing war against Cimon, who was proving himself a very competent general and was laying the foundations of the Athenian empire. In 459 BC, finding himself unable to betray his native city, Themistocles, surely the most brilliant and original leader ever known to Athens, committed suicide.

THUCYDIDES

c. 455–c. 398 BC

ANDREW ROBERTS

THE INCLUSION OF THUCYDIDES IN A BOOK entitled Great Commanders *might seem somewhat quixotic, for Thucydides was a general who failed so comprehensively in battle that he was sent into permanent exile as a punishment. Yet his right to be included stems from his philosophy of warfare, for no thinker before or since has so perceptively enunciated the great truths about what happens to human beings when they come into military conflict. Although those truths are timeless, if we are to understand how Thucydides arrived at them we need to know something of the man himself.*

Because Thucydides spent nearly half his life in exile, and his sole literary work was unfinished at the time of his death, his contemporaries did not write about him, and it

126

was not until the early years of the Roman Empire, half a millennium after his death, that his fame was really established.

From occasional references in his own writing we can surmise that he was probably over 30 years of age when he was elected a *strategos*, one of Athens' ten generals, for the year 424. That locates his birth somewhere in the mid-450s, and makes him a contemporary of some of the greatest Greeks of the ancient world, including Socrates, Phidias, Sophocles, Euripides and Aristophanes. He admired Pericles and knew Alcibiades. The Parthenon was built during his lifetime.

We know that Thucydides' father was called Oloros and that he was distantly descended from the ancient kings of Thrace, where his family still owned gold mines and had some political influence. He himself was an Athenian citizen, however, hailing from one of the 139 *medes* (constituent villages) called Halimous, which was to be found 4 miles from the city on the coast (near to today's Athens airport). From his background and the occasional political references in his work, we can assume that Thucydides was an aristocrat with marked oligarchical tendencies.

Apart from being of a sufficient age to attend the Athenian assembly at the outbreak of the Peloponnesian War in 431 BC, and possibly catching the plague of the late 420s – his description of the symptoms is thought too detailed to be anything other than first-hand – little can be even guessed about Thucydides until his election by the *demos* (the enfranchised) as a *strategos*. Sent to relieve the city of Amphipolis in the northern Aegean, he was outmanoeuvred by the great Spartan commander Brasidas, and subsequently condemned to exile by the Athenians, a sentence that he most probably served in Thrace until his death some time in the early 390s. We can picture him living in comfortable exile among the olive groves there, a disappointed ex-general thinking himself ill-used by the *demos*, and writing what is today the greatest historical work ever penned, *The History of the Peloponnesian War*.

The History of the Peloponnesian War

Thucydides tells us he began his *History* as soon as the Peloponnesian War broke out in 431 BC, rightly 'expecting that it would be a great war'. He went about it in a thoroughly professional manner, interviewing survivors, collecting the texts of important documents, noting down speeches and adopting an accurate chronology of campaigning season by season. The historian Dr G. B. Grundy was convinced that Thucydides also visited Syracuse and walked the battlefields of the Sicilian campaign very shortly after the Athenian defeat there in

413. As Thucydides himself put it, he trusted in 'laborious investigation' rather than mere memory.

Where Herodotus would use absurd exaggeration to make his points – such as claiming that 5,283,320 Persians invaded Greece – Thucydides generally produced believable figures for amounts of tribute and numbers of ships and men. Herodotus' history of the Ionian Revolt, rather like Homer's history of the Trojan War, was more about literature and morality than objective history, while Thucydides' (by him untitled) *History of the Peloponnesian War* tried hard to relate, in Ranke's phrase, *'wie es eigentlich gewesen ist'* ('how it actually was'). Of the verbatim speeches that pepper his work, Thucydides wrote that he attempted to get 'as close as possible to the general gist of what was actually said'.

What also sets Thucydides apart from other ancient Greek writers – especially Homer and Herodotus – is his very modern attitude to human motivation. He excised the traditional supernatural explanations entirely; gone are the stories of gods, dreams, omens and curses. Instead the actions of the Athenians, Spartans and their respective allies are presented as having been actuated by fear, greed, ignorance, opportunism, stupidity, the desire for honour, the lust for glory, the defence of markets, occasionally by idealism, and all the real motives for which men have gone to war throughout the centuries.

This is one of the only accounts of warfare in the ancient world – Xenophon and Julius Caesar being the other two – written by a professional soldier, and although he rarely comments on the pity of war (beyond writing in Book III of the 120 youths lost in a disastrous Aetolian mission as 'the finest men whom Athens lost in the whole war'), the work can and should be read as a tragedy.

What is certainly tragic is that the great work breaks off suddenly in Book VIII while covering the events of 411 BC, despite the fact that in earlier parts of the same volume there are mentions of Athens' final catastrophic defeat in 404. He could not possibly have wanted to finish his great work with the phrase: 'As soon as Tissaphernes arrived at Ephesus he sacrificed to Artemis,' but if there were further books after the eighth, they have not survived.

The Moral of the Work

Thucydides has much of value to say about politics, especially the limits of democracy; about the horrors of *stasis* (civil war), especially in Corcyra in Book III; and about the morally corrosive effect of war, which diverts human progress down vicious channels towards a kind of utter hellishness where new methods of exacting retribution are constantly discovered. Although Might and Right occasionally overlap, he teaches, they are entirely separate from one another.

In Book III, Thucydides makes plain the moral of his great work, which is that:

> In peace and prosperity states and individuals have better sentiments, because they do not find themselves confronted suddenly with imperious necessities; but war takes away the easy supply of daily wants, and so proves a violent teacher that brings most men's characters down to a level with their fortunes.

Such a phenomenon has been found again and again throughout history. War has stripped away the humanity from humans, reducing mankind to what King Lear calls 'unaccommodated man … no more but such a poor, bare, fork'd animal'. The scenes of brutality witnessed during such struggles as the Thirty Years War, the Retreat from Moscow and Operation Barbarossa bear testament to Thucydides' iron law of war, which he believed would remain true 'as long as human nature stays the same'.

Lord Macaulay believed that the seventh book of Thucydides' *History*, covering the hubris and nemesis of the Sicilian expedition, represented the highest achievement of human art. Thomas Hobbes wrote that the whole work provided 'profitable instructions for Noble men and such as may come to have the managings of great and weighty actions'. Writing in the darkest days of the Second World War, in 1942, the great Harvard classicist John H. Finley equated the Athens–Sparta struggle with that of the Allies versus the Axis. In the context of 'a world in which armed nationalism is at its height', he wrote that each generation must study afresh the great authors of the past, 'because each will find in them certain qualities that its predecessors overlooked or failed to emphasize, and the statement has a special force in regard to Thucydides'.

The Melian Dialogue

Thucydides invented the concept of realpolitik, which came to its apogee in his notorious Melian Dialogue of 416 BC, in which his theme was the essential amorality of relations between states. It is, of course, impossible at this distance of time to gauge the exact extent to which the speeches quoted as verbatim by Thucydides actually represent his own views or those of the speakers, despite his protestation of objective accuracy, but the speeches of the Athenians and Melians have a tautness, eloquence and literary quality that are remarkable even for that period of fine rhetoric.

Athens' great maritime power meant that in the

summer of 416 BC, the weaker Aegean island of Melos lay at her mercy. Before she attacked, however, her generals sent envoys to state the case for the island to become a tributary vassal state of the Athenian empire. Refused permission to address the popular assembly, the Athenians presented their case to the magistrates and oligarchs, expressed in uncompromising form in Book V of Thucydides' work:

> The strong do what they can and the weak follow. We will show you that we are here for the benefit of our empire and what we are going to say now will be aimed at preserving your city. We wish to rule over you without trouble and we want you to be spared to our joint advantage.

In answer, the Melians offered benign neutrality, to which the Athenians replied with contempt: 'Your hostility does not harm us. Your friendship would be a sign to our subjects of weakness; your hatred is a sign of our strength.' When the Melians answered that their destruction would send a dangerous message to Athens' other subject peoples, their interlocutors argued that in fact the opposite was the case, because Athenian imperialism rested on the terror of the subject peoples rather than their love. Melian protestations that the gods would not allow the destruction of the righteous brought forth this cynical rejoinder: 'We think that the gods apparently and men demonstrably carry their rule as far as their power extends by a necessary law of nature. We did not make this law, nor are we the first to use it.'

After the Melians rejected Athens' demands, and decided to fight for their independence, Thucydides baldly recorded how 'The Athenians killed all the adult Melian men that they captured; the women and children they enslaved. Then they occupied the island themselves, subsequently sending five hundred settlers.' Such was the tyrannical reality of Athenian imperialism; nor was Melos the only place where the entire male population of a city was put to the sword.

The Sicilian Expedition

Retribution for Athens' cruelty on Melos, Scione and elsewhere, came in the shape of the Sicilian expedition, the story of which is told in Books VI and VII. It forms by far the longest campaign sequence in Thucydides' work and there is some internal evidence to suggest it was originally written as an entirely separate book. Earlier in the work, Thucydides had described an unsuccessful Athenian expedition against Sicily in 427 BC under Laches, but eleven years later:

the Athenians resolved to sail against Sicily with larger forces than those which Laches and Eurymedon had commanded and, if possible, to conquer it. They were for the most part ignorant of the size of the island and of the numbers of its inhabitants, both Hellenic and native, and they did not realize they were taking on a war of almost the same magnitude as their war against the Peloponnesians.

These failures of intelligence Thucydides put down to 'the people' of Athens, rather than to Nicias, the rich commander of the expedition, who had originally argued against it in the assembly. Was this, as some historians have assumed, a case of class comradeship between fellow millionaires, or might the expedition really have been undertaken by an over-excited *demos* in a spirit of wild overconfidence? Certainly its main advocate was one of the most mercurial, vain, charismatic, reckless but undeniably brilliant men in classical Greek history, Alcibiades the Younger, whom Thucydides is thought to have known personally. The Athenians were ostensibly sailing to help their Sicilian allies, the Egestians, stay free of the hegemonizing influence of the town of Syracuse. But as Thucydides clearly alleges, what they really wanted was to bring the whole island under their imperium. They appointed Nicias, Alcibiades and the elderly but adventurous Lamachus as the three commanders of the expedition, notwithstanding Nicias' avowed opposition to the scheme.

Once appointed against his will, Nicias then argued that the whole expedition ought to be a massive effort of 100 triremes and 5,000 hoplites (infantrymen). He hoped to dull its appeal to the assembly, but his proposal met with general acclaim and thus had exactly the opposite result. As Thucydides recorded, 'whoever was opposed kept quiet, lest by voting in the negative he appear unpatriotic'. As a result, the largest fleet and army ever raised by Athens – eventually comprising 134 triremes and 5,100 hoplites, including contingents of allies and mercenaries – set sail in the summer of 415 BC in three squadrons, each under a *strategos*.

On arriving in Sicily, the Athenians discovered that they had been tricked by the Egestians, who were not in fact able to pay for the expedition as they had promised. The three generals then disagreed amongst themselves over the next course of action: Nicias wanted to attack the Egestians' enemy in the city of Silenus and then return to Athens; Alcibiades wanted to raise a Sicilian army against Syracuse; while Lamachus wanted an immediate attack on Syracuse.

After initially following Alcibiades' plan, which largely failed, the Athenians set up camp at Catana, midway between Naxos and Syracuse. Desultory skirmishing ashore resulted in the Syracusan cavalry drawing first blood when they attacked some Athenian light infantry. In the winter of 415 BC, the Athenians made a bold attack on Syracuse. Having lured the Syracusan army away to attack Catana, the Athenians entered the Grand Harbour of Syracuse in a dawn assault, and occupied a strongpoint opposite the temple of Olympian Zeus. When the Syracusans returned, a set-piece battle ensued, in which the Athenians lost fifty men to the enemy's two hundred. The victory could not be pressed home because for some unaccountable reason the Athenians had brought no cavalry to Sicily, whereas the Syracusans had plenty. The next day, Nicias returned to Catana to sit out the winter, requesting that cavalry be urgently sent from Athens. The Syracusans meanwhile built an extra wall around their city and protected the entrance to the Grand Harbour with sharpened stakes under the water.

The following spring (414 BC) saw the Athenians unsuccessfully attacking the Syracusan fort of Megara, capturing and burning Centoripa in central Sicily, and receiving 250 cavalrymen from Athens, who absurdly enough arrived without their horses. Nicias' surprise attack on Syracuse the next morning resulted in the Athenians once more taking an advantageous strategic position, albeit at the cost of Lamachus, who was killed in battle. Nicias then settled down to besiege a seemingly doomed city.

In exile in Sparta, Alcibiades unveiled to his hosts the Athenian plans to conquer Sicily, Carthage and Italy, before they returned in force to lay waste to the Peloponnese. To forestall such a disaster, Sparta dispatched her talented admiral Gylippus with a small force to try to relieve Syracuse.

Once Gylippus landed at Himera on the north coast of Sicily, he was joined by the forces of various anti-Athenian cities, in total over one thousand seven hundred men. In a lightning attack, he arrived at Syracuse just as the inhabitants were considering suing for peace, and caught the Athenians so much by surprise that he was able to enter the city unscathed. Under the cover of skirmishing over the next few weeks, Gylippus was able to build enfilading walls that prevented the Athenians from investing the city, thereby effectively raising the siege. Cut off from a regular water supply on the headlands outside the city, the situation for Nicias started to look bleak, as he explained to the Athenian assembly in a dispatch in the winter of 414 BC, pointing out that he was no longer the besieger but the besieged, and begging for reinforcements.

Whereas Gylippus was an enterprising and

resourceful commander, Nicias was a cautious and nerve-wracked one, whose heart had never been in the campaign from the start. As the Spartans seemed to win the upper hand, neutrals started to support them rather than the Athenians. Even when the Athenians voted to send out another large expeditionary force under the daring general Demosthenes, they could not turn the tide. Attacks by siege engines on the enfilading wall outside Syracuse were forced back, with the engines being set on fire by the Spartan and Syracusan-allied Sicilian defenders. Even when Demosthenes managed to start pulling the wall down after a flanking movement during a daring night attack, the Athenians were finally dispersed with heavy losses.

Sickness in the low-level marshy Athenian camp outside the city walls led to demoralization, even though in sheer numbers of ships they still had clear superiority. In defiance of Demosthenes' advice to withdraw to Catana or Thapsus, Nicias resolved to continue the half-siege of Syracuse. When finally he changed his mind and ordered an embarkation, there was an eclipse of the moon, which convinced the troops that it was ill-omened. The humanist Thucydides despised such superstition, but accurately recorded its dire result for the Athenian expeditionary force.

After a disastrous naval defeat, the Athenians

attempted to escape to Catana, harried by their enemies on both flanks and the rear. Demosthenes' force was cut off, nearly destroyed and then forced to surrender. Nicias surrendered to Gylippus the next day as his troops, maddened by thirst, drank from the River Assinarus even though it was flowing thick with the blood of their comrades killed upstream.

A very few Athenians managed to escape to Catana and safety, but Thucydides' gripping account shows how the vast majority of both expeditionary forces were killed in action, executed (including Nicias and Demosthenes), enslaved or died of exposure in prison-caves. The power of Athens was broken for ever, and with it the power of Greece.

ALCIBIADES

c. 452–404 bc

ROBIN WATERFIELD

ALTHOUGH ALCIBIADES OF ATHENS was a skilled battle-field commander who lost very few of the many engagements in which he was involved, he shone especially before and after battles – at diplomacy, negotiation and fund-raising for his troops. These aspects of warfare, often overlooked by historians, enabled him to keep Athens' hopes alive for a number of years in the Peloponnesian War, even when the situation seemed altogether hopeless.

Too much is made of Alcibiades' alleged treachery; it is more plausible to see him as more or less loyal to his native city – or at any rate to a version of it in which he himself could hold power. With or without him, Athens was destined to lose the Peloponnesian War (431–404 BC), but without him Athenian history in the last quarter of the fifth century BC would have been considerably less colourful.

Alcibiades was always destined for greatness. He was born no later than 452 BC into one of the wealthiest and most powerful families of classical Athens, and after his father's early death was adopted by no less a person than Pericles, who for over twenty years was the leading politician of the city. With this background, Alcibiades could well have stepped into his guardian's shoes, but his scandalous playboy lifestyle – involving heavy drinking, multiple affairs with members of either sex, and near-sacrilege – was a constant hindrance to his evident ambition.

Entry into Public Life

Alcibiades came of age in the early years of the Peloponnesian War between Athens and Sparta. Even as a child he had shown his ambition and arrogance, and since warfare was all he knew, it was warfare that he chose to be the field in which he would rise to greatness. He served in a couple of battles in the early years of the war, but his first major coup was to stir up conflict at a time of temporary peace. In 421 BC, Athens and Sparta negotiated a truce after ten years of open warfare and half a century of cold war. This irritated Alcibiades and the other Athenian hawks. For fifty years Athens had held a maritime empire, which had enriched the city hugely and had made it the most powerful state in Greece, at least the equal of Sparta with its network of alliances and supremacy at land battle. Alcibiades wanted to see the empire not just maintained, but expanded, both for the continued enrichment of his native city and to give himself a greater field of endeavour.

The peace between Sparta and Athens was fragile, since neither side was in a position to fulfil its promises. Alcibiades' opportunity came in 420 BC, at a summit meeting in Athens consisting of the Athenian authorities and delegates from both Sparta and a few of its Peloponnesian neighbours, who were undecided whether to enter into an alliance with Sparta or with Athens. Alcibiades put his rhetorical skills to work and so thoroughly discredited the Spartan representatives that Athens immediately entered into an alliance with Argos and the other Peloponnesian states.

With such a threat on its doorstep, Sparta was bound to try by military means to recover Argos and the other dissident Peloponnesian states. While Sparta hastened to reassure and retain its existing friends, Alcibiades, who had been chosen as one of Athens' ten generals (a post subject to annual re-election in democratic Athens), spent much of 419 BC touring the Peloponnese, strengthening the Athenian–Argive alliance and persuading others to join it. His immediate goal was to try to force Corinth, Sparta's most powerful ally, to withdraw from the Peloponnesian alliance. He strengthened the Athenians' position at the western mouth of the Gulf of Corinth, and tried to persuade Argos to threaten Corinth by land also, although sabre-rattling by Sparta on Argos' borders dissuaded that venture.

Having achieved relatively little, Alcibiades was not re-elected as a general for 418 BC, and when it came to a battle between the two sides, he was present only in an ambassadorial role, to strengthen the allies' resolve. At the Battle of Mantinea, Sparta crushed a combined force of Athenians, Argives and others; the Athenian alliance collapsed and all the dissident Peloponnesian states promptly went over to Sparta. Although Alcibiades' Peloponnesian policy had failed, he was able to boast that he had brought the Spartans to the brink of defeat, and had forced them to risk all on a single battle; and that he had done this without seriously endangering Athens, since the battle had taken place far from the city.

The Sicilian Expedition

Even though Athenian and Spartan forces had clashed at Mantinea, both sides tacitly agreed to overlook this and to try to preserve the tattered peace treaty. Alcibiades had other plans. Having fought off his political enemies, and not least because of his actions in the Peloponnese, by 416 BC he had emerged as leader of the Athenian hawks. He also excelled gloriously at the Olympic Games of 416, when he achieved the unparalleled feat of entering seven teams for the prestigious four-horse chariot event and coming first, second and fourth. He was at the height of his influence in Athens.

The Athenian empire consisted largely of Aegean states, but many Athenians had long entertained hopes of expanding westward, into the Greek cities of Sicily and southern Italy. Apart from anything else, grain was plentiful there and Athens constantly suffered from a shortage. The pretext came in the winter of 416–415 BC, when a number of small Sicilian cities appealed for Athenian help against Syracuse, which wanted to establish hegemony over the entire island.

The debate in the Assembly was personal and furious, but in the end Alcibiades prevailed, and was chosen, along with two of his fellow generals, Nicias and Lamachus, to command the expedition. The size of the armada showed that Athens wanted not just to curb Syracuse, but to establish a powerful presence on the island. Though Syracuse was a Spartan ally, the Athenians were well aware of Spartan reluctance to campaign abroad, and they had no reason to doubt that they would be successful.

However, just a few weeks before the expedition sailed, a terrible omen rocked the city. On a single night, a great many of the herms of the city – squared blocks of stone personalized only by a bearded head of Hermes and an erect phallus – were defaced. This was sacrilege of the highest order, and smacked of a conspiracy of some kind, even if its purpose was a complete mystery. Was it a drunken prank or politically motivated? The subsequent inquiry rapidly became a witch-hunt as fears spiralled out of control. In the course of the investigation it was revealed that this was not the only sacrilege that had taken place in the city: on a number of occasions, aristocratic men had mocked the Eleusinian Mysteries, one of the most sacred and secret rites, by performing some of the rituals out of context and before an uninitiated audience.

Alcibiades was certainly implicated in the latter sacrilege, but the terrified Athenians so compounded the two scandals that it was commonly supposed that he and his circle had also been involved in the mutilation of the herms; Alcibiades' ambition was well known, and it was assumed that he was intending to replace democracy with a narrow oligarchy or even with tyranny. The armada therefore set off with this dark cloud hanging over it.

The expedition's first purpose was to win over as many

of the southern Italian and Sicilian states as possible, and with the help of Alcibiades' negotiating skills the Athenians began to achieve moderate success. But then an official ship arrived from Athens with orders to relieve Alcibiades of his command and to bring him home to stand trial. Alcibiades jumped ship, however, and made his way to Sparta, where he took up residence in the enemy heartland. Meanwhile, back in his native city, the Athenians cursed him, condemned him to death in absentia, and confiscated all his property.

In Sparta and Sardis

To his credit, Alcibiades did little to harm his native city during his stay in Sparta. He advised the Spartans to help the Syracusans, but in the event they sent only a small force. The Athenian defeat there was due to Athenian incompetence, not to Alcibiades' advice. He also recommended that the Spartans establish a permanent fortification close to Athens, rather than employing their old tactic of invading once a year for a few weeks, so as to threaten agriculture and generally make life difficult for the Athenians, who were no match for the Spartans on land. The Spartans duly fortified Decelea, but this was a tactic they had been contemplating for a while, so again Alcibiades' contribution as a traitor was slight.

Alcibiades spent two years in Sparta. This was a quiet period for him, but he then fell out with one of the two Spartan kings (whose wife he was rumoured to have seduced) and found it prudent to move on. He chose to go to the court of Tissaphernes, the Persian king's satrap in central Asia Minor. Persia had long been hovering on the margins of the war. The Persians claimed the Greek cities of Asia Minor as their vassal states, and had lobbied for their return ever since losing them sixty-five years earlier. They were poised to enter the war, and were prepared to finance whichever side took their fancy. Sparta desperately needed their help, because without them they could not afford to build and maintain the navy they needed to combat the Athenians at sea. The Athenians needed them because by 413 BC they had lost an entire fleet and thousands of men in Sicily. Moreover, in the wake of this disaster, some of their most important subject states seceded from their empire and deprived them of income.

In the early part of his sojourn in Asia Minor, Alcibiades helped Tissaphernes and his more northerly colleague Pharnabazus in their efforts to spread the coastal Greek cities' rebellion against Athenian domination. This enabled him to ingratiate himself with the Persian satraps at the same time as blunting the Spartan king's hostility towards him. But the Athenians were surprisingly quick at rebuilding a fleet, and once they had made the island of Samos their base of operations in the Aegean, they managed to staunch the potentially lethal haemorrhage of rebel states.

At this point, once again, Alcibiades helped his native city. The Persians had to decide which side to support, and Sparta was the natural choice, not just because Athens had been crippled by the Sicilian disaster, but also because Athens had been at the forefront of resistance to Persia since the start of the fifth century. Alcibiades, however, persuaded Tissaphernes to offer tepid support to both sides, arguing that he should play them off against each other and come down firmly on one side or the other only when it was clear where the advantage lay.

Tissaphernes followed Alcibiades' advice, and Athenian hopes began to rise a little. Alcibiades took advantage of this to enter into secret negotiations with the Athenian commanders on Samos. He convinced them that he could bring the Persians into the war on the Athenian side, but only if he was restored to power in Athens. Since this was impossible under the current regime, which had cursed him and condemned him to death, a regime change was the first prerequisite.

There was plenty of disaffection amongst the aristocrats of Athens against the democracy, but it was far from universal, whether on Samos or in Athens itself.

Nevertheless, the oligarchs on Samos stirred up matters in Athens until there was a coup, and in 411 BC the democracy was replaced by an oligarchy known as the Four Hundred. The single most important reason for the success of this coup was the prospect of the war's ending as quickly as possible with the Persian help that Alcibiades had promised. What most people did not know, however, was that Alcibiades was unable to do this: he had promised the Persians not only that they would regain their long-lost coastal territories but also that they would have the right to patrol the Asia Minor coast with their Phoenician fleet. While the Athenian oligarchs were prepared to go along with the first provision, they flatly refused to countenance the second.

Restoration, Second Fall, and Death

A desire to end the war quickly was not, however, the Athenian oligarchs' main reason for establishing the Four Hundred; they were simply committed oligarchs. But the troops on Samos remained democratic, and their leaders were also committed to ending the war as quickly as possible. Ironically, it was they who recalled Alcibiades from exile, since they too were convinced by his promise of Persian aid. The Athenian fleet wanted to sail to Athens and restore the democracy, but Alcibiades persuaded them not to: he knew that would leave the eastern Aegean undefended against the Spartans, and he also dreaded civil war.

Alcibiades abandoned the oligarchs, however, and said that he would negotiate only with a more moderate regime in Athens. Such was Athenian faith in Alcibiades' powers as a war-leader that this was one of the main levers that caused the downfall of the Four Hundred in Athens. Alcibiades was again Athens' darling, but he chose not to return home immediately. Although he held no official position, he was the effective leader of some of the Athenian forces in the Aegean, and he used them to good advantage.

By the end of 411 BC, the Spartans were dominant in the Aegean and, even more importantly, in the Hellespont. They had proved capable of absorbing any minor defeats the Athenians could inflict on them, and their control of the Hellespont meant near-starvation for the Athenians at home: in the classical period, Athens was never self-sufficient in grain and other produce, which was imported from the fertile Black Sea region. Spartan dominance also encouraged discontented members of the Athenian empire to secede, and every such secession was a further blow to the Athenian war effort, since they were losing much-needed revenue.

But in 410 BC, Alcibiades was instrumental in destroying the Spartan fleet at the Battle of Cyzicus. Cyzicus was a critical Athenian possession in the Propontis, with strategic harbours facing both east and west. When it fell early in 410 BC to a combined sea and land attack by the Spartan general Mindarus and the Persian satrap Pharnabazus, the Athenians knew that they had to recover it, or Athens would soon be desperately short of grain. But they had only forty ships in the region, so they sent urgently for their most experienced generals and reinforcements from the Aegean. Within a week or so, the Athenians had eighty-six ships, to match the Spartans' eighty.

The Athenians sailed towards Cyzicus under cover of darkness, so that Mindarus would not know their true numbers, and moored off the island of Proconnesus. Alcibiades kept all the local fishermen on land, again because secrecy was critical to his plan. In the morning they set out for Cyzicus in driving rain, and divided their forces into four parts: Alcibiades, Theramenes and Thrasybulus remained at sea, while Chaereas was put in charge of a land force.

Alcibiades sailed towards the western harbour of Cyzicus with forty ships, and Mindarus, assuming that this was the entire Athenian Hellespontine fleet, took the bait and sailed out in full force. Alcibiades feigned retreat and drew the Spartan fleet towards the Artace headland, behind the heights of which was hiding the rest of the Athenian fleet. At the appropriate moment, Alcibiades had his ships wheel around, while Theramenes and Thrasybulus pounced from behind the promontory. Mindarus had enough time to avoid being trapped, but not to make it back to the safety of Cyzicus harbour. Instead, he headed for land at Cleri, where Pharnabazus had his army.

Alcibiades pursued Mindarus and destroyed some of his ships. Hand-to-hand fighting began on the shore, with the Athenians hampered by fighting in the water against men on dry land. Thrasybulus therefore came up to support Alcibiades, while Theramenes landed further west and joined forces with Chaereas. This land army arrived just in time to save Alcibiades' and Thrasybulus' troops from defeat, and after a hard battle Pharnabazus ordered his men to retreat. Not long afterwards, Mindarus himself was killed, and the dispirited Spartans abandoned their ships and fled. The remaining Spartans just had time to send a typically laconic message back home before abandoning Cyzicus: 'Ships lost. Mindarus dead. Men starving. No idea what to do.'

Over the next three years Alcibiades led or took part in a number of engagements that enabled the Athenians to regain control of the Hellespont. This was a complete turnaround: even after the Sicilian catastrophe, and despite political opposition at home, Alcibiades enabled Athens to recover for three whole years, and even to hope once more for ultimate victory – so much so that they rejected a Spartan offer of peace after Cyzicus.

Buoyed by his successes, in 407 BC Alcibiades returned in splendid style to Athens, where he was welcomed with adoration as the saviour of the city. All the charges against him were dropped, the curses were revoked, and his property was restored to him. Naturally, he was elected general and he soon returned to Samos to prosecute the war against the Spartans and to bring rebel states back into the Athenian fold. But by now Alcibiades had met his match in the new Spartan commander Lysander, who was not only a brilliant strategist and tactician, but had also endeared himself to Cyrus, the Persian king's son, who had been sent west from Persia to see to Athens' downfall. Lysander took advantage of Alcibiades' absence on a fund-raising campaign to defeat his lieutenant at the Battle of Notium, and Alcibiades was powerless to retaliate. His ineffectiveness made it possible for his enemies in Athens to arouse hostility against him, and in 406, only a few months after his restoration, he was once again banished.

This time he retired to private estates in the Thracian Chersonese. He played no further part in the war except, in a probably apocryphal story, to offer advice to the Athenian generals before the final battle of the war at Aegospotami, not far from his estates. The advice was ignored, the battle was lost, the empire crumbled, and in 404 Athens was rapidly starved into submission. Only a few weeks later, under circumstances that must remain for ever obscure, Alcibiades was murdered in Phrygia.

XENOPHON

c. 430–c. 354 BC

ROBIN WATERFIELD

XENOPHON OF ATHENS was a prolific writer who is best known, in military terms, as one of the leaders of the so-called 'Ten Thousand' Greek mercenaries who journeyed east on an ill-fated expedition to topple the Persian king and replace him with his brother. He himself wrote the only surviving account of the expedition, which is the world's first eyewitness campaign narrative. Although his military career was short, after retiring he continued to reflect upon his experiences as a commander and this led him to develop a theory of leadership, which features in his account of the expedition, with portraits of himself and other generals at work. These ideas also crop up in other works. His importance, then, is not just as a practitioner, but also as a theorist.

The famous expedition lasted two years (401–399 BC), and then Xenophon chose to stay on for a few years as a mercenary commander, with the remnants of the Ten Thousand, fighting for the Spartans first against the Persians in Asia Minor, and subsequently, more briefly, on mainland Greece fighting for the Spartans against other Greek states, including his native Athens. But by then he had been formally exiled from Athens, for his anti-democratic and pro-Spartan tendencies.

Xenophon was born into a well-to-do Athenian family, and was rich enough to serve in the Athenian cavalry. He probably helped the Thirty Tyrants police Athens during their brutal but shortlived regime (404–403 BC), and it was during this time that he got to know the philosopher Socrates. The restoration of the democracy in 403 BC, with which he was not in sympathy, helped to trigger his decision to travel east with Cyrus, the younger brother of the Persian king Artaxerxes II. His time as a mercenary ended in 394 or 393 BC, and after that he lived as a gentleman farmer on an estate in Scillus, in the western Peloponnese, under Spartan protection. Most of his books, which range from history to technical treatises on matters such as hunting, estate-management and cavalry command, were written during his twenty or so years at Scillus. At some point the Athenians repealed his banishment, but he chose not to return to Athens and ended his days in Corinth.

The Anabasis

Intermittently, Cyrus had held a command in the Persian territories of Asia Minor, but he wanted more. When he decided to try to take the Persian throne from his brother, he began to recruit Greek soldiers, because they were the best in the known world – the best-equipped and, thanks to the Peloponnesian War (431–404), the most experienced. By the time his plans came to fruition in 401, he had about ten thousand six hundred Greek hoplites (heavily armed infantry), and about two thousand three hundred peltasts (light infantry) from the margins of the Greek world. He also had at least the same number again of native troops, under the joint command of himself and his uncle Ariaeus.

The journey east (the *anabasis*, 'the march up country') was not too arduous, but it was the longest such march undertaken before Alexander the Great. They marched some 1,700 miles, at a fairly leisurely pace, and met Artaxerxes in battle near a village called Cunaxa, somewhere in the desert west of modern Baghdad.

Artaxerxes commanded an army of forty-five thousand. Most of the king's men were foot soldiers, from all over the empire, and the dreaded Persian archers, but there were also hundreds of cavalrymen and dozens of scythed war chariots. Cyrus' men, perhaps thirty thousand in all, largely recruited from Asia Minor, were outnumbered. But Cyrus was not unduly worried about this, because he had Greeks on his side. Cyrus' battle formation disposed the Greeks on the right wing, himself in command of the centre, and his trusted Persian second in command Ariaeus on the left.

When the enemy were about half a mile away, the Greeks advanced. They started at a walk, but the phalanx began to bulge, and those who were being left behind picked up speed to catch up with the others. Soon they were all running forward. But before they reached the Persian lines, the Persian left wing, under the command of Tissaphernes, turned and fled. It was a feint! Tissaphernes had his men draw the Greeks further from the battlefield than they should have gone. They were supposed to circle back and outflank Artaxerxes' centre.

With the Greeks off the immediate battlefield, Artaxerxes' cavalry galloped forward, followed by the infantry, in an attempt to encircle Cyrus' right flank, now exposed by the forward movement of the Greeks. Cyrus had to act quickly to come up with a significant counter-threat. He spotted the Persian royal standard with its spread eagle, and led his elite horsemen in a reckless, headlong gallop straight for his brother. They broke through Artaxerxes' cavalry, but at the cost of

Cyrus' death, which meant that the battle was lost, whatever else happened.

Meanwhile Cyrus' left wing, commanded by Ariaeus, also fared badly. Their attention was divided, since they were constantly in danger of being outflanked by the longer Persian line. At first they resisted as best they could, but the news of Cyrus' death broke their spirits and they fled all the way back to the staging-post where they had spent the previous night. A desperate fight took place among the baggage carts of the Greeks, where their plucky camp followers seized whatever weapons came to hand and fought off the marauding Persians.

The Battle of Cunaxa was lost, which left the Greeks in a desperate situation. They had no paymaster and were deep in hostile territory. They offered themselves for employment by Artaxerxes, but were rejected. Having decided not to surrender, they had no choice but to try to get back home, but they could not return by the route they had taken, since they had exhausted the supplies there. They had to head more or less directly north, aiming to strike the south coast of the Black Sea, then head west for familiar Greek territory around Byzantium.

Up to the mountains of northern Iraq and southeastern Turkey they were shadowed by Tissaphernes, who was on his way to take up Cyrus' former post in Asia Minor. There were occasional skirmishes, but no pitched battles, because Tissaphernes had other plans. First he suborned Ariaeus, and so deprived the Greeks of their allies; then he convinced Clearchus, the Spartan general who had the most authority among the Greek commanders, of his good intentions, and tricked most of the senior officers into a conference with him, at which they were arrested; they were taken to Babylon and killed. If Tissaphernes had hoped that this alone would be sufficient to make the army vulnerable, he had reckoned without Xenophon, who persuaded the Greeks to choose new generals, including himself, and continue north. Tissaphernes was now content to let the winter climate and the hostile tribes of the mountains finish the Greeks off, and he turned west for Asia Minor.

The Greeks had to make their way through some of the most rugged, mountainous terrain in the world, in winter. Xenophon instigated some tough but necessary decisions, such as shedding all non-essential baggage and the cumbersome carts on which much of the baggage had been transported by lumbering oxen. At a later stage, he even insisted that the men abandon their prisoners, who when sold into slavery were one of the main sources of income for mercenaries. These decisions were essential to conserve supplies and fodder, which were hard to come by in the winter mountains.

The Ten Thousand had to fight not just the appalling

weather, but running battles and skirmishes with almost every tribe they came across. The terrain was never suitable for traditional Greek hoplite tactics, and Xenophon and his fellow commanders quickly had to learn to be flexible, in order to endure the constant harrying from Persian troops and mountain guerrilla fighters; in order to take a fortress built into a cliff and a hilltop stronghold; and in order to cross rivers against strong opposition and fight with their backs against ravines.

Matters did not improve much once they reached the Black Sea – their first sight of which, and their cry 'The sea! The sea!' was so memorably recorded by Xenophon. They encountered Greek settlements there, but there were still long stretches of non-Greek coastline, and in fact their worst losses were sustained in Bithynia, when about one thousand men died in battle in one week. By the time they reached Byzantium, several thousand Greek mercenaries had been lost since Cunaxa, and countless camp followers had died too.

Moreover, on the Black Sea, the motivation of the army changed from mere survival to profit. Under the influence of greed, the army began to fall apart again into its various contingents, and they alienated every single Greek town they came to, culminating in their storming and temporarily occupying Byzantium, until Xenophon made them come to their senses. The Spartans, who were at that time the masters of the Greek world, naturally wanted them out of the way – either back in their various homelands, or employed by them for their own purposes, with a distinct preference for the former option.

Serving Under the Spartans

By the end of the journey, Xenophon had emerged as the general most trusted and respected by many of the mercenaries. In fact, when they reached Sinope, and the mercenaries decided that things would go better with a single leader, it was Xenophon they nominated. But by then they were back in the Greek world, so Xenophon diplomatically made way for the senior Spartan officer among them. This episode sums up his main contribution to the campaign as a whole: in the face of potential rifts caused by divergent goals, by differences in nationality, by lack of discipline, greed and disillusionment, he bolstered morale and kept things from falling apart.

Some of the men trickled home from Byzantium, but Xenophon took several thousands of them to serve for the winter of 400–399 BC, under the Odrysian Thracian warlord Seuthes. Seuthes was in the process of expanding his personal holdings in what is now northern Greece and Bulgaria, with a view to making himself the most powerful ruler in the region. By the time this campaign had come to an end, the fragile peace between Sparta and Persia had broken down, and they were at war. The Spartans therefore changed their minds about the undesirability of Xenophon's men, and offered them employment as they set about trying to drive Tissaphernes out of Asia Minor. They intended to replace the former Athenian empire with an even more extensive one of their own.

Xenophon and the remnants of the Ten Thousand fought over the next three years under Thibron and then Dercyllidas. Their *esprit de corps* and experience made them one of the Spartans' most valuable units, though their loyalty was to Xenophon and to themselves, rather than to the Spartans as such. But the war did not go well until one of the Spartan kings, Agesilaus II, was sent out in 396. He was a brilliant tactician and strategist, especially in his use of large-scale ruses, and he waged a remarkable campaign against both Pharnabazus in the north and Tissaphernes in central Asia Minor. His successes included victory in a major battle against Tissaphernes outside Sardis. Xenophon was later to write a eulogistic biography of Agesilaus.

Tissaphernes fell from grace and was assassinated on the orders of Artaxerxes, but any hopes Agesilaus had of conquering Asia Minor were dashed by the Persians' judicious distribution of cash on the Greek mainland, where resentment of Sparta was running high. Politicians were bribed, recruitment financed, and a coalition of Greek states went to war against Sparta. In 394 Agesilaus and his men, including Xenophon, were recalled from Asia Minor to meet the more immediate threat at home. It is not known whether Xenophon actually took part in any of the battles that the Spartans fought against the Greek coalition, which prominently included his fellow Athenians, though he was certainly present at the ghastly Battle of Coronea in 394. But soon after that, Xenophon's brief military career came to an end.

Theory of Command

Leadership is a recurrent topic in Xenophon's works and was a live issue for debate among fourth-century intellectuals. The theory of leadership that Xenophon developed, initially as a result of his experiences and observations while campaigning in the east, goes somewhat as follows.

The first principles of any organization consisting of leaders and subordinates are that subordinates should be obedient and should meet with good leadership. These are in fact two sides of the same coin, because the only true obedience is willing obedience, and obedience is given willingly to a good leader. The essential ingredient of good leadership is knowledge, specifically knowledge of how to recognize and work for the good of the subordinates. A true leader, then, is analogous to a shepherd, who takes care of his flock, rather than being a dictator, concerned only to enhance his own wealth and position, or a demagogue, who is pulled this way and that by the whims of his community. A true leader finds the balance between leading and being led.

Successful rulers, in Xenophon's opinion, know how to care for the interests of their subjects better than the subjects themselves do. Aristocratic self-confidence is a huge advantage here, and Xenophon seems to have believed that true leaders result from a combination of nature and nurture. Certainly not everyone can do it. Good leaders lead by example and show that they are flexible and imaginative in devising the means of attaining the common good and the safety of their subjects, and strong enough to stand up to aggression and wrongdoing. 'The good' may of course vary between different forms of organization: what is good for a household may not be what is good for an army. But, generally speaking, a leader works to increase and improve his community.

In a military context, this means that the leader has to not only ensure the safety of his troops and guarantee them pay and provisions, but also enhance their military capacity and do his best to ensure success on the battle-field. In most ancient military contexts, it also meant making sure that they returned home richer than they left, so the leader had to provide them with opportunities for plunder. But the improvement of subordinates also has a moral dimension: all Greek political theorists believed that moral improvement was possible for human beings chiefly in a communal setting, interacting with others. And so, in a military setting, a good general sets an example to his men by his own self-discipline and even self-denial, until, hopefully, they too learn discipline and are not motivated by greed, and refrain from plundering too much or inappropriately.

Such a leader is immediately attractive to his subjects, who, as a result, respect and honour him, and obey him. Willing obedience is best, but in emergencies it may also be generated by compulsion or emulation or a sense of shame or of duty. Ideally, the leader uses praise and rewards to teach his subordinates, but at times punishment is required. However it comes about, the vertical virtue of obedience to a superior is chiefly a means of instilling discipline in his subordinates, the horizontal virtue of being able to work with others. This in turn raises morale, the value of which, especially in military success, Xenophon recognized with exceptional clarity.

A good leader needs more specific characteristics, though: courage (Greek generals were not just tacticians, but fought in the front rank), intelligence, tactical and strategic skill, self-discipline and piety; the ability to act slyly; accessibility to his men, and knowledge of their strengths and weaknesses; the ability to negotiate with foreigners and in general to communicate well. Of these qualities, self-discipline is the most critical, because, as a good Socratic, Xenophon saw self-discipline as the foundation of all moral virtue, including the ability to do good to others, or to inculcate self-discipline in them. Deficient leaders, on the other hand, lack the determination and strength of moral certainty. They fail to find the correct balance between coercion and the instilling of willing loyalty; they are too swayed by personal motivations; they do not tell men off when they are making mistakes, but buy them off instead with rash promises; they cause divisions in the army; and they ignore the omens sent by the gods.

Xenophon was not so naive as to think that even a perfect leader would always arouse willing obedience from all his subordinates. But a good leader is prepared to take the time to inculcate discipline in his men, to channel their competitiveness, and to develop their virtues. In the meantime, a certain degree of negative reaction from soldiers is just something a leader has to expect and use his skills to overcome, just like any other hazard of leadership.

PHILIP II
OF MACEDON

382–336 bc

ROBIN LANE FOX

KING PHILIP OF MACEDON was the greatest military inventor and army-trainer in the ancient Greek world. His new model army conquered from the Danube to Sparta in southern Greece, from the area around modern Dubrovnik to the west coast of the Black Sea. Philip was a master tactician and a courageous leader in battle. His new type of army was retained by his son and was a main reason for Alexander's great victories in Asia. Philip's army units remained dominant in the Greek army for the next 150 years; he is the founder of Hellenistic warfare.

Philip's genius is still overshadowed by that of Alexander, his glorious son. Philip was also unlucky in his contemporary historians. The most productive, Theopompus of Chios (*c.* 387–320 BC), lived for a while at Philip's court in Macedon, but wrote maliciously about Philip's extravagance, vice, and the supposed sexual profligacy of his courtiers. He recognized Philip as a 'man such as Europe has never borne', but even this comment may have been hostile. We know this work only in a few later quotations, but it underlies the Latin historical epitome by Justin (*c.* AD 350) which is our best brief source on Philip's campaigns. Although Theopompus called his long history work the *Philippica*, in recognition of Philip's importance, he was not a military historian. For accounts of Philip's battles we have to look to much later Greek collections of military stratagems and anecdotes (especially Polyaenus', *c.* AD 162) and the brief secondary narrative of Diodorus of Sicily (*c.* 20 BC) whose sources are uncertain and were not eyewitnesses. The discovery in 1977 of the great royal tomb, surely Philip's own, at Vergina in Macedon revealed contemporary weapons and a great painting of the king and his young royal pages armed and out hunting. Other archaeological finds have helped our understanding of Philip's military reforms and preferred weaponry.

King Philip's Early Military Career

Philip took command of the Macedonian kingdom in northern Greece at a time of extreme crisis (359 BC). The previous king had been killed in battle and much of the kingdom's western sector had been overrun by victorious Illyrians. Philip was aged 23 and at first was only the regent for an even younger nephew. He probably did not become king until 356 BC. The young Philip had already gone as a hostage to the Illyrians and then to the Greek city-state of Thebes in the 360s BC. There he had observed the greatest Greek generals of the age, especially Epaminondas, and the training of the Thebans' citizen army, famous for its cavalry and infantry formations, up to forty-eight ranks in depth. He was well educated, and as ruler of Macedon deployed the basic units of cavalry and infantry in a new way. His cavalry were to charge, armed with specially long spears, and his unusually equipped infantry were to advance against enemies who were broken by the 'shock and awe' of galloping horsemen.

After victories over the neighbouring barbarians in the northwest and north (359–358 BC), Philip attacked walled Greek cities on or just beyond the eastern borders of his kingdom. He had inherited siege machinery from previous kings, but his engineers improved it and Philip applied it to no less than thirty-two Greek towns in the north, including, between 357 and 354 BC, four of particular importance: Amphipolis, 357 BC; Potidaea and Pydna, 356 BC; and Methone, 354 BC (during the siege of which he lost his eye to an arrow from a catapult). These conquests gave him well-watered farmland, which he gave to Macedonian settlers, many of whom became new recruits for his cavalry on receipt of this good horse pasturage.

From 354/3 BC until July 348 BC, Philip, responding to an initial invitation by Thebans and Thessalians, fought a 'sacred war' which they had initiated against the lesser power of Phocis in central Greece. After a major victory at the Crocus Field in Thessaly in 352 BC, Philip settled the war by artful diplomatic skill, avoiding a major battle. Meanwhile he had captured and flattened the big Greek city of Olynthus on his eastern borders. Its walls had defied his siege engines for a year until the city was betrayed from within. The ruins are our best-preserved town plan of a fourth-century BC Greek city. They contain missiles inscribed with offensive words that were thrown by Philip's troops.

From Peace to War

In the summer of 346 BC, Philip, ever the diplomat, made peace with many of the Greek states, including the Athenians, who had been antagonized by his various sieges in the north. It was, as he knew, only a temporary measure while he secured Macedon's borders with the barbarian north and east. His greatest conquests lay here, beyond Greece. We follow Philip nowadays in the hostile speeches of the democratic Athenian orator Demosthenes, but thirteen of Philip's twenty-three years of campaigning were spent in the barbarian plains and mountains, where we know him only through anecdotes.

His increasingly centralized standing army allowed him to campaign abroad even in winter. The open plains of Thrace (approximately modern Bulgaria) were well suited to the massed ranks of his infantry, armed with long pikes (*sarissai*), and the galloping tactics of his cavalry. Perhaps Philip had devised them with the open terrain of Thrace and western Asia in mind.

At least since the late 350s his ultimate aim had been the invasion of the old Persian Empire in Asia. An invasion would require control of the Hellespont between Europe and Asia, which the Athenians kept open as the vital route for their city-state's grain ships. Philip knew, as they did, that they would fight to keep control of it. Their city had formidable long walls and a potentially big navy. Philip's fleet was still very small and the Athenian walls would be impregnable, even to his improved artillery, siege towers and arrow-shooting machinery.

In 345 BC he marched northwest into Illyria and from 341 to 339 BC he campaigned against the cavalry and lightly armed infantry of the Thracian tribes. He even reached the eastern end of the River Danube. In July and September

340 BC he besieged the two important Greek cities of Perinthus and Byzantium on the nearby Sea of Marmara but failed, significantly, to take either. The attack on Byzantium damaged his deteriorating alliance with Thebes, Byzantium's old ally, in central Greece.

Late in 339 BC, Philip returned to central Greece for what he had always known would be his ultimate test there, a war with the Thebans and Athenians, who had finally combined against him. After entering central Greece in early winter by an unexpected route, Philip's army encamped near the small Boeotian town of Chaeronea. After an inconclusive winter of diplomacy Philip finally engaged in battle on the plain. On 22 August 338 BC he won a hard-earned victory, reputedly by a deceptive infantry manoeuvre and a decisive charge by one wing of his cavalry led by his son Alexander. The Battle of Chaeronea was indeed fatal to liberty, as poets later said. It ushered in the Macedonian kings' domination of the Greek city-states for more than one hundred and fifty years.

Philip's final victory over the large Greek army led by the Athenians and Thebans exemplifies the problems in reconstructing his battles. The site has been identified as the narrow plain between the River Cephissus and the acropolis of Chaeronea in Boeotia. Both sides had been waiting for several months and it was only in mid-August 338 BC that the Greek army took up a battle position. They chose it so as to limit the scope for Philip's cavalry to make an outflanking manoeuvre. The river and the hills protected the Theban infantry on the right and the Athenian infantry on the left respectively. If the line broke, the Cerata pass offered the Greeks an escape route to the southeast.

Typically we have two contradictory sources for the size of Philip's army. One says he was outnumbered, the other that he had 30,000 infantry and 2,000 cavalry, outnumbering the enemy. More than 60,000 troops were probably engaged, a battle far bigger than any in western Europe in the medieval period. Our only overview of the battle is the abbreviated version of Diodorus, three centuries later. He credits Alexander with leading the cavalry on Philip's left wing in a decisive charge against the Greek infantry. Anecdotes preserved by Polyaenus credit Philip's infantry phalanx with a deceptive manoeuvre. They marched back as if in retreat, heading for high ground (which is not visible on the site) and when the Athenian infantry rashly pursued them Philip is said to have exclaimed, 'The Athenians do not know how to win a victory,' and to have ordered his retreating phalanx to halt and march forwards again with their *sarissai* unbroken. This manoeuvre is hard to accept in such a controlled fashion, but it would account for the breaking of part of the Greek line and the scope for a decisive cavalry charge into it.

The combination of anecdotes and contradictory sources typifies almost all ancient battles and the problems of reconstructing them. Nobody had a total overview and promptly wrote it up; participants knew only what was happening hand-to-hand around them. The battle site of Chaeronea has archaeologically verified burial places. A mound on the Macedonian left contained cremated bodies, spear-points and coins, presumably for the Macedonian dead. A commemorative stone lion marks another mass burial place, probably containing 254 bodies of the Theban Sacred Band (linked by homosexual pairing, it was said). The sight of the bodies of these brave men, who opposed Alexander on the Greek right wing, caused Philip to weep.

Philip followed up his victory by campaigning against the still hostile Sparta, by another campaign into Illyria (probably in 337 BC) and by launching an advance invasion into Persian-ruled Asia under his senior generals in summer 336 BC. He was murdered, however, during wedding celebrations at the ancient Macedonian capital of Aigai (Vergina) in autumn 336 BC. The murder was almost certainly related to discontent in his family over the most recent of his polygamous marriages and the birth of another son. It was left to Alexander, nearly two years later, to follow up Philip's first moves in Asia and to carry them as far as India, probably much further than Philip had ever thought possible.

Philip's New Model Infantry

In 359 BC Philip had inherited a small kingdom with a long tradition of good cavalry but no trained or centralized infantry, no supporting units of lightly armed troops and only a simple style of siege train. His military reforms relied on changes in the Macedonians' social order and he gave new titles to the military units he created. Names like 'Royal Foot Companions' and 'Royal Shield Bearers' bound them closely to the king, not to the local nobles they had served as personal retainers. He also gave many of them new lands from his ever-increasing conquests and thus won them away from their local loyalties. Captives taken in war became slaves who would work the land and mines in his expanding Macedon. The royal infantry was then trained intensively for campaigning throughout the year (including winter). Traditionally the summer month of harvesting had been inauspicious for campaigning because Macedonians needed to gather in their crops. Philip's new army was freed from work on the land and could fight in any month.

The reforms were complex and needed years to perfect. He planned a battle line whose central block was to be his famous phalanx of infantrymen armed with very long spears, the *sarissai*. A *sarissa* was at least 16 feet long and was made of two lengths of tough wood, preferably from the Cornelian cherry tree (*Cornus mas*), which was already used for cavalry spears by Persians in western Asia. The two pieces were held together by a central metal tube. One end carried a balancing butt-spike that could be rammed into the ground when making a stand. The *sarissa* had to be held with both hands, and when nearly horizontal the first five ranks' metal points would project beyond the front line. The central ranks could hold their *sarissai* upright so as to intercept arrows and missiles. By trained manoeuvres, the phalanx would present *sarissai* vertically, face about, then lower them in the rear ranks and march in retreat. Sideways manoeuvres were also possible, directed by trumpeters. Alternatively a *sarissa*-armed phalanx could halt and present a wall of protruding spear-points on all four sides of the rectangle. The soldiers in the front and back ranks were the finest and were paid more highly.

Sarissa-armed infantry wore leg armour, at least in the front and back ranks, metal helmets (the 'Phrygian' type, with a forward-curving crest, was popular) but no metal breastplates. They had a small convex shield slung on the neck and left shoulder by a strap, as both hands were needed for manoeuvring the long spear. The basic infantry unit began as one of ten ranks, but eights and sixteens were soon developed. Later Greek tactical manuals identify basic units of 256 men (16 x 16) in a phalanx but they may only be theoretical reconstructions. The phalanx was made up of battalions (*taxeis*) which were locally recruited according to cantons in Macedon and led by a local prince or noble. Each *taxis* was probably around one thousand five hundred strong and at least seven *taxeis* made up a phalanx at battle strength.

Later authors compared this phalanx with the Greek battle lines described in Homer's *Iliad*, but Homer was not Philip's source for it. He devised it as one part of a carefully planned line. Its long wall of sharp, slim spear-points kept off attackers with its greater outreach, but it was most useful when moving on level ground. Its unprotected right flank linked with the highly trained unit of Shield Bearers, who carried bigger metal shields and wore full body armour while carrying spears and swords. They numbered three thousand in Philip's battle-plan and became the supreme military unit in all ancient history during their service with Alexander. They were also used for pursuits and dangerous 'special operations' on rough and steep ground. Presumably they could take off some of their armour to increase their flexibility on these missions.

The New Style of Cavalry Warfare

On their right and on the phalanx's left Philip stationed cavalry in pointed formations, wedge-shaped ones for his Macedonian Companion cavalry, diamond-shaped ones for his Thessalian Greek allies. These pointed formations increased the speed of turning, as horsemen focused on their immediate leader and turned as he did, like birds, watchers said, who were flying in formation. The cavalry wore no stirrups and no toe-straps. They sat on padded saddlecloths which were sometimes the skins of wild animals. Their legs are shown in art as unprotected and they carried no shields, although they wore metal breast-plates and a protective leather 'skirt' from the waist to mid thigh. Their helmets were metal, fluted round the rim in the Boeotian Greek style, and they carried a sword for close combat, the feared *kopis*, which was a very sharp slashing instrument. In their right hands they carried a long spear, the *xyston*, up to 9 feet long, which gave them a longer reach than their enemies. So long as an enemy had no stirrups, a frontal charge with a *xyston* was manage-able, as recent reconstructions of Macedonian battles by film armies have proved. It is most effective to ram the *xyston*'s long metal point into an opponent's shoulder just by the collarbone. The spear is not easily extractable by galloping on and pulling on its shaft when past the enemy. After using it, therefore, the cavalryman resorted to the sword, or *kopis*. A wedge-shaped charge with spears at the ready would often be enough to scatter enemies in terror.

These cavalry charges were trained to turn at an angle and strike into the centre of a line which was already breaking when attempting to avoid being outflanked. Previous Greek armies used cavalry only to fight opposing cavalry or to pursue infantry who were already in flight.

A Balanced Army

Balance and variety were the principles of Philip's new battle line. It was an integrated whole, to which Thracian javelin throwers, Greek slingers and Cretan archers added the element of the long-range missile. Experts in artillery were brought in from Greek Thessaly in order to develop the torsion power of arrow-catapults and bigger and better siege towers. Dogs, even, were used in pursuit, while breeding mares were imported by the thousand. Stallions must have been carefully controlled in special royal studs to maintain the development of the best warhorses.

Philip led his cavalry in person, sustaining several serious wounds. Like his diplomacy, his tactics were often cunning. Twice he allowed letters announcing his troops' imminent withdrawal to be intercepted by the Athenian general Chares. On the first occasion Chares was deceived and believed him. On the second occasion he wrongly chose to believe the message again, a neat double bluff by Philip. His army's mobility depended on extreme discipline and drill. Servants were severely limited in camp, while forced marches with heavy supply packs and tents were frequent. It was said that hot baths were banned in Macedon except for women who had just given birth.

Philip seldom ended a battle on the battlefield, the usual Greek practice. In the tribal non-Greek world it was crucial to capture the king and his few courtiers by pursuit. Philip would follow up at the gallop for many miles, a practice which he passed on to Alexander. His rebalancing of cavalry and infantry, the *sarissai*, the shock charges, and the array of missiles and these long pursuits made battle with him a new and terrifying experience for conventional Greek armies.

ALEXANDER THE GREAT

356–323 BC

ROBIN LANE FOX

ALEXANDER THE GREAT was the supreme conqueror in the ancient world. An acknowledged military genius, in three battles he defeated huge Persian armies and took the western and central parts of their empire in Asia. He then pressed on into India, aiming for the edge of the world. His personal leadership, strategic boldness and tactical ingenuity are unsurpassed, whether on the flat plains of Mesopotamia or on the peaks of the Himalayan range. He died, from uncertain causes, when he was only 32.

Even in antiquity, people argued whether his success owed more to luck than skill. The truth is that great commanders create their own luck. Alexander owed much to his father Philip's new model army and to the trained units and experienced officers Philip had prepared for him. We know far more about Alexander's campaigns than about Philip's and so we may underestimate Philip's example. An experienced army, which a much-adored king has created, is not easy for a young heir to lead. Alexander inherited a balanced army the subtle variety of which could easily have been misapplied by a lesser tactical mind. No previous Macedonian king had died peacefully from natural causes. His older officers would not have hesitated to kill him and replace him if he had failed them. Alexander was only 20 when he began leading a great army to victory. In thirteen years he was only defeated once, by the weather and dry terrain on his march home through southeastern Persia's fearsome Makran desert.

Alexander's Early Career

When his father Philip was murdered in the autumn of 336 BC, Alexander became king of the Macedonians and promptly asserted his role as leader of the Greek alliance that Philip had founded. His first year required campaigning to retain Thrace (approximately, modern Bulgaria) as far as the River Danube, which his troops crossed on skins of leather stuffed with hay, a time-honoured method in

Asia. He deployed his father's cavalry and famous infantry phalanx with distinction against loose formations of rebellious tribes. His infantry's exceptional training showed in their advance through fields of standing corn, flattening the crops by a disciplined sideways movement of their long *sarissa* spears, which they wielded in formation with both hands. When the tribesmen released wagons at them down a steep hill, they were quick to close ranks behind a wall of shields, the bearers of which crouched to the ground and caused the wagons to fly up and over their unit's bodies. A rebellion in the Greek city of Thebes caused Alexander to march with exceptional, but characteristic speed south and issue the rebels with an ultimatum. They refused, so he besieged and took the city, levelling it to the ground and selling the thirty thousand Greek survivors into slavery. Throughout his career Alexander was utterly destructive of opponents who refused or went back on his offers in return for surrender. He was also a master-besieger, unlike his father Philip. From 332 BC onwards he was helped by siege machinery improved by his engineers, who applied torsion-power to enable catapults to throw rocks, not arrows. However, machinery alone never won him a city. His night attacks, 'special operations' and dispersed assaults on sections of wall were essential factors.

In the spring of 334 BC, Alexander invaded Asia and

paid his respects at ancient Troy, where weaponry said to belong to Homer's Achilles was given to him in honour of his self-publicized rivalry with the great hero. It accompanied him into battle as far as India. The Homeric values of personal prowess in combat and individual courage were profoundly rooted in Alexander and were well adapted to the semi-Homeric Macedon in which he had grown up. He never asked of others what he would not risk himself. He even put care of their wounds before his own. He led by example in the front line, inspiring his men with a faith in his fortune and invincibility.

His invasion was matched with an effective political 'spin'. Like Philip, he claimed to be avenging the Persians' past sacrileges in Greece (back in 480–479 BC). He was liberating the Greek cities in Asia under their rule, to most of which he granted democracy, the opposite of rule by small pro-Persian cliques. In May 334 BC, he won his first victory by a bold charge across the Granicus river in modern northwest Turkey. Persian cavalry held the far bank but they were pushed back by an audacious assault by Alexander's cavalry. The infantry phalanx was less effective, being hindered by the river.

Alexander's genius became clear in November 333 BC at the huge Battle of Issus, near modern Iskenderun and the southeast Turkish coast towards Syria. The

Persian king Darius had mustered a vastly greater army, but unintentionally passed north of Alexander's, which was hidden by the intervening Amanus mountains. Alexander then heard that his enemy was advancing down into his rear, threatening to push him out into a wide open plain where their numbers would be decisive. Brilliantly, he decided to turn his men round, march them back up the coast in a narrow formation and then line them across an enclosed plain where the sea and the hills guarded his two wings from encirclement. He regained surprise by this forced night march, countered the Persians' superior numbers and won a remarkable victory by an angled cavalry charge that drew off and weakened the Persian centre. Again, the main infantry phalanx and their long *sarissa* spears split apart on rough ground broken by a river. Again, this victory was a cavalry triumph. The deceptive shuffling of his battle line before combat began, his personally led charge on his horse Bucephalas (as at Chaeronea for his father Philip in 338 BC) and his inspiring decision to turn back and fight on narrow terrain made the Battle of Issus one of Alexander's masterpieces. As ever, he showed a brilliant grasp of space and the potential of terrain.

Other strategists might have pursued Darius directly into Asia, even though many more troops and many walled cities would have protected him there. Instead,

Alexander attended deliberately to his coastline. He had disbanded his inferior fleet in the summer of 334 BC. In order to hinder the Persians' fleet, he set about capturing their main naval bases, including Tyre, which he took after a massive siege, and then Gaza after another. His machinery was now fearsome, including siege towers and collapsible bridges up to 100 feet high. Diades, his chief engineer, was remembered as the 'man who took Tyre with Alexander'. His troops included many skilled carpenters and woodworkers, trained by their years in Macedon's forests. Alexander even made them connect the island of Tyre to the mainland by an artificial causeway, which is still visible, more than half a mile across the sea.

Sieges always brought out the boldest and most ingenious side of him. His overall strategy, however, was even bolder: to take Egypt, return to Tyre and then wait for most of the summer of 331 BC while Darius gathered the biggest possible army – which Alexander wanted to knock out in one engagement. The plan was immensely daring, pitting his forty-seven thousand men against at least four times as many under Darius. These exact numbers were added as special effects to the remarkable film reconstruction of this, the Battle of Gaugamela in northern Iraq, for Oliver Stone's film *Alexander* (2004). They give us a visual sense of its scale for the first time. As at Issus or in his father Philip's battles, Alexander's winning manoeuvre was again an angled cavalry charge on the right wing, led by himself, cutting back into the enemy centre which he had destabilized. The charge was supported by many minor tactical tricks, by a reserve phalanx line behind his main one, by the concealment of slingers and light troops on foot amongst units of cavalry, by the ability of one half of the phalanx to stand fixed and firm in a central rectangle although their other half had broken. Inevitable outnumbering on his left wing meant that Alexander had to abandon pursuit of Darius and return. The foul smell of the dead soon caused him to abandon the site.

He was now being called the 'King of Asia'. It remained to capture Darius and show where Asia ended.

Fighting in Asia

Alexander never had to cope with a separate political parliament: he was general and politician in one. True to his initial publicity, he took revenge and burned down the big Persian palaces at Persepolis in early 330 BC. Like many great commanders, he often drank heavily when off duty. At Persepolis, drink helped along a riotous evening of destruction.

Before capturing Darius' dead body, Alexander changed his tone and presented himself as Darius' respectful heir, and from July 330 BC as the punisher of Darius' murderers. In reality he wanted to conquer all Asia, even beyond the Persian empire's boundaries. The aim took him through astoundingly steep and difficult landscapes, including a crossing of the snowbound Hindu Kush mountains. The next four years (330–326 BC) were typified by hardly believable mountain marches, by sieges of sheer rocks beyond the Oxus river, by a more open and fluid style of warfare and an absolutely implacable assault on all 'terrorists', or local rebels if they went back on their initial surrender. From the winter of 328 BC, Alexander's army was more often split into divisions which fought under his increasingly experienced officers. None the less, the most spectacular sieges were all led by his example, supported by the veteran Shield Bearers he had inherited from Philip and by the fearsome Agrianian–Thracian javelin men. The troops were driven by Alexander's intrepid example, the increasing promise of bonuses and the knowledge that their skills of besieging, bridging and mountaineering had already triumphed over the impossible. They even believed they were following the tracks of the ancient Greek god Dionysus and Heracles the hero.

In the late spring of 326, Alexander's army reached the River Hydaspes, now the Jhelum, one of the broad Punjab rivers of northwest India. It was held on the far bank by a major army of Porus, the Indian king, complete with war chariots and many war elephants. Alexander began by waging a month-long war of nerves. He marched to and fro on his riverbank under darkness, making noises as if he was planning to cross. He wore down his opponents by deception, and only then launched one part of his army in small boats by night, leaving another part downstream to mislead Indian observers. Fearful storms broke out, but enough of his cavalry, his veteran Shield Bearers and part of his phalanx crossed to take control of the far bank. Fortunately the rains impeded the Indian advance unit of war chariots.

The Indian army was preceded by a long battle line of war elephants. Archers with longbows and cavalry were the main Indian strengths. Alexander had planned for each arm of war. He sent part of his cavalry with his general Coenus on a wide outflanking gallop to the left: the reasons for it have become clearer after Oliver Stone's recent film reconstructions of a cavalry charge against a live elephant corps. Against an elephant line, horses will pull away to the left in fright, even if they have lived for a while in the company of elephants. Alexander's plan built on this tendency and turned it to advantage as a wide outflanking movement which then cut round into the main Indian army's rear.

Elephants are also prone to panic when attacked from behind.

The elephant line was then driven back by Alexander's Shield Bearers on foot, armed with special axes and cutters so as to slash the beasts' trunks and legs. They panicked and withdrew into their own lines behind them, compounding a chaos which a part (or probably, all) of the phalanx in its *sarissa*-led formation could then sweep into disarray. Alexander, as usual, led a simultaneous cavalry charge, drawing off the Indian cavalry on his right wing.

One source for the Battle of Hydaspes implies that only a few thousand of Alexander's army crossed the river and engaged in battle. The implied length of the Indians' elephant line makes such a small force most unlikely and the support of the rest of Alexander's troops has surely been omitted from this one shortened narrative. Certainly posterity remembered him as a great elephant-conqueror. After his death, the coins of his successor in Egypt, King Ptolemy, showed a portrait of Alexander wearing a symbolic headdress of an elephant's head. It had been a memorably planned victory against a river, the weather and a novel enemy. Alexander followed up by sparing King Porus because of his bravery and reappointing him as ruler, but now under his victor's command.

In India the snakes and the monsoon rains dampened Alexander's misplaced aim of reaching the 'edge' of the world at the mouth of the River Ganges. His troops refused to march on, which threw Alexander into a rage; but eventually he accepted it.

Their return home from the River Beas in the Indian Punjab took them in specially built ships down the River Indus. Since 330 BC, Alexander had been recruiting troops from his new subjects. His returning army was now more than one hundred thousand strong and was mostly non-Macedonian, including Indians and many Iranian cavalry, especially their fine horse archers.

During the return march home it is wrong to see him as addicted to battle and slaughter or straining to punish the men who had refused to fulfil his aims. He had to fight hard against Indian tribes, who were known to be warlike and were keen to block and defeat him. He continued to lead by example, even leaping alone off the battlements into a host of Indians inside a walled city. He was then badly wounded in the chest by an Indian arrow. These risks were not new or desperate: they had always been part of his style.

His one major disaster followed his recovery. It was due to his miscalculation of the weather. He marched his fittest men home by the coastal route through the Makran desert, although he knew it to be a harsh landscape. Part of his plan was to dig wells for the fleet, which would then follow and meet him. Arguably, the other part had been for this fleet to bring a stockpile of supplies by sea for the army. Adverse winds detained the fleet's departure, leaving Alexander already in the desert with no supply line. His losses were heavy, but they are not quantifiable. As many as half of the troops that were with him may have been lost.

He returned to Babylon, but in the spring of 323 BC was planning yet another land and sea operation, this time against the Arabian peninsula. Here too the winds at sea might have worked against him, but before setting out he died (June 323 BC) from uncertain causes. Poisoning was rumoured, but is most unlikely as he lay sick for more than a fortnight. It is possible that he had caught a malarial fever.

Alexander's Aims and Planning

The makeup of his army remained essentially Philip's, as described on pp. 170–84. In 323 BC he was experimenting with Iranian archers in the centre ranks of the phalanx, but *sarissai* were still crucial in the front and back ranks. Cavalry charges in pointed formations were his supreme shock tactic, reinforced by Persian horsemen, whom he added into his all-conquering Macedonian Companion units. His wish for an 'army of the best', whatever its origin, provoked a Macedonian mutiny, but he did not abandon it. The identity, but not the structures, of his army thus changed considerably by the end of his life. The one addition was a corps of war elephants, always ridden, however, by Indian experts.

His dash and brave example were important, but his tactical ruses, his bold 'grand strategy' and his sense of the spatial possibilities on a battlefield and the imperatives of supply were crucial. Even the Makran march had had a double supply plan, though it failed badly. Supplies were partly carried in ox-drawn wagons, partly looted from local stockpiles and livestock. Water sources were a crucial determinant of the route of his men and especially his horses. They have still not been traced systematically along his line of march. Increasingly, women accompanied the march too, at least ten thousand of them by 325 BC. Traders came as well, one reason for the high debts which the troops contracted over and above their regular pay.

Even after turning back in India, the troops revered Alexander as invincible. He himself believed he was guided by the god Zeus, to whom he had a special heroic relationship as Zeus' son. His achievements were indeed superhuman and their style was long invoked and imitated by his successor-generals. Even in his lifetime, Greek admirers and hopeful flatterers gave him honours equal to those of the gods. He had excelled even the mythical deeds of Heracles.

HANNIBAL

c. 247–183 BC

TOM HOLLAND

COMPILING LISTS OF GREAT GENERALS is an exercise that even great generals themselves have been known to enjoy. A celebrated example took place in 193 BC, when the two most brilliant commanders of their age met during the course of a diplomatic exchange, and one took the opportunity to ask the other who would feature on his own personal hit-parade. The man putting the question was Scipio Africanus, a Roman who only nine years previously had recorded a crushing and decisive victory over the last surviving army of his city's deadliest rival, Carthage; and the man whose opinion he was canvassing was none other than the Carthaginian whom he had defeated on that fateful day, Hannibal Barca.

Yet Scipio put his question in no mood of gloating or triumphalism. He appreciated – none better, perhaps – the full genius of his old adversary: for such was Hannibal's record of victory and devastation, achieved over sixteen years of relentless campaigning, that it had won for him, despite his final defeat, a reputation as the most dangerous enemy that Rome had ever faced. The opinion of such a man, Scipio judged, was well worth having. And so it was, in the words of Livy, 'that he asked his companion who was the greatest general of all time'.

Hannibal's choice was hardly a controversial one: Alexander the Great. At number two, with a due show of modesty, he placed King Pyrrhus of Epirus; and only at number three did he finally nominate himself. Scipio, it is said, laughed at this, and asked his companion, '"What would you be saying had you defeated me?" "In that case," replied Hannibal, "I would certainly have put myself before Alexander and before Pyrrhus – in fact, before every general who had ever lived."' The reply was, as Livy points out, a subtle one, for it succeeded in flattering both men simultaneously – and yet it also reflected, on Hannibal's own part, a haunting appreciation of the essentially tragic nature of his own genius.

He knew that he had been a failure. No matter how many and spectacular his victories had been, the fact that his career had ended in disaster ensured that all his battle honours would serve only as trophies in the triumph of his enemies. It was not Scipio alone who had brought about the ruin of his war plans. Even more fatal had been the unyielding character of the Roman republic itself, a state that had consistently refused to acknowledge any superior, or ever to sue for terms. Hannibal, by opting to declare war upon such an implacable and ruthless foe, had staked everything upon his conviction that it was possible to bring the Roman people to their knees, a miscalculation that in due course would prove as fatal to his city as to himself. Yet what set his failure as a strategist in an even bleaker light was the fact that as a tactician he had indeed shown himself incomparable – for he had inflicted upon the legions a succession of defeats so shattering that any other enemy, set to bleed as grievously as the Romans had, would surely have given up the fight. Had Hannibal combined his ability to win battles with a strategic vision capable of defeating Rome, then he surely would have deserved to outrank Alexander. As it is, even at a distance of more than two millennia, there is one victory of his in particular that has no rival as the very model of the perfectly executed battle plan. Cannae, where some seventy thousand Romans were enveloped and wiped out by Hannibal's vastly outnumbered forces, remains the single engagement of the pre-modern era that is still capable of serving as an inspiration to commanders today. From August 1914 and the German attempt to execute the Schlieffen Plan, to 1991 and Norman Schwarzkopf's strategy of encirclement during the first Gulf War, Hannibal's example has loomed large in the minds of many a twentieth-century general. That is more than can be said for any other commander from the ancient world – even Alexander himself.

Like Father, Like Son

Indeed, for all the lip-service that he paid to Pyrrhus, Hannibal has a far worthier claim to be considered Alexander's heir than any Greek. Like his great predecessor, he struck fearlessly into the very heartlands of his enemy; he combined cavalry with different classes of infantry to devastating tactical effect; and he had a god-like taste for defying the very elements. In one other obvious way as well, Hannibal's career was a striking echo of Alexander's: both were the greater sons of great commanders. Just as Philip of Macedon had done, Hannibal's father bequeathed to his heir both a formidable army and a ferocious sense of mission. Hamilcar Barca had well understood what it took to fight the Romans. War between Carthage and the upstart republic had first broken out in 264 BC, and had raged, amid escalating slaughter, for more than two decades. The principal campaigning theatre had been Sicily; and the most impressive commander operating there on either side had been

Hamilcar. Although in the end it was the Carthaginians who had been brought to defeat, Hamilcar himself had remained unvanquished in open battle; and he never quite shook off a sense of resentment at being obliged to lower his arms. Resolved to see his city restored to its former pre-eminence, Hamilcar duly began to scout around for new horizons. In 237 BC, he set off for Spain.

This was a bid of some desperation, for the army available to him was limited, and Spain itself notoriously savage, swarming with barbarous tribes. Naturally, then, before leaving on such a perilous venture, Hamilcar made sure to seek the blessing of his city's gods. Hannibal, then only 9 years old, was taken by his father to watch the sacrifice. After Hamilcar had poured out a libation, he turned to his son, and asked if he too wished to embark for Spain. Hannibal, who is said to have possessed precisely 'the same vigour in his look, and the same fire in his eyes' as his father, did not hesitate. Then came a fateful moment. Hamilcar took his son by the hand, led him up to the altar, and commanded him to swear, upon the bloody remains of the victim, 'never to bear goodwill to the Romans'.

It was a promise that Hannibal would never forget. From that moment on, his life, like his father's, had a single purpose. Arriving in Spain, his aptitude for warfare was soon being forged amid the breaking of the natives to

Carthaginian power. Carving out a new empire in the west was very much a family project: after Hamilcar's death in 228 BC, the result of a tribal ambush, his son-in-law Hasdrubal took command of the imperial enterprise, successfully pushing the reach of his dominance ever northwards, expanding the size of the army and establishing a cadre of officers of quite exceptional experience and ability. Chief among these was Hannibal himself, who, as commander of horse, was responsible for the training of a cavalry arm that would prove itself more proficient than any since the time of Alexander. By the time Hasdrubal was murdered by a disgruntled Spaniard in 221 BC, and Hannibal stepped up to replace him, the Carthaginian empire in Spain was possessed of a killing force that might have served to make even the Romans pause.

Elephant Man

Except that it did not. In 219 BC, when Hannibal attacked Saguntum, a Spanish city that had long been allied to Rome, a tense diplomatic stand-off culminated the following year in the republic's decision to renew its war with Carthage. The test for which Hannibal had been preparing all his life was now upon him – and he was ready for it. In the previous conflict with Rome, the Carthaginians had been content to fight defensively; this time round, however, Hannibal was resolved to take the attack directly to the enemy. Because the Romans had command of the sea, he knew that he would have to lead his army over the Pyrenees and through the hostile badlands of southern Gaul if he were to reach Italy: an intimidating prospect. Hannibal not only accepted the challenge, however, but positively embraced it – for it was his intention, as he marched on the Romans, to shock and awe them with the sheer Herculean scale of his boldness. This was why, along with heavy infantrymen from Libya, light horsemen from Numidia, slingers from the Balearic Islands, and sizeable contingents of both cavalry and infantry recruited from Spain, he took thirty-seven of the beasts for which his army today is chiefly remembered: elephants. Never mind that they were, as one military analyst cheerfully acknowledged, 'unsuited by their very nature to the demands of combat'; that was hardly the point. Ever since the time of Alexander, elephants had served as the ultimate in military status symbols, lumbering expressions of the taste for gigantism that had long afflicted generals raised in the military traditions of the eastern Mediterranean. None, however, had thought to do what Hannibal, as the climax of his march on Italy, intended to attempt: to lead them, and all his army, over a mountain range as towering and bleak as the Alps.

What followed remains even today perhaps the most

totemic exploit in all military history. To that extent, at least, Hannibal's ambitions for his Alpine crossing were more than met. That a general would lead war elephants across the roof of the world in pursuit of his burning hatred did indeed serve to astound the Romans, who were generally, as a people, unwilling to be astounded by their opponents. Yet Hannibal paid grievously for what was, essentially, a propaganda stunt. It was true that the Romans were expecting him to take the low road, and had been planning accordingly; but the advantage Hannibal accrued by outflanking them was as nothing compared to the losses that he suffered amid the snows. He had left Spain that summer of 218 BC with, at a rough estimate, some sixty thousand men; of these, by the time that he finally debouched into northern Italy, a bare twenty-five thousand were left to him. Losses on such a scale appeared devastating to all of Hannibal's hopes. It had never been any part of his plans to invade Italy with so small a force. Even though he sought, with a mounting degree of success, to recruit the local Gauls to his standard, he knew that even the hardiest of them were not the equals of the seasoned veterans he had lost on the road to Italy. There must have been many in his ranks, then, who dreaded that their great bid to overthrow Rome was doomed to failure almost before it had begun.

'Hannibal Ad Portas!'

But if so, their spirits were soon to be spectacularly raised. Whatever the strategic failings that had marred Hannibal's journey from Spain, his arrival on the Romans' very doorstep provided him at last with an opportunity to engage in what he did best: winning battles. His first brush with the Romans took place near the River Ticinus, by the Alpine foothills, and even though the engagement was little more than a skirmish, the Roman cavalry were routed and their commander, a consul by the name of Scipio, severely wounded. A few weeks later, amid the bitter cold of late December, Hannibal won an emphatic victory on the banks of a second river, the Trebia. Out of a Roman army of forty thousand men, some three-quarters were killed or captured: a morale-sapping demonstration to the defeated of what they were up against in Hannibal.

The concealment of troops behind the enemy's line, a brilliant exploitation of the terrain of the battlefield, and a climactic encirclement: Trebia had featured them all. So too, the following year, would an even more devastating victory. In the summer of 217 BC, as Hannibal headed south, he brilliantly outmanoeuvred a Roman army that had been stationed to block his crossing of the Apennines, and then headed on southwards, merrily burning and looting as he went. The Romans – up to thirty thousand of them in all – naturally set off in hot pursuit. In due course, on the evening of 20 June, they caught distant sight of their quarry by the banks of Lake Trasimene. The following morning, impatient to get to grips with the invaders, they advanced hurriedly through an early morning fog towards the Carthaginian rearguard. On one side of them stretched the waters of the lake, and on the other a line of hills. It was, in other words, the perfect spot for an ambush – and Hannibal was not the man to waste such an opportunity. The fog grew thicker; the legionaries blundered along the lakeside road; and Hannibal gave the order for the jaws of his trap to close. The legions found that they were entirely surrounded. In the resulting massacre, all but the Roman vanguard, some six thousand men, were wiped out. Such was the horror of the slaughter that even an earthquake went unregarded.

From that moment on – with a single, disastrous exception – the Romans bound themselves to the grim and inglorious strategy of refusing battle to Hannibal. The general who first formulated it, Quintus Fabius Maximus, would end up being given the derisive nickname of 'the Delayer' for his pains; but, as time would show, he had correctly identified the fatal weakness in the invader's strategy. Ironically enough, the Battle of Cannae, the most extraordinary victory of Hannibal's entire extraordinary career, only served to emphasize it: for even after inflicting upon the republic the greatest calamity in its history, he could not force a final victory. Bled of manpower though Rome had been, Hannibal's reserves were more anaemic still. By the spring of 217 BC, he had already lost all but one of his elephants; and over the decade and a half that followed Cannae, disease and desertion progressively accomplished what the legions no longer dared to attempt. Simultaneously, every source of reinforcements was being methodically denied him. Not only was a second Carthaginian invasion of Italy, led by Hannibal's brother, annihilated, but a Roman expeditionary force succeeded in conquering the Barcid empire in Spain. The general who pulled off this feat was none other than the son of the consul who had been wounded beside the Ticinus, Scipio; and by 204 he was ready to embark on the invasion of the Carthaginian homeland that would serve to win him his nickname of 'Africanus'. Hannibal, frantically summoned back from Italy, met Scipio's army in the summer of 202, outside the town of Zama. He lost.

That single defeat ended the war. Carthage no longer had the manpower to continue the struggle, and when its conqueror's terms were delivered, Hannibal advised his countrymen to accept them. What he had failed to achieve as a commander he now sought to accomplish as a statesman: to ensure the survival of his country. The Romans, however, fearful of him still, forced him in 195 BC to leave Carthage; and from that moment on he endured a wretched and spectre-like exile, 'an eagle plucked of all its feathers', forever being harried from foreign court to foreign court by Roman agents. When he eventually died in 183 BC, it was by his own hand: his enemies had cornered him at last. Their inveterate hatred of him, of course, ranked as the greatest compliment that they ever paid a foe. A failure, in the final reckoning, he may have been; but the Romans would never forget that in Hannibal, in the scale of his exertions and in the scope of his ambitions, they had met the opponent who was most like themselves.

A Perfect Battle: Cannae

The Battle of Cannae was Hannibal's masterpiece. The Romans, having initially agreed to avoid open combat with the invader in the wake of their defeat at Lake Trasimene, had in due course wearied of such an inglorious policy. Accordingly, in the summer of 216 BC, they set about raising the largest army that the republic had ever put into the field: eight whole legions, some eighty thousand men in all. At their head rode the two heads of state, the consuls. No effort was spared in their effort to wipe out Hannibal once and for all.

Nothing daunted, Hannibal himself eagerly seized the opportunity to offer his enemies battle. As the Romans advanced southwards into Apulia, he stationed himself on an open plain near the town of Cannae, where his cavalry would be able to operate at peak effectiveness. Even though one of the two consuls refused to risk an engagement amid such terrain, the command that he held with his fellow-consul was a rotating one, and his colleague was set on battle. Accordingly, on 2 August 216 BC, the order was given, and the legions left their camp. They outnumbered their enemy two to one.

Hannibal, confronted in the centre by a massive block of infantry, but on his wings by only six thousand untrained horsemen, had opted to weaken his own centre, and massively to strengthen his wings. As the legionaries advanced, they found Gauls and Spaniards arrayed against them in a curving bulge. Inevitably, the sheer weight of Roman numbers was soon serving to push the bulge flat and then back – drawing the densely ranked legionaries ever forwards. Simultaneously, however, Hannibal's wings had easily routed the Roman cavalry, and were now poised menacingly on the undefended flanks of the legions. As the Libyan heavy infantry closed in on their sides, so Spanish and Gallic horsemen fell upon their rear. The Romans, completely surrounded, were massacred. By nightfall, if the Greek historian Polybius is to be believed, the battle-field was strewn with more than seventy thousand dead.

Yet if Cannae was the most disastrous defeat in the republic's history, it was also, for Hannibal himself, a fateful tipping point. That same evening, his lieutenants urged him to march on Rome. Hannibal refused, aware that he lacked adequate numbers to storm the city. Yet the opportunity, with Rome swept by panic and denuded of troops, was the best he would ever have. His failure to take it would ultimately prove fatal to all his hopes.

SCIPIO AFRICANUS

c. 236–184 bc

ADRIAN GOLDSWORTHY

PUBLIUS CORNELIUS SCIPIO WAS THE MOST GIFTED Roman general to emerge from the desperate Second Punic War fought between Rome and Carthage. After a series of Roman disasters, he was given command of Spain in 210 BC, and within five years had driven the Carthaginians from the entire Iberian peninsula. He then led the invasion of North Africa, threatening Carthage itself, ending the war with his victory at Zama in 202 BC. He was the only Roman commander to defeat Hannibal in a major land battle.

Scipio trained his men hard. Under his command the Roman legions became better drilled and more confident than ever, able to perform both complex battlefield manoeuvres and surprise night attacks. He was both methodical and meticulous in his preparations for each campaign, gathering intelligence, acquiring local allies and ensuring that adequate supplies were readily available. These were the skills that made possible his bold capture of New Carthage. In Spain he used large numbers of Spanish warriors, although never relying on them too heavily and leaving the more serious fighting to his own troops. In Africa he secured sufficient Numidian light cavalry to give him an advantage over the enemy – an essential to success that he had learned from Hannibal. He also copied the Carthaginian in ensuring that the enemy was deceived about his intentions, and that every move he made was both fast and unexpected.

Scipio's life and career were closely tied up with Hannibal's. A teenager when Hannibal invaded Italy, he served on the staff of his father, was present at the first encounter between the armies in 218 BC, and survived Rome's most serious defeat at the Battle of Cannae in 216. Scipio grew up in a time of war fought against a skilled and determined opponent. Because of this, his generation served on campaign for longer periods than was normal for Roman aristocrats and learned how to soldier in a very hard school. Such men proved to be very capable commanders, and Scipio was by far the best of them.

Yet his career, after the defeat of Hannibal, was largely one of disappointment. Although he commanded an army in one later campaign, his performance was no more than competent and his opponents merely a Gallic tribe. The long years of commanding the army in distant lands were poor preparation for political life in Rome, and he proved an indifferent politician. He eventually died in bitter and self-imposed retirement; in death as in life seemingly linked to Hannibal, who took his own life around the same time.

The Hard School

Scipio was born into one of the wealthy and distinguished patrician families that held a central place in the political life of the Roman Republic. His father was elected consul for 218 BC and given the task of taking an army to Spain to confront Hannibal. En route, he realized that Hannibal had already passed him, heading for Italy, so he sent his brother with the bulk of the troops on to Spain and turned again to the east, to meet Hannibal south of the Alps. The young Scipio came with him as a member of his staff. In November 218 BC, the consul led a force of cavalry and light infantry that confronted Hannibal at the River Ticinus, where it was overwhelmed. The Roman commander was wounded and Scipio, according to family tradition, led a desperate cavalry charge that saved his life.

Scipio was still with the army when the combined forces of the two consuls were smashed at Trebia in December, and in 217 BC may have been present at the disaster at Lake Trasimene, where a Roman army was ambushed by Hannibal and massacred. In the following year he was a military tribune with the Second Legion, part of the massive army sent to confront Hannibal. In August, despite massively outnumbering the enemy, the Romans were almost annihilated at the Battle of Cannae, but Scipio again survived. He rallied groups of other survivors, gaining fame by his dramatic response to a group of young aristocrats who were thinking of fleeing abroad; grasping his weapon, he made them all swear an oath, at sword point, never to abandon the Republic.

In 211 BC, the Romans suffered a serious setback. On recovering from his wounds, Scipio's father had been sent to Spain to hold joint command there with his brother, but following the defection of local allies, both brothers were killed. A year later, when he was still only in his mid-twenties, Scipio applied to succeed them in the Spanish command. Despite the fact that the Republic normally gave military commands only to elected magistrates in their forties, casualties among the ranks of the Senate had been exceptionally high in the previous few years. No one else appears to have been keen to serve in Spain. In addition, it was felt that the family name would command greater loyalty from the tribes in the peninsula than the distant and unknown entity of Rome. Even so, it is important to remember just how exceptional his appointment was. At a time of crisis, it demonstrated the extent to which the Romans were prepared to gamble.

The Spanish Campaign

Scipio took with him reinforcements to raise the number of Roman troops in Spain to just over thirty thousand. Although massively outnumbered by the Carthaginians, the Roman army was concentrated and disciplined; the Carthaginians, on the other hand, were unable to keep their armies assembled in one place because of the difficulty of feeding them. Almost immediately Scipio decided to launch a bold stroke against the Carthaginian provincial capital at New Carthage (modern Cartagena). According to local fishermen, the lagoon protecting the western wall of the city was fordable in certain conditions. At the start of the campaigning season in 209 BC, discovering that the three Carthaginian field armies were at some distance from the city, he moved rapidly down the coast, his fleet keeping pace with the land forces. The day after arriving, he launched a full-scale assault on the wall facing the main landward approach, his forces fighting hard even to reach the wall in the face of a robust defence from the Carthaginian forces that came out to meet him.

Scipio kept the attack going for several hours. Only once the tide had fallen did he dispatch a force of five hundred men to ford the lagoon. Virtually all of the defenders had been drawn away to face the 'main' Roman threat and these five hundred men were able to use ladders to climb the wall. They then followed the wall round to the main gate, while the forces outside renewed their assault. The Carthaginian defenders panicked and fled, allowing the Romans to open the main gate. Scipio then led a reserve force to seize the citadel and other key points in the town. It was a remarkable victory, showing the tribes that it was possible to beat the Carthaginians.

Scipio took possession of the enemy treasury, along with many other resources. There were also hostages in the city, from the noble families of many of the Spanish tribes, kept there as security for treaties with the Carthaginians. One of the hostages – a beautiful aristocratic woman – was brought to him by his men. In a gesture emulating Alexander the Great, Scipio refused to touch her, instead handing her over to her family with her honour intact. It was a politic as well as a noble gesture. Over the following winter Scipio was able to persuade a number of Spanish leaders to defect to his side, bringing their warriors with them.

In 208 BC, Scipio won a marginal victory over Hannibal's brother Hasdrubal Barca at Baecula, but he was unable to prevent Hasdrubal from leaving Spain to march to Italy. In the event this did not matter, since Hasdrubal was overwhelmed by superior Roman forces soon after he arrived in Italy. The next year was spent in indecisive manoeuvring before the Carthaginians concentrated a great army under Hasdrubal Gisgo and met Scipio at Ilipa. The Romans were heavily outnumbered, and almost half of their force consisted of Spanish allies, whose loyalty was questionable and whose effectiveness was low. Yet Scipio's legions and their Latin allies were well drilled. For days the armies confronted each other, lined up with their best troops in the centre and allies on the flanks; neither side choosing to risk a battle.

Having lulled the enemy into this routine, at dawn the next day Scipio sent his cavalry and light infantry to attack the enemy outposts in front of their camp. While this attack was under way, Scipio formed up his main army, this time posting the legions on the flanks and placing his unreliable Spanish in the centre. Hasdrubal deployed in a hurry, taking up the same formation as before. He was stunned when he saw the Roman wings marching forward towards his weakest infantry on his own flanks. Scipio's Spanish allies deliberately advanced much more slowly, but still prevented Hasdrubal's centre from threatening the Roman wings. The Carthaginians watched, mesmerized, as the Roman infantry manoeuvred, quickly routing these flanks before turning against the better troops in the Carthaginian centre. Hasdrubal's army was utterly shattered. In the following months it was simply a matter of mopping up the few remaining Carthaginian strongholds.

The Invasion of North Africa

After his success in Spain, Scipio returned to Rome and was elected consul for 205 BC. Although he was still below the legal age for this office, his recent successes made the electorate and other senators willing to make an exception. Scipio then lobbied successfully to be given command of an army that would invade North Africa and threaten Carthage itself. The invasion was launched from Sicily, and at the heart of the army were two legions formed from the survivors of Cannae and other Roman defeats – now very experienced soldiers whose drill, Scipio made sure, was up to his high standard.

In 204 BC, Scipio landed and camped outside the town of Utica. He was soon afterwards joined by Masinissa, a Numidian prince, who brought with him a force of cavalry. Contingents of these superb light horsemen had been some of Hannibal's most effective troops, but after service with the Carthaginians in Spain, Masinissa had become disgruntled and was persuaded to defect. Masinissa commanded only a small force, but they soon proved their worth, luring some enemy cavalry into a carefully laid ambush. Scipio started to besiege Utica, and two large Carthaginian armies soon approached, one led by Hasdrubal Gisgo, the other by Syphax, the Numidian king, an ally of Carthage and a bitter enemy of Masinissa. Throughout the winter the two forces camped about 7½ miles apart and watched the Romans. Early in the spring of 203 BC, Scipio divided his army into two and launched carefully prepared night attacks on the separate enemy camps. The camps were burnt, and the panicking enemy soldiers were either cut down or dispersed. It was a spectacular success.

The Carthaginians took some time to regroup, allowing Scipio to strengthen the fortifications of his own camp and build substantial granaries to hold the supplies of captured enemy grain. Eventually, combining a newly arrived contingent of mercenary Celtiberian warriors from Spain with the survivors of the earlier disaster, Hasdrubal and Syphax mustered an army roughly equivalent in size to the Romans'. Scipio attacked immediately, confronting them in what became known as the Battle of the Great Plains. The Celtiberians formed the centre and put up stiff resistance. On the wings the Roman cavalry and Masinissa's men swiftly overwhelmed the enemy horsemen. The infantry on the wings – in the main survivors of the night attacks on the camps at the beginning of the year – soon joined them. Scipio's legions were up against the Celtiberians, but while the first line kept them pinned down, the second and third manoeuvred to strike at both flanks of the mercenaries. Then they too were driven off or destroyed.

This new disaster forced the Carthaginian leaders to summon Hannibal and his army back from Italy to confront the invader. In a display of confidence, Scipio ordered that some captured enemy spies should be shown around his camp and then released to make their report. After a brief attempt at negotiation, the two armies met at Zama and for the first time in his career Hannibal was utterly defeated. Aware that there was no possibility of forming another army, he returned to Carthage and told the political leaders that they had no alternative but to make peace.

The Battle of Zama

Hannibal brought back with him from Italy his surviving veteran soldiers. However, the bulk of his army consisted of recently raised troops of questionable quality. He was outnumbered in cavalry, with many of the superb Numidian light horsemen now fighting for the Romans. Hannibal did have some eighty war elephants, more than he had commanded in any previous battle, but unfortunately most of these animals were also recently acquired and not fully trained. His army in 202 BC was thus anything but the flexible, well-disciplined force with which he had won his great victories. Facing him, Scipio had a smaller, but homogeneous, confident and well-trained army. He also had four thousand Numidian cavalry and some six thousand skirmishers on foot, brought by Masinissa.

Hannibal deployed in three lines, with his veterans at the rear. He hoped that the charge of the war elephants would disorder the Roman line, which would then be worn down by his infantry until the time came for his veterans to deliver the *coup de grâce*. Scipio's legions were in the normal three lines (*triplex acies*). However, rather than station the individual maniples in the conventional chequerboard pattern, he drew them up directly behind the unit in front, thus creating wide lanes running through the middle of his infantry formation.

The battle opened with the elephants charging forward en masse. Stung by the missiles from Roman skirmishers, some panicked and turned back to trample their own horsemen on the wings. Others charged on, but instead of hitting the Roman maniples, they took the easiest path and ran down the lanes between them, to be picked off and killed behind the lines. Scipio's veterans were disciplined enough to remain in their maniples and let the animals run past them. The elephant attack failed utterly.

In the meantime, the Roman and Numidian cavalry charged on both wings, overwhelmed their Carthaginian counterparts and pursued them off the field. In the centre, the Roman front line struck the foremost of Hannibal's infantry lines. The Carthaginians resisted stubbornly, but after a time were driven back. There was some confusion as units from the first line withdrew and the second line was reluctant to let them pass. After a further struggle the Carthaginian second line was also routed. That these two lines failed to support each other properly showed clearly that the Carthaginian army had not had sufficient time to train together or integrate its contingents.

Hannibal's veterans had not moved from their position and closed ranks, preventing any of the fugitives from forcing their way through. The Roman first line was by now tired, and had probably already been reinforced by maniples from the second line. In another impressive display of discipline, the Romans halted and reformed. All three lines were merged to form a single block, much like the traditional phalanx formation. This then lumbered forward into contact with the veterans. A fierce combat ensued, which was only ended when the Roman cavalry returned and attacked Hannibal's veterans in the rear. Having superiority in cavalry gave Scipio a marked advantage from the start. But he also effectively countered each of Hannibal's tactics. Hannibal's army was utterly broken, having lost twenty thousand dead and almost as many taken prisoner.

Fading Glory
Scipio returned to Rome and celebrated a spectacular triumph. He also took the surname Africanus as a permanent reminder to others of his great victories. Now in his late thirties, he was at the age when a senator would normally

begin to seek high offices and the chance for military command. But he had already fought and won great campaigns. Elected consul for a second time for 194 BC he was given command of an army campaigning against the Gallic tribes of the Po valley. Two consuls were sent to the region and the bulk of the fighting seems to have fallen to his colleague. Scipio may have led a series of plundering expeditions, but achieved little. Furthermore, the situation had changed since the Second Punic War. There were now plenty of Romans who were eager for military commands, and he was granted only a single year in his post before being replaced.

Perhaps Scipio's last chance to achieve something comparable to the victories in Spain and Africa came when he accompanied his younger brother Lucius in the campaign against the Seleucid ruler Antiochus the Great, a command given to Lucius largely because Scipio announced that he would go with him. Yet in the event Scipio played only the most minor of roles and was not present at the great Roman victory of Magnesia in 190 BC. The reason given was illness, but perhaps he chose not to be there so that his brother could win glory for himself.

Lucius celebrated a great triumph on his return to Rome, but both he and his brother were accused of misappropriating state funds during the campaign. Neither was convicted, but simply being brought to trial was a major humiliation. Soon afterwards Scipio retired to a country estate and never again took part in public life. His grandson by adoption, Scipio Aemilianus, would destroy Carthage in 146 BC.

JUDAH MACCABEUS

c. 190–160 bc

MARTIN VAN CREVELD

PERHAPS the strangest thing about Judah Maccabeus is the way he is remembered: as a glance at publishers' catalogues will confirm, only a handful of books have been written about him; on the Internet, many of the hits refer not to him but to the oratorio that bears his name, Judas Maccabaeus – *written by George Frideric Handel in 1746 to a libretto by Thomas Morell, and containing the celebrated passage:*

> See, the conquering hero comes!
> Sound the trumpets, beat the drums.
> Sports prepare, the laurel bring,
> Songs of triumph to him sing.

See the godlike youth advance!
Breathe the flutes, and lead the dance;
Myrtle wreaths, and roses twine,
To deck the hero's brow divine.

See, the conquering hero comes!
Sound the trumpets, beat the drums.
Sports prepare, the laurel bring,
Songs of triumph to him sing.
See, the conquering hero comes!
Sound the trumpets, beat the drums.

Sources about Judah are relatively abundant; in addition to the two Books of Maccabees – apocryphal texts originally written in Hebrew during the second half of the second century BC but surviving only in Greek translation – we have several shorter ancient accounts of his deeds. Still we know nothing of his youth, other than that he was the third son of a priest, Matthathias the Hasmonean, and that the family lived in the village of Modiin in Judea, not far from where Tel Aviv airport now stands. His name, Judah (Judas is the Greek version), means 'Knows God'; his nickname, Maccabeus, may have derived from *makevet*, or mallet, so probably meant 'the hammerer'.

Judea was, at the time, governed from Antioch, in Syria,

by the Seleucid king, Antiochus IV Epiphanes ('Surrounded by Light'). His father, Antiochus III, had been badly defeated by the Romans at the Battle of Magnesia in 190 BC, after which his kingdom began to disintegrate. In 170 BC, Epiphanes usurped the throne from his brother Seleucus, and in order to consolidate his power he then prohibited Jewish practices and demanded that religious worship focus on himself.

In 170 BC and again two years later, Antiochus IV invaded Egypt. The second campaign in particular was a great success; the king got as far as Alexandria, the capital. However, at the city's outskirts he was met by a Roman envoy, who summarily ordered him to turn back, a grievous blow to his power and prestige. In 167 BC, the very next year, Matthathias raised the standard of revolt against him. When he died in 166 BC, Matthathias designated Judah, rather than either of Judah's older brothers, to be his successor.

The Judean Revolt

The first blows of revolt were directed not against the Syrian occupiers but against fellow Judeans. Apparently not everybody was delighted to join the sons of Matthathias; at one point, altars of idol worship had been destroyed and some 'Hellenizing' Jews forcibly circumcised.

The first Seleucid response was commanded by Apollonius, who was possibly the governor of Samaria. He, and what today would be called 'the forces of order', appeared at Modiin in the spring of 166 BC. Modiin being situated in a plain, the rebels were unable to resist their heavily armed enemy, and fled to the nearby hills. While details are scant, apparently Judah relied on classic guerrilla tactics, fighting at night, selecting suitable places, and taking the enemy by surprise. We are told in I Maccabees that he 'made quite a number of the enemy flee ... and the fame of his courage spread everywhere'.

The victory over Apollonius was quickly followed by another skirmish. This time the Seleucid commander was one Seron, who was probably in charge of some garrisons along the coast. Seron committed the error of marching his troops into the mountains by way of Beth Horon, a route that, until a modern highway was built there a few years ago, had always been notoriously hard to travel and easy to block. The sources say Judah had about six thousand men with him – which, modern scholars believe, was considerably more than Seron had. In any case eight hundred of the royal army died, possibly including Seron himself, while the rest fled back the way they had come.

Clearly, a pattern was being established. The Seleucid

army was a powerful war machine, consisting mainly of heavy infantrymen who carried long pikes and operated in a phalanx. It also included light infantry, however – the only element that was really useful outside the plain – as well as heavy and light cavalry. We have no idea what kinds of units Apollonius and Seron commanded, because the prime purpose of our main sources, I and II Maccabees (which all the rest seem to have used), was not to provide military detail but to record and praise the ways of God.

The Road to Jerusalem

By this time Antiochus had realized the revolt was more than a minor affair. To deal with it, he therefore dispatched a relative, Lysias, who was governor of the western part of his kingdom. In September 165 BC this led directly to what was probably Judah's greatest triumph: the Battle of Ammaus.

Although Ammaus was not the largest battle Judah fought, it changed the nature of the revolt he led. Fortunately, an account of the battle was preserved in I Maccabees, containing information so detailed that modern scholars have speculated that the author may have participated in the battle.

The Seleucid king Antiochus IV was angered by the defeats of his commanders Apollonius and Seron. Having appointed Lysias as his commander, he gave him 'forty thousand men and seven thousand cavalry to go to the land of Judea and devastate it'. He also had some elephants, the tanks of the ancient world, though our sources do not say how many there were.

Along with his subordinates, Ptolemy, Nicanor and Gorgias, described as 'men of valour from among the king's friends', Lysias marched south into the land of Israel. He set up camp at Ammaus, very close to Latrun (where fierce battles were fought during Israel's 1948 War of Independence). There he was joined by auxiliary forces from Philistia and Edom. Also present was a throng of merchants with money to buy the expected Jewish prisoners and chains to put them in.

Judah's first move was to raise the morale of his troops, which had been lowered by the mighty host brought against them. Jerusalem was, at the time, in the hands of a Seleucid garrison; it was 'desolate as a desert'. Accordingly, he assembled his men at Mitzpah, a hill further to the north, where there was 'a place of prayer'. They put on sackcloth, fasted and prayed. Judah then harangued them:

> Gird yourselves and be valiant men, and be ready
> against the morning, that you may fight with
> these nations that are assembled against us and our

sanctuary. For it is better for us to die in battle than to see the evils of our nation and of our Holy Places.

Gorgias must have heard about the ceremony, or perhaps the Jews deliberately spread the news. Taking with him five thousand infantrymen and a thousand cavalrymen, he launched a night march to take the rebels by surprise – only to find their camp empty. As he spread out to seek them in the hills, Judah and his men, probably about six thousand in number, evaded him and marched west until they took up positions south of Lysias' main base. Again Judah harangued his men, then gave the signal to attack.

The enemy fled, and the Syrian camp was soon taken and set alight. Realizing that Gorgias' force remained intact, however, Judah managed to prevent his men from dispersing and plundering it; apparently he had them well in hand. Soon after, light being reflected from shields showed that Gorgias was coming to the rescue. However, when Gorgias realized what had happened to the rest of the force he, in turn, fled.

And Judah returned to plunder the camp and they seized much gold and silver and cloth dyed blue and marine purple and great riches; and

returning they sang hymns and praises to
Heaven, for he is good, for his mercy endureth
for ever.

By enabling Judah to switch from guerrilla to regular
warfare, the victory at Ammaus changed the nature of the
struggle. Lysias' army, though it had been shattered, was
not annihilated. The Syrian commander succeeded in
rallying his forces, and, while the sequence of events that
followed is not completely clear, November–December of
165 BC found him leading another large-scale expedition
against the Jews.

Wary of the mountains, this time Lysias took an altogether different route. Starting from Philistia, he marched
east by way of Beer Sheba, then turned north and headed
for Hebron and Beth Lehem, reaching all the way to Beth
Tzur (today a Palestinian Arab village on the southernmost
outskirts of Jerusalem).

Judah was waiting for him, but no major battle took
place. Antiochus was, at the time, campaigning against
the Parthians far away, where he died of disease. The
Seleucid postal services, consisting of mounted messengers working in relay, were efficient, and the news apparently reached Lysias even as he was preparing for his
assault on Jerusalem. The army thereupon retreated, and
its commander hastened to Antioch to look after the

succession of the late king's son, Antiochus V, who was a mere child.

The citadel of Jerusalem was known as Akra or Hakra. One hundred and seventy years later, it was where Jesus was imprisoned; in 164 BC it was firmly held by a Seleucid garrison. Still Lysias' retreat enabled Judah to enter the temple – which for years had been used for idol worship – and purify it, in a ceremony which gave rise to the modern Jewish festival of Hanukkah, when candles are lit in commemoration. In the words of the song that is sung on the occasion:

> O mighty stronghold of my salvation,
> to praise You is a delight.
> Restore my House of Prayer and there
> we will bring a thanksgiving offering.
> When You will have prepared the
> slaughter for the blaspheming foe,
> Then I shall complete with a song of hymn
> the dedication of the Altar.

Lysias, however, did not give up. The next year saw Judah and his men, who had grown from a band of guerrillas into a semi-regular army, engaged in an attempt to reduce Akra by means of siege machines. In telling us how powerful Lysias' force was, I Maccabees grows positively lyrical: 'from other kingdoms and from islands of the sea mercenary armies came to him. And the number of his armies was a hundred thousand foot and twenty thousand horsemen, and elephants thirty-two trained for war.' Considering the state of the Seleucid kingdom, the true figure was probably less than half that.

This time the encounter took place a little further to the south, not far from the village of Beth Zeharia, named after the biblical prophet. First came the elephants, which had been 'saturated with blood of grape and berries to rouse them for war'. Each of these moving fortresses was surrounded by a thousand heavy infantry and five hundred picked horsemen. Each elephant carried a wooden castle with four men in it, plus the mahout (elephant driver); a good example of combined arms at work. Following the normal Hellenistic pattern, the remaining cavalry was distributed on both wings to provide cover. 'And all trembled who heard the sound of their throng, and the strides of the throng and the clank of the weapons for the camp was very large and heavy.'

The ensuing battle was sharp, but short. Judah's brother Elazar sacrificed himself, diving under one of the elephants, killing it with his sword and then being crushed as it fell. This act of heroism notwithstanding, there was no resisting Lysias' superior force. Soon the Jews found themselves besieged in the Temple Mount, so recently liberated, with nothing to eat; many of Judah's men deserted. No doubt they would have succumbed, but again luck came to their aid. Back in Syria, a certain Philippus, who commanded the Seleucid army in the east, had marched on Antioch in an effort to wrest the kingdom for himself. In the end, Lysias was able to overcome him, but only at the cost of giving Judah a much-needed respite.

Last Battles

By this time the revolt had been going on for four years, the first two of which had been marked by considerable military successes. Guerrilla warfare on its own could not liberate the country, however, and once the Seleucids were able to bring even part of their mighty forces to bear – the rest were tied down in Iran – only the death of Antiochus IV and the ensuing troubles saved Judah and his men. Nor did Lysias' victory over Philippus end the kingdom's difficulties. Only in 162 BC did a new ruler, Demetrius I, succeed in consolidating his control.

A new commander, Bacchides, was sent out. Apparently Judah had learnt the lesson of Beth Zeharia in the previous campaign; his men, for all their courage, were not yet ready to face the full might of a well-organized, well-armed and well-led Seleucid army. Accordingly, when Bacchides appeared in front of Jerusalem, he gave up the city without a fight.

At this stage, Bacchides appears to have considered the war as good as won; he even appointed a new high priest. Leaving a garrison at Akra, he marched from Jerusalem to the hills to the north, apparently with the intention of combing them. However, once again outside events intervened. The military situation in Babylonia was deteriorating, forcing Bacchides and some of his forces to go there. To fill his place he appointed a former subordinate, Nicanor, *strategos*.

Nicanor tried to negotiate with the insurgents, but to no avail. Next, apparently fearing that his inferior forces would be bottled up in Jerusalem, he decided to leave the city and offer battle in the mountain plateau to the north; there, some reinforcements reached him. We know nothing about their strength, or Nicanor's. However, they must have come through Samaria by way of the present road that leads from Jenin to Nablus and Ramallah.

The two armies met at Adasa, the exact location of which remains unknown, in March 161 BC. Nicanor 'fell first in battle' (the thirteenth of the Jewish month Adar being thereafter called 'Nicanor Day'). His troops, dispirited by their commander's death, fled wildly to the west. Their route was the same one followed by Seron five years earlier, only in the opposite direction. As the inhabitants of the surrounding villages came out and joined in the pursuit, the survivors' plight grew worse and few of them can have survived. Nicanor's own body, or parts of it, were brought to Jerusalem in triumph and displayed on stakes.

The next year, 160 BC, brought Bacchides back to Judea. This time he chose to march by a completely different route, namely the one leading south from the Sea of Galilee through the Jordan valley; next, turning west at Gilgal (where Joshua had once camped), he ascended the mountains to reach the same mountain plateau where Nicanor had been defeated.

The encounter took place at Elasa, a few miles northwest of Adasa. Attempting to explain away the defeat that was to come, I Maccabees grossly exaggerates Bacchides' strength while under-reporting that of Judah's army; still there is no doubt that the Seleucid force was much the stronger. When Judah's staff advised a retreat, however, his response was defiant: 'If our end is near, let us die bravely for our brothers!'

For the first time, we get a glimpse of Judah's tactical dispositions. Following the normal Hellenistic pattern, he deployed his light troops, armed with bows and slings, in front. The cavalry occupied the wings, while his infantry held the centre. Likewise Bacchides had his phalanx in the centre with cavalry on both wings.

Bacchides himself commanded his powerful right wing, which was standard Hellenistic practice. Apparently

Judah felt he had only one chance: namely, to stake every-thing on a single throw by concentrating his best men against Bacchides. Coming under attack, Bacchides, resorting to a manoeuvre that had been executed many, many times before, carried out a feigned retreat, drawing the Jews after him. This enabled the phalanx to march into their rear: 'and the battle grew harder, and many fell dead of these and of these, and Judah fell, and the remaining fled'.

The Aftermath

From the beginning of the revolt, Judah proved himself a tough, resourceful commander and a master of guerrilla warfare. Probably his greatest successes were the early ones. Later, as he engaged in regular warfare, things became more difficult; in part, this was because much of the time he simply could not match the enemy in terms of numbers and armament. Twice, in 163 and 162 BC, he was saved only by his enemy's internal difficulties. In his last battle he was overwhelmed by superior forces and, fighting to the end, lost his life.

His death was a grave setback, but it did not end the revolt. His remaining brothers took over; in the end, thanks as much to the internal difficulties besetting the Seleucid kingdom as to their own abilities, they prevailed. The Hasmonean kingdom survived for just under a century, but in 64 BC was occupied by the Roman commander Pompey. With that, the curtain was drawn on Jewish independence for a period lasting more than two thousand years.

POMPEY

106–48 bc

ADRIAN GOLDSWORTHY

GNAEUS POMPEY was one of Rome's greatest generals, who won victories in Italy, Africa, Spain and Asia. Contemporaries compared him to Alexander, and he was especially delighted when the dictator Sulla gave him, too, the name Magnus or 'the Great'. His career was exceptional in every way, for unlike other Roman commanders he held no political office until he was in his late thirties, instead spending most of his early life on campaign. Pompey broke most of Rome's political rules, and spent as much time fighting other Romans as he did foreign enemies. This made it all the more ironic that he died as the defender of the Republic, fighting Julius Caesar.

Pompey's exceptional skill was in organization and planning. He had immense talent for raising and training troops, setting a personal example, even when in his late fifties, by drilling with his soldiers. Still more impressive was the scale of organization that he displayed in combating and defeating the pirates in the Mediterranean in 67 BC. Furthermore his armies rarely faced serious supply shortages; when they did, it was usually because of decisions taken by others over whom he had no control. In this he contrasted markedly with Caesar.

As a battlefield commander, however, Pompey lacked Caesar's finesse. He had immense courage, being inclined throughout his life to lead heroic cavalry charges after the manner of his hero Alexander. On one occasion, however, he had to flee, abandoning his horse, and only escaped because the pursuing enemy fell to bickering over his mount and its rich harness. Worsted on several occasions on the battlefield, Pompey usually learned from his mistakes. Yet his aim was always to gain such a massive strategic advantage that a battle was either unnecessary or its outcome a foregone conclusion.

The Private Army

In his teens, Pompey served on the staff of his father, Pompeius Strabo, in the Social War fought from 91 BC to 89 BC against Rome's rebellious Italian allies. His father avoided taking sides during the civil war that followed immediately after this, but died suddenly – struck by lightning, according to one story. Pompey himself came under suspicion from one of the sides in the war, and so resolved to join the other, led by Sulla. He did not arrive empty-handed, but raised two legions from the population of his family's vast estates, paying for their wages and equipment out of his own pocket. He later added a third legion to this private army. As he marched to join Sulla, he encountered several enemy forces, all poorly trained and most abysmally led. Pompey routed them easily at every encounter. He became one of Sulla's most trusted subordinates, sent to region after region to overwhelm the enemy there. Within a few years he had fought in northern Italy, Sicily and North Africa.

Pompey's soldiers were fiercely loyal, but were not always under his full control. They mutinied when they felt that Sulla had slighted their commander, and were only restored to discipline after Pompey threatened to kill himself. Sulla – who made himself dictator in late 82 or early 81 BC – soon after dubbed him 'the Great' and allowed him to celebrate a triumph. He also arranged for him to marry his stepdaughter (although she died not long after the wedding).

Other people, however, had a lower opinion of the youthful general: older subordinates of the dictator were jealous of the favour shown him, and neutral observers felt that Pompey revelled far too much in power and took excessive pleasure in executing his defeated Roman enemies – it was at around this time that he gained the nickname of the 'young butcher'.

Sulla resigned his office in 79 BC and died a year later. As Pompey still had his army, the Senate decided to make use of it to defeat an attempted coup by the consul Lepidus in 78 BC. Pompey suppressed the rebellion with his usual speed and ruthlessness, and was then sent to Spain to fight against Sertorius, one of Sulla's rivals, who had refused to surrender. It was the first time that Pompey and his army had come up against a well-trained and competently led enemy, and in the first encounter Pompey was ambushed and completely outfought. Pompey learned from his experiences, however, realizing that it was better to attack Sertorius' inept subordinates and avoid confronting the man who had dubbed him 'Sulla's pupil'.

Although Pompey had for the first time been granted formal power as a proconsul by the Senate, there was little enthusiasm for this tough campaign from the elected magistrates, and on several occasions Pompey complained that he and his army were being inadequately supplied. Despite this, he and his fellow commander Metellus finally defeated the enemy – helped considerably by the assassination of Sertorius by jealous rivals. Pompey returned to Italy in 71 BC, where he managed to encounter and destroy a fragment of Spartacus' slave army that had survived defeat by Crassus, and began to display a petty tendency to boast about finishing wars already won by others. Finally, at the age of 36, he decided to enter the Senate, but despite being still under age, was determined to start at the most senior level by becoming consul. The Senate felt unable to resist either his popularity or the armies which he and Crassus kept camped outside Rome, and both were elected consuls for 70 BC in a landslide victory.

The People's General

Pompey revelled in his popularity, celebrating a second triumph. (Crassus, on the other hand, despite having prevailed in a gritty campaign against the slave army, was granted the lesser honour of an ovation.) Pompey had fame and massive wealth, but little experience or skill in political life. Within a few years he sought fresh military glories to reinforce his position, and in 67 BC was granted an extraordinary command by popular vote – something normally allocated only by the Senate. The exceptionally influential and popular could, however, bypass the magistrates and go straight to the People's Assembly. Pompey's challenge was to deal with the pirates infesting the Mediterranean, a task previously attempted by others but with inadequate resources and inevitable lack of success.

Pompey, however, was given massive authority, along with men, ships and money on a lavish scale. The war was won in a matter of months.

Piracy had been a serious problem throughout the Mediterranean since the start of the first century BC. Kidnappings were common – two Roman praetors with their attendants were once abducted from the Italian coast – and frequent attacks made on ships or coastal communities, including Ostia, the vital port which dealt with the huge amounts of grain needed to feed Rome. In 67 BC Pompey was voted an extraordinary command to deal with this, with power superior to that of provincial governors, to encompass the entire Mediterranean coast for a distance of 50 miles inland. His forces totalled 120,000 infantry and 5,000 cavalry, as well as a fleet of 500 warships. To assist him he had no fewer than twenty-four legates (or senior generals), many of them highly experienced.

Organization was always Pompey's great strength. He divided the Mediterranean into thirteen regions – six to the west and seven to the east of Italy. Each area was controlled by a legate, backed by strong forces, ordered to pursue only within his own zone. Pompey himself led the main strike force of sixty ships, which would attack the pirates anywhere they were found. In the spring he began in the western sectors, and within forty days had swept them free of pirates with apparently little fighting. The pirates had not been faced with serious Roman opposition for decades and appear to have been completely unprepared for this sudden concerted onslaught.

Operations took a little longer in the east, which had less land directly governed by Rome and thus more pirate strongholds. From the beginning Pompey knew that it was useless to sweep the sea of raiders if their coastal bases remained secure, and his land forces played a vital role in capturing enemy strongholds. Siege equipment had been prepared, but again there was less fighting than had been anticipated. In most cases the approach of a determined Roman force was enough to prompt a surrender. Once again Pompey confirmed his reputation for stealing other men's glory by accepting the surrender of some pirate strongholds in Crete, placed under siege by another Roman commander.

The Romans could be utterly ruthless in punishing defeated enemies yet at other times lenient. For the pirates, Pompey had judged from the beginning that a permanent solution required conciliation. Accordingly, those who surrendered were not enslaved, but were transported and settled in new communities on better land, the aim being to enable them to feed themselves and their families without resorting to piracy. The east was settled in forty-seven days. Although Pompey claimed to have captured 846 vessels, some of these were no doubt very small. Some twenty thousand prisoners were resettled, one of the cities in Cilicia to which they were sent being renamed Pompeiopolis in his honour.

Publicly Pompey now asserted that he wanted a chance to enjoy a peaceful life, but it was abundantly clear that he was eager for another grand command. A second bill in the People's Assembly put him in charge of the war against King Mithridates VI of Pontus. Sulla had beaten the king in an earlier war, but had negotiated a peace that allowed him to return to face his rivals in Italy. Conflict had soon restarted, and the Romans had again come very close to total victory under the leadership of Lucullus. The latter had enemies in the Senate, however, who were able systematically to starve him of resources, allowing Mithridates to recover.

Pompey was once again given all the men, supplies and money that he needed. In 66 BC, he confronted Mithridates in western Pontus, a region on the southeast coast of the Black Sea, but the latter was forced to withdraw when his food supplies ran out. As usual, Pompey was far better prepared and pursued the enemy. The Pontic cavalry was lured into an ambush and badly cut up. In spite of a numerical superiority, Pompey was determined not to take risks and blockaded the enemy army, building a line of fortifications 19 miles in length. His men starving, Mithridates withdrew again, escaping under cover of darkness. In the days that followed, Pompey force-marched his men and got ahead of the enemy column. In the ensuing ambush the king managed to escape, but his army was effectively destroyed. Soon afterwards Mithridates' ally, King Tigranes of Armenia, surrendered.

Mithridates was beaten and fled to a stronghold in the north of his kingdom. Pompey showed little interest in capturing or killing him, being eager for further military adventures before the war was formally concluded and he was forced to lay down his command and return to Rome. An attack on one of his army's winter camps by a force of Albanians prompted Pompey first to invade this kingdom, and then extend his operations into neighbouring Iberia and Colchis. He then intervened in a civil war raging between rival members of the Hasmonean dynasty in Judea, backing one claimant and besieging Jerusalem, capturing the city three months later. He then moved south against the Nabatean Arab kingdom of Petra, his campaign coming to an end only when news arrived that Mithridates had committed suicide.

Pompey had added great swathes of territory to Rome's empire. These operations and those against the pirates were his only campaigns fought against unambiguously foreign enemies, and once the fighting was over he again demonstrated his genius for organization by creating a settlement to administer the new conquests. Much of the administrative structure he created would last for centuries. Not all became provinces, as some remained under the rule of local client kings. However, there was a delay before the arrangements were formally ratified in Rome. When Pompey returned in 62 BC he was granted another triumph – his third – in which he boasted that he had triumphed over Europe, Africa and now Asia, the three continents known to the Greeks and Romans. Yet again he was to display his lack of skill at political manipulation, however, and he did not seem to know how to deal with political opponents.

Civil War

A few years later, Pompey secretly allied with Crassus and Julius Caesar, forming what is known to scholars as the First Triumvirate. Caesar was elected consul for 59 BC and forced through the legislation sought by his two colleagues. Pompey secured the ratification of his eastern settlement and grants of farmland for the discharged veterans who had fought under his command. He also married Caesar's daughter Julia to cement the alliance. His new father-in-law then left for Gaul in 58 BC to begin a five-year command, later extended to ten.

The alliance was always a little uneasy. Pompey and Crassus disliked each other intensely. They came close to a split in 56 BC, but were reunited and again shared the consulship in 55 BC. Pompey was given command of all the armies in Spain, although he never went to the peninsula and instead remained just outside Rome to oversee events. Crassus went to Syria, and from there launched an invasion of Parthia, where he was killed in 53 BC. Julia died in childbirth at around the same time, weakening the bond with Caesar. As the time approached for his Gallic command to end, there was growing tension between the two former allies, Pompey being unwilling to accept Caesar as an equal. When asked what he would do if Caesar chose to fight, he disdainfully replied 'What if my son should attack me with a stick?' He also boasted that all he had to do was stamp his foot and legions would spring out of the soil of Italy. Eventually mutual suspicion, and the confident expectation that the other side would back down, led to war.

In January 49 BC, Caesar marched a legion across the border of his province – the little River Rubicon – into Italy. More troops followed. Pompey and his allies had raised many soldiers, but they were still untrained and no match for Caesar's veterans. Unlike his opponent, he was also saddled with many prominent senators who demanded important commands, but refused to obey his orders. Pompey decided that he must abandon Italy and create a massive army in the eastern Mediterranean, so that he could then return and dispose of Caesar. As Pompey himself put it, referring to Sulla's successful invasion of Italy from Greece in 83 BC – 'Sulla did it, why can't I?' Apart from some serious losses when his subordinates disobeyed his orders, his retreat was well managed, the bulk of his troops being safely evacuated from Brundisium in spite of Caesar's attempt at a blockade.

For the rest of the year Pompey concentrated on mustering a very large army in Greece, backed by strong naval forces. Although unable to catch Caesar's invasion fleet at the end of the year, they made it difficult for him to receive reinforcement and supply convoys. Caesar twice attempted to capture Pompey's main supply depot at the port of Dyrrachium. On the second attempt Pompey arrived first, and the two armies then sought to blockade each other, building long lines of fortifications on the high ground. Caesar's smaller army was on the outside, furthest from the sea, and struggled to complete their more extensive line, although they managed to repulse a series of attacks by the Pompeians. However, a major assault launched by Caesar a few days later ended in a costly failure. He commented that the enemy would have won an outright victory 'if only their leader was a winner'. Yet Pompey was content to wait. There were clear signs that his strategy of starving the enemy into submission was working; with his army desperately short of food and no prospect of beating the enemy, Caesar withdrew from the coast.

In August, Pompey was persuaded by the many senior senators with his staff to risk battle outside Pharsalus (see also pp. 265–6). Although a break with his strategy, it is possible that he felt the time was at last ripe. Relying on his greatly superior cavalry to outflank the enemy line, he was dismayed when this was routed, and would seem to have had no other clear idea of how to beat the enemy. Soon afterwards he fled the field. It was a lacklustre performance, perhaps explained by his age – he was now 58 – and by the fact that he had not been on campaign for over a decade before the Civil War began. Pompey escaped and took ship for Egypt, perhaps still hoping to rebuild an army there. On rowing ashore in a small boat he was greeted by officials of the boy King Ptolemy XIII, one of whom had served under him in his eastern campaigns before taking service as a mercenary in the Egyptian army. At a signal, Pompey was cut down and beheaded. Caesar arrived a few days later, but refused to look at the head when it was presented to him. Despite the nature of his death, Pompey was given a funeral that befitted his status, and his tomb was a landmark in Alexandria for many years.

JULIUS CAESAR

100–44 BC

ADRIAN GOLDSWORTHY

CAIUS JULIUS CAESAR was Rome's most famous and successful general. In eight years of intensive campaigning from 58 to 51 BC, he conquered Gaul (roughly modern France and Belgium), crossed the Rhine into Germany, and twice landed in Britain. Backed into a corner by his political enemies at Rome, he then defeated them in the Civil War (49–45 BC) fought all around the Mediterranean. The Romans believed that he fought more battles than any other commander, won all his campaigns, and only suffered two serious setbacks, both of which proved temporary. Caesar was also a writer and consummate propagandist. His Commentaries *on his own operations in Gaul and the Civil War were recognized from the start as one of the greatest expressions of the Latin language. Their clear, dispassionate and fast-paced narratives are models of how military history should be written. Napoleon was just one of many famous commanders who acknowledged that he had learned a good deal from them.*

Like Napoleon, Caesar was a charismatic leader, able to inspire an almost fanatical loyalty in his soldiers. The stubborn determination of his legionaries carried his army through a number of desperate situations. It is also fair to say that Caesar's skills as a commander were often most spectacularly displayed when he was obliged to extricate himself from problems of his own creation. He was always bold, and at times apparently rash. Roman generals were expected to be aggressive, and Caesar's audacity is sometimes deceptive. He took risks – famously starting the Civil War with a gambler's comment 'the die is cast' (*iacta alea est*) – but only after he had done everything possible to strengthen his own position. If delaying would not improve his situation but would strengthen the enemy, then Caesar attacked even if the odds were against him. He was never wasteful with the lives of his men.

Caesar was very generous with promotions, plunder and praise. His officers, the famous and formidable centurions, he knew by name, emphasizing their heroism in his *Commentaries*. Caesar imposed a rigorous training regime on his army, but led by example. According to Suetonius, he would often order his men to keep a watchful eye on him, and then slip quietly out of camp, expecting them to catch up and follow him on a tough route march. He did not worry about formal discipline in rest periods, however, and was no martinet. When he spoke to his legionaries, he always addressed them as 'comrades'. When he faced two serious mutinies during the Civil War, the second one led by his favourite Tenth Legion, Caesar broke the mutineers' spirit with just one word, calling them 'civilians' instead of 'comrades'. Soon the veteran legionaries were begging him to decimate them – executing one soldier in ten – as long as he would take them back into his service. Ultimately, however, his men always trusted him, believing that, with Caesar in charge, they would win. He boasted that he was lucky, something the Romans felt was one of the most important attributes of a general. In his campaigns he made mistakes, and took big risks, but in the end he always won. For the Romans that was all that mattered.

Early Career

Caesar was born into a Republic riven by increasingly violent political rivalries. While he was in his teens, the first civil war erupted and saw Rome itself stormed three times by Roman armies. The young Caesar played no active part in this brutal conflict, but in its aftermath he angered Sulla the dictator and spent some months as a hunted fugitive. His mother and her influential relatives managed to secure him a pardon, and he was sent as a junior officer to the Roman province of Asia (80–78 BC). Here he quickly demonstrated his courage, being awarded Rome's highest decoration, the civic crown (*corona civica*) at the siege of Mytiline. However, a diplomatic mission to the court of the allied King Nicomedes of Bithynia led to scandal, when Caesar was rumoured to have become the old king's lover. Despite always denying the story, the gossip was to dog him for the rest of his life.

Caesar returned to Rome in 78 BC. By this time the Roman army was effectively a professional force, but led by aristocratic officers who interspersed periods of military service with civil and political posts. Caesar, too, embarked on this course, and for the next twenty years his career was a broadly conventional one for a young senator. He also spent some time studying rhetoric and oratory with famous lecturers in the Greek east. On one of these trips he was captured by pirates and held for ransom. Caesar charmed his captors, but promised that after his release he would return and have them all crucified. When the ransom arrived he did just that. With no authority to do so, he raised a force of ships and men from allied cities and swooped down to capture his former captors. The pirates were duly crucified, although as a gesture of mercy he had their throats cut first. In 74 BC he was on another study trip when a raiding force sent by King Mithridates of Pontus attacked the Roman province of Asia. Caesar rushed east, organized an army from the local allied cities and chased the enemy out of the province. Again he had no authority to do this, but his actions were widely praised, demonstrating both his skill and his immense self-confidence.

Caesar was building an impressive reputation which helped him climb the political ladder at Rome (at the same time gaining a less reputable name as a serial seducer of other men's wives). In either 72 or 71 BC he was elected to the post of military tribune – effectively a staff officer – and seems to have served against Spartacus and his army of rebellious slaves. It was another decade before he won a significant military post, when he was made governor of the province of Further Spain in 61 BC. He was massively in debt, having spent far beyond his means to win fame and popularity, and needed a successful and profitable campaign in Spain to restore his reputation and keep his creditors at bay. The province was garrisoned by two legions, but he quickly raised the equivalent of another and led the army on a series of aggressive operations against the border tribes.

Caesar won his victory and was awarded a triumph – a formal parade through the heart of the city of Rome

– when he returned at the end of 60 BC. However, his political opponents made sure that this honour would prevent him from standing for election for the consulship, Rome's most senior magistracy. In consequence, Caesar gave up his triumph, was elected to the consulship and formed a secret alliance with Pompey and Crassus, the two most powerful men in Rome. Together the three dominated politics for a year. Caesar's reward was a five-year command of the Gallic provinces and Illyricum. This was later extended to ten years. Still facing staggering debts, Caesar desperately needed to win victories on a vast scale.

Intervention in Gaul

Caesar may well have originally planned to fight a campaign in the Balkans, advancing from Illyricum to attack the Dacian kingdom. Instead an opportunity presented itself when the Helvetii, migrating from their homeland in what is now Switzerland, sought permission to pass through Transalpine Gaul (modern Provence). Caesar refused, fortified the line of the River Rhône, and repulsed all attempts to cross it by force. When the Helvetii turned away, Caesar answered an appeal for protection from the Aedui, a Gaulish tribe allied to Rome, and pursued them. An attempt at a night attack failed because of poor scouting, but soon afterwards Caesar managed to surprise one isolated convoy of the migrants and cut them to pieces. When his allies failed to supply him with sufficient grain, Caesar withdrew towards the Aedui's capital at Bibracte. The Helvetii took this as a sign of weakness and massed their army to attack him. But they were beaten back, suffering massive losses, the survivors being sent back to their homeland.

Later in 58 BC, Caesar turned on the Germanic war-leader Ariovistus, again claiming that he was responding to an appeal for help from Rome's allies. There was nearly a mutiny when the Roman army heard rumours of the ferocity of the German warriors. Caesar announced that he would press on, even if only the Tenth Legion accompanied him. The Tenth were flattered, and the rest shamed into following. In a brief campaign Ariovistus was brought to battle and utterly defeated. In 57 BC, Caesar answered another appeal for help and turned northeast to confront the warlike Belgian tribes. A stand-off between the two armies was broken when the tribal army ran out of food and had to disperse. Caesar began attacking the tribes individually, but they managed to re-form their army and surprised him with a large-scale ambush beside the River Sambre. In a desperate and confused battle, Caesar rushed to his right wing and, in his own words:

He ... took a shield from a man in the rear
ranks – he had come without his own –
advanced into the front line and called on the
centurions by name, encouraged the soldiers,
and ordered the line to advance and the units
to extend, so that they could employ their
swords more easily.

In the end the day was saved – but only when troops from
his victorious left wing were sent back into the fray by one
of his subordinate commanders.

In 56 BC, Caesar's operations were smaller scale – for
much of the year he was preoccupied with political matters
– although he did smash the navy of the Veneti, a tribe
living on the Atlantic coast and famous for their seaman-
ship, having constructed a fleet in order to do so. In 55 BC,
an attempt by some German tribes to migrate into Gaul
provoked a ferocious response, and all were massacred.
Caesar followed up this success by crossing the Rhine, the
legionaries building a bridge in just ten days, then led his
men over the river and devastated the nearest fields before
returning to the west bank. The bridge was then demol-
ished. It was a vivid demonstration to the Germans, to
show how easy it was for Caesar to reach them in their
homeland.

Late in the year, Caesar took two legions across the

Channel to Britain. The Romans landed and established a base, but soon afterwards most of their transport ships were wrecked in a storm, and Caesar was barely able to repair enough to get back to Gaul. In 54 BC, he returned to Britain with a much larger force, driving north and crossing the Thames. The Britons harassed him, but were persuaded to come to terms by his attacks on their main towns. However, once again the Romans lost many beached ships to a violent storm and were only just able to escape. Militarily neither expedition to Britain achieved much, while both came close to disaster. Politically, however, they were staggering successes, capturing the imagination of the Roman people.

Rebellions

In the winter following his second British expedition, Caesar was faced with the first of a series of rebellions. One and a half legions were massacred by rebellious Belgian tribes, and another garrison besieged. Caesar led two under-strength legions and some cavalry – in total fewer than seven thousand men – to break the siege. In 53 BC, he led a series of punitive expeditions, ravaging the lands of the tribes responsible until all submitted.

In the winter of 53–52 BC, an even wider and more serious rebellion erupted throughout Gaul. The rebels were led by Vercingetorix, a talented young chieftain who was able to impose much tighter discipline on the tribes than they had displayed in the past. Caesar was initially wrong-footed, but responded with characteristic aggression by launching counter-attacks against tribes who joined the rebels. Vercingetorix planned to deprive the Romans of supplies and starve them into submission rather than risk a battle. He therefore withdrew in the face of Caesar's advance, harassed his foraging parties, and ruthlessly burnt the towns and grain stores in the Romans' path.

The townsfolk of Avaricum pleaded to be allowed to defend their strongly fortified home, yet it was stormed by Caesar after a siege lasting just four weeks. As a terrible warning to others, the town was sacked and its people massacred. Caesar then pursued Vercingetorix to the town of Gergovia. A plan to launch a limited attack on the Gauls' camp went wrong when his eager soldiers pursued too far and began to assault the town itself. They were then swept out and suffered heavy losses when the bulk of the Gaulish army came up. Caesar withdrew and the Gauls rather over-confidently chased him. An attack by the Gaulish cavalry on the Roman column was repulsed, prompting an immediate reversal as the Gauls retreated. Caesar followed.

The Gauls camped outside the hilltop town of Alesia and sent messengers to all the tribes to muster a great army to come to their rescue. Caesar surrounded the hill with

11 miles of fortifications – a line of circumvallation. He then built a second, even longer line facing outwards – a line of contravallation. A massive Gaulish army eventually arrived. As it attacked from the outside, Vercingetorix led his own men in repeated attempts to break out. Eventually there was a final day of desperate fighting around a fort sited at the weakest spot in the Roman lines. Caesar fed in reserves, and then led in his last troops to break the Gaulish attack. Vercingetorix surrendered the next day. The rebellion was not fully suppressed for another year, but the Romans systematically defeated the few recalcitrant tribes. Intensive diplomacy accompanied the military operations, for Caesar was always aware that this was the only way to create a lasting peace.

Civil War

By 49 BC, Caesar's former ally Pompey had become much closer to his opponents. Determined to prevent him from returning to public life and enjoying the fame and wealth of his Gallic victories, they backed Caesar into a corner. Rather than see the end of his public career, Caesar was willing to fight a civil war. In January 49 BC, he crossed the River Rubicon and in a matter of weeks overran Italy. He then went to Spain, forcing the Pompeian army to surrender at Ilerda. At the end of the year he crossed to Macedonia to confront Pompey himself. An attempt to capture the enemy supply base at Dyrrachium ended in failure after weeks of effort.

Defeated at Dyrrachium, Caesar withdrew from the coast into Thessaly, where he was cut off from any supplies or reinforcements from Italy. Pompey pursued him and finally, on 9 August 48 BC, under strong pressure from the senior senators with his army, offered battle outside Pharsalus. Caesar's army mustered 22,000 infantry and just 1,000 cavalry. They were veterans, but were heavily outnumbered by the enemy's 45,000 infantry and 7,000 cavalry.

Pompey's cavalry was the greatest threat. The battlefield was an open plain, but Caesar was able to secure his left flank on the River Enipeus. His right flank was exposed and Pompey concentrated 6,500 horsemen on his own left: his plan was simple – overwhelm the thousand or so Caesarean cavalry, then swing round to roll up Caesar's infantry. All Pompey's less experienced infantry had to do was defend their position until this occurred.

As usual, Caesar's legions were in three lines of cohorts (the *triplex acies*). As the enemy formed up, he took one cohort from the third line of each of his legions and stationed them behind his own horsemen as an extra fourth line. These were masked by his own horsemen and so invisible to the enemy. The battle opened with Caesar's legions advancing, expecting the enemy infantry to come forward to meet them. In a remarkable display of discipline, Caesar's veterans halted when they saw that the enemy were not moving. They re-formed, before resuming the advance and charging into contact.

Meanwhile, Pompey's cavalry had charged forward and driven back Caesar's cavalry on the right wing. In the process the massed Pompeian squadrons lost much of their order and merged into one. Although well mounted and confident, these horsemen were inexperienced and not well disciplined. When the cohorts of the fourth line came through the clouds of dust and attacked them, the Pompeian cavalry stampeded to the rear. Caesar's fourth line now swung round against the left flank of the Pompeian infantry. Under pressure from the front and the flank, these troops began to give ground, then collapsed into rout.

Losses were always disproportionately heavy for the side that fled in an ancient battle. Pompey's army was virtually destroyed, losing at least 6,000 dead – Caesar himself claimed that 15,000 were killed – and 24,000 taken prisoner. The Caesarean army lost just 200 men, in addition to no fewer than 30 centurions, officers who led from the front and so tended to suffer very high casualties. The Battle of Pharsalus was a remarkable victory.

Pompey fled to Egypt, but was murdered by the boy king, Ptolemy XIII. Caesar arrived shortly afterwards and soon became involved in the civil war between the king and his older sister and wife Cleopatra VII. Famously smuggled into Caesar's presence – actually in a laundry bag rather than a carpet – she quickly became his lover. Unsurprisingly Ptolemy could not match her negotiating power and Caesar eventually defeated and killed him. He then spent months cruising the Nile with Cleopatra, and it was not until late in 47 BC that he again stirred himself, going to Asia to defeat King Pharnaces at Zela. It was in celebration of this rapid campaign that he coined the expression *veni, vidi, vici* – I came, I saw, I conquered.

Given time to regroup during this lull, Caesar's Roman enemies had massed a new army in Africa. He crossed there and, after an initial near reverse at Ruspina, crushed the Pompeians at Thapsus in 46 BC. The final campaign of the Civil War took place in Spain, and was concluded by the victory at Munda in 45 BC. Caesar returned to Rome and made himself dictator for life. He planned a major expedition, first to Dacia and then to Parthia (equivalent to modern Iraq and part of Iran). However, although he had won the war, he failed to make a success of the peace. On 15 March 44 BC he was assassinated by a group of senators.

ARMINIUS

c. 18 BC–AD 21

ADRIAN MURDOCH

THE BATTLE OF TEUTOBURG FOREST was the greatest military setback that the Roman Empire was ever to suffer. 'The heaviest defeat the Romans had endured on foreign soil', wrote a contemporary Roman historian of the battle in September AD 9 that saw Germanic warriors wipe out three legions, three cavalry battalions and six auxiliary units under the command of Publius Quinctilius Varus. Arminius, commander of a loose coalition of Germanic tribes, achieved what no other opponent of Rome ever managed. The Carthaginian Hannibal, the Gaulish leader Vercingetorix or Boudica, queen of the Iceni, to name just three who dared challenge Rome, were all eventually punished and their territories absorbed into the Roman world. But Arminius stopped the Roman Empire in its tracks and halted any imperial pretensions east of the Rhine.

The emperor Augustus' plaintive and heart-rending cry 'Quinctilius Varus, give me back my legions!' as he paced his palace on the Palatine Hill in Rome is well known, but so serious was the loss of Legions XVII, XVIII and XIX that the few survivors of the battle were banned from ever setting foot in Italy, the legions themselves were never replaced, and the Rhine became a barrier between civilization and barbarism that was never willingly crossed even in late antiquity.

Little wonder that Arminius himself soon turned into a mythologized figure of German might. He became, in turn, the personification of German resistance to Catholic Italy, a symbol of the struggle against France in the nineteenth century, one of the voices of German nationalism and ultimately Nazism. A massive statue of Arminius, the 174-feet-tall Hermannsdenkmal near Detmold, remains one of the more popular tourist attractions in Germany. He is as popular today as he ever was, thanks to the discovery in 1987 of the battlefield itself, near the town of Kalkriese in Lower Saxony, by an amateur British archaeologist – a find justifiably trumpeted in one German newspaper as 'a second Troy'.

First Contact with Rome

Arminius is a difficult man to characterize. Everything we know about him comes from inevitably hostile Roman authors, most of them writing a hundred years or more after the events took place. As a result, virtually every fact given here is open to debate.

To give just one example, it is not known for certain what Arminius was actually called, though most accept that what has come down to us is a Latinization of either a familial name or an honorific. *Erman* or *ermen* is an old Germanic word meaning roughly 'the eminent' – not implausible for a boy born into the ruling elite. Nor is it certain what he was called by the Romans. There was a convention that auxiliaries of the period took on the name Julius, so it is plausible that he was called Gaius Julius Arminius, but there is no universal agreement about the spelling of his name in the manuscripts either. Sometimes he is Arminius, sometimes Armenus.

The son of an aristocrat called Segimerus, Arminius was born in roughly 18 BC, around the time that the Romans started giving serious consideration to a conquest of Germany. His tribe, the Cherusci, dominated the area that roughly corresponds to the southern part of the modern state of Lower Saxony, between the River Elbe to the east and the River Weser to the west. Archaeological research in what was Cheruscan territory remains in its infancy. Because of the nationalist associations that tainted Arminius from the nineteenth century up to the Second World War, little work was carried out on native settlements in Lower

Saxony post-war until recently. But archaeological research since the mid-1990s has painted a picture of a predominantly agrarian countryside dotted with isolated farmsteads or clusters of farms.

Apart from an occasional passing mention, the Cherusci do not enter recorded history until the turn of the millennium, when Arminius was in his late teens. For the next three years, the tribe was a participant in, though not an instigator of, a serious revolution (one Roman historian calls it 'a vast war') that gripped Germany. Following restoration of peace in AD 4, the tribe seems to have been an ally of Rome until AD 9.

In the Service of Rome

From the time of Julius Caesar onwards, Celtic tribes provided the Roman army with auxiliary soldiers to serve as lightly armed infantry or cavalry. There is no doubt that the supply of troops was a condition of the peace treaty that the future emperor Tiberius signed with the Cherusci in AD 4.

It is certain that in his early twenties Arminius was an officer in the Roman army, seeing action somewhere in the northern Balkans during what are known as the Pannonian uprisings, the revolts that shook the empire after AD 6. The Roman historian Tacitus writes that Arminius 'served ... as commander of his fellow-countrymen', the senior officer of an auxiliary corps. He clearly distinguished himself. Arminius' service record was significant enough for him to have earned not just coveted Roman citizenship but promotion to equestrian status, the admired middle class.

No sense of his own feelings towards Rome emerge, but this period of Arminius' life certainly provided the military groundwork for what was to come. Above all, it allowed him to know his enemy. At its most basic level he became fluent in Latin. Much more importantly, Arminius learned how the Roman army worked and saw its tactical innovations in action. It is easy to forget that for the Cherusci the majority of warfare of the period involved tribesmen fighting tribesmen – conflicts which have left no mark on history. Arminius' strength as a tactician and strategist was to find ways of using the very different Germanic mode of warfare to beat the technologically advanced Romans.

Home Again

In around AD 7, Arminius left Roman service to return to his homeland. Rome may even have interfered to encourage Arminius' return to act as some kind of standard-bearer for Roman civilization. The new governor of Germany, Publius Quinctilius Varus, was attempting to speed up the Romanization of the province, and he wanted as many pro-Roman allies and senior Germanic voices around him as possible. It was one of the great failings of Roman imperialism that it never considered the possibility that someone who had once tasted the fruits of its civilization might ever reject it.

Arminius may have had some cachet because of his Roman experience but he was not universally welcomed. It took him, after all, two years to establish his position and engineer the attack on the Romans. At the time of his return there were at least three factions, or perhaps more accurately two other nobles, vying for influence in Cheruscan politics. All three had significant followers and were related to each other either by blood or by marriage.

Arminius came to represent the anti-Roman point of view. His uncle Inguiomerus was undecided. And Segestes remained consistently pro-Rome throughout. His influence and support for Rome throughout the period is a reminder that Arminius was not leading a universally popular rebellion. The relationship between Arminius and Segestes is given an additional twist after the Battle of Teutoburg Forest, when Segestes' daughter Thusnelda eloped with Arminius while betrothed to another man.

The Revolt

What tipped the young Cheruscan commander into revolution? The Greek historian Cassius Dio gives two reasons: first, the Germans were given orders 'as if they were actual slaves of the Romans'; and second, that 'Varus demanded money as he would from subject nations'.

The first was an unpalatable loss of freedom. A change from being an ally of Rome to a conquered nation meant that Cheruscan troops, for example, would now be subject to Roman discipline, pay and conditions. But the second reason was conclusive. All the costs of Romanization were borne by the province itself. The bills for roadworks, for buildings and for towns, landed on the desks of local worthies. Resentment was fuelled by the continuous presence of the Roman army in their territory. There were, of course, some economic benefits – for local businesses that supplied the camps with food, goods or amatory services – but for the most part the Romans were loathed. It is also safe to assume that the Roman soldiers were not at their most sensitive towards natives in the young province after years of warfare.

By September AD 9, disaffection and resentment had spilled over into active revolt, and Arminius, the 27-year-old Roman officer, mutinied against his commanders, keeping his plans secret by pretending to be loyal until the trap was sprung.

Arminius' skill as a commander was to make the Romans fight inefficiently. The Battle of Teutoburg Forest remains a master lesson in how to neutralize the technological advantages of a superior war machine.

Arminius planned to ambush the Roman army and its retinue in what is now Lower Saxony, when it was marching west through what it believed to be friendly territory. He sprung the trap with calculated finesse. The Cheruscan leader had arranged an uprising to draw out the Roman army. News of the revolt was significant enough for Varus to lead the army in person, but not so important as to awaken suspicion.

The challenge for Arminius was how best to counteract the might of the Roman legions. Both sides were fairly evenly matched numerically. Arminius could count on approximately fifteen thousand men while the Roman commander Varus was leading a force that was around fourteen thousand strong. In a pitched battle, however, the lightly armed German forces were no match for heavily armed legionaries protected by a new, light and flexible segmented armour called *lorica segmenta*. What Arminius did was to play to the strengths of the Germanic warriors.

The first attack happened east of Kalkriese, at the end of a day when the Roman soldiers were tired. The initial targets for Arminius' men were the Roman cavalry – a strike that immobilized and demoralized the Romans, quite apart from causing them huge logistical problems.

The weather helped. Persistent storms waterlogged the Roman legionaries, while the unarmoured, spear-carrying Germanic warriors carried on their guerrilla attacks unencumbered.

The next morning, Varus led the three legions towards

a narrow pass called the Kalkrieser-Niewedder-Senke, where the main west–east routes from the mid-Weser to the lower Rhine converged. It was the perfect spot for an ambush, a narrow corridor, some 4 miles long, but because of the high water-table at the time, only 200 yards wide. It was bounded by the Kalkriese Berg to the south and the Great Moor to the north. The analogy of a lobster pot has been used to describe the pass – the Romans could get in, but not out.

Archaeological evidence has revealed that the spot for the ambush had been well planned, with arc-shaped turf walls and sand ramparts built along the side of the hill. These preserved the element of surprise for the Germans and also narrowed the path, so that the Romans had no chance to form their impregnable legionary lines that had seen off so many enemies.

Trapped, and with no means of escape, the remainder of Varus' army was soon massacred. Varus committed what the Roman historian Cassius Dio calls the 'terrible yet unavoidable act' and killed himself. Arminius had won.

After the tactically brilliant and definitive ambush at Teutoburg, virtually all the Germanic tribes joined Arminius' call. Every Roman settlement east of the Rhine was overrun. Even nascent towns such as Waldgirmes, an assimi-lated civilian settlement in the Lahn Valley discovered in 1993, were either abandoned or destroyed. The Germans wanted to erase any trace of the hated invaders. Only one

Roman stronghold, the camp of Aliso (usually equated with the camp at Haltern) made any attempt to hold out, but that, too, was assaulted and then burned to the ground in the autumn. Little wonder that the German historian Theodor Mommsen described Arminius' campaign as the turning point in Germany's national destiny.

But for all Arminius' skill as a tactician, his great flaw as a commander was his lack of a sense of strategy. What was he trying to achieve? He cannot be spoken of as a liberator of Germany; that is too Roman a perspective. It is too much even to suggest that he was trying to unite Germany east of the Rhine. He appears to have had no imperial ambitions at this time. His aim, quite simply, was to stop the Romans from setting up a province between the Rhine and the Elbe.

After Teutoburg

Rome's reaction to this military debacle was massive mobilization. The Rhine armies were boosted from five to eight legions under the command of Tiberius throughout AD 10 and 11. A new chapter began in AD 13 with the appointment of Germanicus, Tiberius' nephew and heir to the throne, as governor and commander-in-chief. His commission was to consolidate his uncle's work, to repair the damage caused by Varus and to pursue and punish Arminius. In all three he proved to be an abject failure.

Germanicus' lack of success, however, was not really down to Arminius so much as his own incompetence. In the years immediately after Teutoburg, the Cheruscan leader was strangely passive. He did not, for example, capitalize on the revolt among the Rhine legions, caused by news of the death of Augustus on 19 August AD 14. Instead, Arminius seems to have been preoccupied with internal politics, a power struggle that resulted in the imprisonment of Segestes.

For most of AD 15, the initiative remained with Germanicus. He embarked on a series of retaliatory campaigns against Arminius' allies, recaptured two of the three legionary standards that had been lost at Teutoburg, and buried the Roman dead on the battlefield. It took the Roman liberation of Segestes and the capture of Arminius' pregnant wife Thusnelda to shake Arminius from his torpor and to unify the Cherusci again.

Throughout the autumn of AD 15, the Cheruscan leader continually harried the Romans though deliberately without engaging them on the battlefield. It was only disunity among the Cheruscan high command that saved the Romans from an even greater debacle at the end of the year – the loss of a further four legions – after they were ambushed in a repetition of the manoeuvre deployed at Teutoburg. Arminius' final attack plans were vetoed by his uncle Inguiomerus, which suggests that Arminius' position was not as unassailable as many have presumed. The legions escaped and the Germans were routed. On balance, though, the year was one of success for Arminius. He might have been thwarted in his endgame, but he had won a great deal of Roman booty and had inflicted significant losses on the enemy.

The Battle of Idistaviso

With Roman patience and money running out, it was clear that AD 16 would be decisive. Arminius was forced to confront for the final time what he called the 'cowardly runaways from Varus' army' at the Battle of Idistaviso, an unidentified site along the River Weser, possibly somewhere near Minden.

That it came to pitched battle is curious. Up to that point, what had made Arminius outstanding as a commander was his ability to minimize Roman military supremacy. It is tempting to suggest that Arminius found himself overruled at Idistaviso by his fellow commanders, as he had been the previous summer. Whether because of this or through overconfidence, Arminius' battle formation showed how much he had developed as a military thinker. Despite the fact that this was his first set battle, his deployment was professional and notably Roman in style. He and the Cherusci kept to the higher ground with other tribes to the fore, the River Weser to his left and forest to the right to keep the Roman attack front narrow.

None the less it was a disaster. Arminius was injured in the first moments of the battle and the Germanic tribes were routed. A subsequent engagement resulted in further German losses. Yet on that inconclusive note, Roman involvement on the eastern side of the Rhine ended. Germanicus' plea for one more campaign fell on deaf ears (Emperor Tiberius had a campaign in Armenia to fund) and he was recalled to Rome.

The Final Years

His defeat at the Battle of Idistaviso marked the beginning of the end of Arminius' power. Despite the recall of Germanicus, Cheruscan warriors began to move east, away from any future Roman threat. This migration brought the settlers up against the Bohemian king Maroboduus. By AD 17, war had broken out between the two commanders. Arminius was hailed as victor and an isolated Maroboduus had to appeal to Tiberius for sanctuary.

For Arminius this should have been the greatest moment of his life, the consolidation of his power. He had won. The Romans had been pushed back to the other side of the Rhine and his greatest rival was gone. But his victory and subsequent attempt to unite the tribes proved to be his undoing. He was 'aiming for royalty', writes Tacitus. As soon as Arminius began to demand authority for its own sake, he lost his power; he had become simply another oppressor.

An attempt by a disgruntled Germanic chief to get the Romans to sponsor an assassination attempt on Arminius was rejected by Emperor Tiberius. But it was an indication of how unpopular he had become. Arminius was faced with a civil war and was soon murdered by a member of his family under somewhat murky circumstances. We do not know who killed him or how he died, though it is a tidy coincidence of history that he and Germanicus died in the same year.

His obituary at the end of the second book of Tacitus' *Annals* is one of the most extraordinary pieces of Latin prose to come down to us. In a few sentences, the historian manages to capture, with incredible pathos, both the admiration and revulsion the Romans had for their most successful opponent.

Make no mistake, Arminius was the liberator of Germany, one too who defied Rome, not in her early rise, as other kings and generals, but in the height of her empire's glory. The battles he fought were indeed indecisive, yet he remained unconquered in war. He lived for thirty-seven years, twelve of them in power, and he is still the subject of song among barbarous nations, though to Greek historians, who admire only their own achievements, he is unknown, and to Romans not as famous as he should be, while we extol the past and are indifferent to our own times.

TRAJAN

ad 56–117

ADRIAN GOLDSWORTHY

TRAJAN WAS PERHAPS THE GREATEST, and certainly the most famous, of Rome's soldier emperors. He was the last great Roman conqueror, and during his reign the empire expanded to its greatest geographical extent. After the period of expansion under Trajan, the Roman Empire switched to a more defensive posture. Trajan's successor Hadrian is famous for building Hadrian's Wall in northern Britain, as well as other frontier defence systems.

Trajan's most important and lasting conquest was the occupation of Dacia, a powerful and wealthy kingdom in what is now Romania, which had inflicted a number of humiliating defeats on the Romans in the last decades of the first century AD. Later in his reign he embarked upon a massive offensive in the east, aimed probably at the complete conquest of Parthia. Some gains were made and a new province created in Mesopotamia, but widespread rebellions in other recently occupied territories erupted within a few years. In addition there was a major revolt by Jewish communities within the Roman Empire. Many of the new gains were abandoned before Trajan died, and Mesopotamia was later given up by Hadrian. On several occasions over the next two hundred years, the Romans managed to regain some of the lost territories, these often being a source of friction between the empire and its Parthian, later Persian, neighbours.

The Romans remembered Trajan as one of the best emperors they had ever had, setting him alongside Augustus. Although his martial achievements contributed a good deal to this, it was also due to his reputation for justice, generosity and good administration. He was one of the emperors who made the second century AD, according to Edward Gibbon, '... the period in the history of the world, during which the condition of the human race was most happy and prosperous.' We know more about his wider achievements and the broad trend of his campaigns than we do about the details of his command style. As far as we can tell, he led in the conventional way for a Roman general. Like Julius Caesar, Trajan wrote *Commentaries* describing his campaigns, but only a single sentence of these has survived. However, we do have some literary accounts, as well as evidence from archaeology and the reliefs depicting his Dacian Wars on Trajan's Column, which still stands in Rome today.

Trajan's Rise to Power

Trajan's family lived in Italica in Spain and boasted that they were descended from the veteran soldiers settled in the colony there by Scipio Africanus at the end of the Second Punic War. The family were part of the local aristocracy, and in time began to enter imperial service and enjoy distinguished careers. Trajan's father was a senator – we do not know if he was the first in his family – and commanded the Tenth Legion Fretensis during the suppression of the Jewish rebellion against Nero in AD 67–70. This army was led by Vespasian, who emerged as the victor from the civil war that followed Nero's suicide in AD 68. As emperor, Vespasian granted Trajan's father the post of legate (governor and army commander) in Cappadocia and later the even more prestigious province of Syria. During this time he successfully dealt with a border dispute with the Parthians.

Trajan's own early career was typical for a man of his

social class. In his late teens he became a senior tribune (*tribunus laticlavius*) in one of the legions commanded by his father. Tribunes were essentially staff officers. For some men it was merely a necessary step in a political career and they spent as little time with the army as possible, and certainly no more than a year. Others, like Trajan, were far more enthusiastic and chose to extend their service. In his case he took a posting to a legion on the Rhine frontier. It was not uncommon for men to serve as tribunes for three years. Trajan was supposed to have held this rank for a decade, although this may well be an exaggeration. He certainly took soldiering seriously and used his time to learn as much as possible. A speech in his honour later claimed that: 'Through ten years' service you learnt the customs of peoples, the localities of countries, the opportunities of topography, and you accustomed yourself to cross all kinds of river and endure all kinds of weather ...'

A keen horseman – like many aristocrats from Spain, he was addicted to hunting – it was said that he became an expert in all military drills and weapons handling, although again this was a fairly conventional compliment. It is unclear how much fighting was involved in his father's border dispute with the Parthians or whether the son was directly involved. Trajan certainly saw active service on the Rhine, and from the beginning displayed unusual skill.

He was an enthusiastic and serious-minded soldier, but no Roman aristocrat was ever a professional military man. Like anyone else pursuing a senatorial career, he held a series of civil posts. His next spell with the army did not come until he was 32, when he was posted as legionary legate to command the Seventh Legion Gemina at the city of Legion (modern León) in Spain. It was a peaceful province with little prospect of active campaigning, but in AD 89 he and his legion were sent to deal with the rebellion of a governor on the Rhine against the unpopular emperor Domitian, second son of Vespasian. The revolt sputtered out before Trajan arrived, but he remained on the Rhine for some time and led a successful punitive expedition against the German tribes on its eastern bank.

In the next decade Trajan was made provincial legate, commanding first one of the German provinces, and then Pannonia on the Danubian frontier. In Pannonia he fought and defeated part of the Sueves, a numerous Germanic people divided into many sub-tribes and famous for wearing their hair in a topknot. When Domitian was murdered in a palace conspiracy in AD 96, the 40-year-old Trajan had a good reputation for his character and military skill. The Senate appointed one of its elderly members, the childless Nerva, to become emperor. Insecure – he faced strong pressure from the Praetorian Guard to execute the conspirators who had killed Domitian – Nerva adopted Trajan as his son and heir. It was a popular choice. More importantly, Trajan was at the head of an army that could be expected to back his claim.

Wars with Dacia

Nerva died in AD 98 after a reign lasting less than two years. Trajan's succession was generally popular, but he may have realized that some great achievement would help to strengthen his position. Under Domitian the Dacian king Decebalus had raided across the Danube into the Roman provinces, on one occasion defeating and killing a provincial legate. Roman expeditions to exact punishment for these attacks had enjoyed mixed fortune. One column commanded by the praetorian prefect Cornelius Fuscus was virtually annihilated by the Dacians in AD 86. In the end, Domitian concluded a peace treaty in which he agreed to pay Decebalus an annual subsidy, as well as supplying him with military engineers to supervise the building of fortifications, and artillery. The emperor claimed victory, but this was widely seen as a major humiliation and contributed further to Domitian's unpopularity.

The heartland of Dacia lay in Transylvania, and many of Decebalus' strongholds, including his capital at Sarmizegethusa Regia, lay in the Carpathian mountains. Dacia was rich in gold and other mineral deposits, and had contact with old Greek colonies in the Black Sea. Its many fortified towns and outposts reveal an ingenious blend of indigenous, Hellenistic and Roman building techniques. Decebalus was a very strong king, and no Dacian leader had had as much power since the middle of the first century BC. His victories over Domitian strengthened his position. He not only controlled the Dacians, but also drew allies from neighbouring peoples, including the fierce Germanic Bastarnae and the Sarmatians, who were famous for their heavy cataphract cavalry. Encouragement was also given to Roman troops to desert and take service with the king.

Trajan seems to have resolved on a war with Dacia from very early on in his reign. Troops from all over the empire were massed along the Danube and in AD 101 the Romans invaded. Nine out of the thirty legions then in existence were represented, even if some were only present as detachments. There were also substantial forces of regular auxiliaries, along with irregular units of Germanic and British warriors, as well as Numidian light cavalry. Trajan supervised the operations in person. At first there seems to have been little fighting, the Dacians withdrawing in the face of this onslaught and abandoning some of their forts. The Romans pushed forward to secure the Iron Gates pass in the Carpathians.

The first major battle seems to have been fought at Tapae, where a strong Dacian force tried to block the Roman advance. There was heavy fighting – the Dacian two-handed curved sword known as a *falx* made a strong impression on Roman observers – before the Romans were victorious. Trajan's Column in Rome shows the emperor overseeing this engagement and others. It was not his job to fight hand to hand, but to supervise from close behind the fighting line, committing reserves and encouraging the troops. It was important for Roman soldiers to feel that they were closely observed, and conspicuous bravery would be rewarded as readily as cowardice would be punished. Trajan's Column often shows the emperor rewarding or encouraging his men. Twice auxiliary soldiers present him with severed heads taken from enemies they have killed. In a later battle we hear of a wounded cavalryman who was evacuated to the field hospital, but then told that he would not survive. Inspired by the emperor, he returned to the battle and died fighting. When the aid stations ran short of bandages, Trajan ordered that his own spare clothes should be torn up and used. He always emphasized that he cared for the welfare as well as the discipline and fighting power of his soldiers.

Trajan was also directly involved in planning, reconnoitring the ground and interrogating prisoners. When the Dacians counter-attacked on the Danubian frontier and raided the Roman frontier garrisons, he went himself with his Praetorians to meet the threat. They travelled by boat along the river, and then hunted down the raiders and destroyed them, before rejoining the main army. Decebalus made several attempts to negotiate, but would not meet the Roman demands and so Trajan pushed on and won another battle. The approach of winter then ended the fighting for that year.

In 102 Trajan advanced again, taking stronghold after stronghold by siege. In the end Decebalus surrendered. At this stage the Romans were not bent on annexation. The king was allowed to remain in power, although a token Roman garrison was installed in his capital. He lost some territory, was made to return all Roman deserters in his service and not receive any more, and would now pay the Romans a subsidy instead of receiving one. Trajan took the title of Dacicus – victor over the Dacians. However, the peace proved to be temporary as Decebalus chafed under these new restrictions. He decided to fight again, and a second war was fought from AD 105–106. This time Trajan's victory was complete and the kingdom was turned into the province of Dacia. An extremely prosperous province, it was soon providing soldiers for the Roman army. One man named Decebalus is later attested as serving in one of the forts on Hadrian's Wall.

The Second Dacian War began in AD 105 when Decebalus seized the commander of the small Roman garrison in the Dacian capital, hoping to use him as a hostage and renegotiate the treaty. He was thwarted when a servant smuggled poison to the officer in question and he committed suicide. It took time for a new field army to be mustered. Trajan was in Italy when the war began and had to travel to the theatre of operations. The army for this campaign may actually have been larger than the force used in the earlier conflict. Two new legions, raised by and named after Trajan himself, were sent to the area.

There were massive preparations, including construction of a road running along the Danube – and where necessary cut into the rock of the cliffs themselves – as well as a great arched stone bridge across the river. As the army mustered, great supply dumps were formed. One historian notes that 'Trajan conducted the war with safe prudence rather than with haste.'

Negotiation with individual Dacian chieftains persuaded many to submit, and also prevented many of Decebalus' old allies from joining him. The Dacians seem to have attacked Roman outposts late in 105, but were driven off.

In 106 the Roman army crossed the Danube and advanced into Dacia. Its target was the capital at Sarmizegethusa Regia, a place of religious as well as political significance, high in the Carpathians. The city was large, situated on a mountain top and defended by a strong circuit wall. The Romans settled down to a formal siege, employing torsion catapults and other siege engines. A direct assault was mounted, which seems to have been only partially successful and may actually have been repulsed. Nevertheless it was enough to provoke the defenders to set fire to the city and escape. It is probable that the location of the site made it very difficult for the Romans to cut off all the paths leading from it. Trajan sent patrols to pursue the fugitives, with specific orders to take Decebalus. Some Roman horsemen led by a junior officer named Tiberius Claudius Maximus caught up with the Dacian king, who cut his own throat before he could be captured. His head was taken back to Trajan and paraded before the army. There were some mopping-up operations, but the war was effectively over. Sarmizegethusa Regia was slighted and abandoned, and Trajan founded a new capital for the province, naming it after himself: Colonia Sarmizegethusa Ulpia. It was situated in the valley at the foot of the Carpathians.

War with Parthia

Trajan celebrated his Dacian triumph with great splendour, using the plundered gold of Decebalus to build a massive new Forum complex in the heart of Rome. At its centre was the column 100 Roman feet high (97 feet 9 inches in modern measurements) which served as a reminder of the height of the hillside before it was excavated to form the site of the Forum. Success in Dacia confirmed the emperor's power and avenged Domitian's humiliating peace treaty. For a few years Trajan seems to have been content to remain at peace. However, in time, tension with the Parthians over the border kingdom of Armenia led him to plan a massive expedition to defeat them once and for all. The desire to emulate Alexander the Great helped to fuel his ambition, but that is not to say that he did not also feel that it would be for the greater good of the empire.

In 114 Trajan led a huge army against the Parthians. Armenia and then Mesopotamia were overrun and both turned into provinces by 115. A year later the Romans marched down the Euphrates to the Parthian capital at Ctesiphon and sacked it. Trajan then pressed onwards, getting as far as the Persian Gulf. He is supposed to have looked longingly at a trading ship sailing for India, realizing that he could not follow Alexander any further. The point was rammed home when many of his recent conquests rebelled and his overstretched army struggled to cope with these new threats. When Trajan was at Babylon he heard of rebellions by the large Jewish communities in Egypt, Cyrenaica and Cyprus, although not curiously enough in Judea itself. Savage fighting involved militias from the Gentile communities as well as regular Roman troops before the revolts were finally suppressed.

As Roman columns moved to confront the various rebel groups, there were a number of reverses. Trajan was reluctantly forced to recognize the Parthian monarchy, abandoning his ambition of occupying the whole kingdom. Probably in 117, he attempted to storm the oasis city of Hatra, but was repulsed. During one reconnaissance of the fortifications, the guard cavalryman next to Trajan was killed by an arrow – the defenders' attention having been drawn by the 60-year-old emperor's grey hair. A siege was mounted, but the harsh climate and problems of supply forced the Romans to withdraw.

Trajan had been ill for some time and soon afterwards suffered a stroke. A few weeks later he died. He was succeeded by Hadrian, although Hadrian's 'adoption' may well have been arranged after Trajan's death in concert with the emperor's widow. Needing to establish himself more securely, Hadrian had no enthusiasm for remaining on campaign in the east. Those territories from Trajan's eastern conquests which had not already been lost were swiftly abandoned.

ZHUGE LIANG

181–234

JONATHAN FENBY

WHAT MACHIAVELLI IS TO EUROPEAN STATECRAFT, the third-century Chinese general and strategist Zhuge Liang is to his country's military history. Known as the 'Crouching Dragon', he is more than a military commander of the Chinese. He epitomizes prized traditional virtues and skills at the start of a protracted period of national division which followed the decline and fall of the third imperial dynasty, the Eastern Han, in 220 and lasted until the Sui dynasty took the throne in 581, restoring unity and paving the way for the great era of the Tang.

Helped by a highly impressive starring appearance in the vast epic saga about the period, the *Romance of the Three Kingdoms*, where he is referred to also as 'Master Sleeping Dragon', Zhuge Liang is seen as a byword for intelligence, a supremely skilled and loyal commander who was also a statesman, a scholar and – highly important given the status of the heavens in Chinese cosmology – an astrologer.

Much of what is attributed to Zhuge lies on the borderline between history and myth; it is virtually impossible in many cases to distinguish between the two.

Techniques and Technology

If Zhuge did not actually possess the supernatural powers granted to him in the stories handed down over the centuries, he nevertheless represents a corpus of military techniques prized by the Chinese both of his time and subsequently. Furthermore, the general feeling is that such an iconic figure should have been able to summon up winds to decide naval battles, whether or not he could actually do so.

On firmer ground, he is credited with having advanced military technology through his inventions, including weaponry, mines and transport equipment. Works attributed to him outline infantry and cavalry tactics based on Taoist principles; one is said to be so finely written that it drew tears from readers – anybody who did not cry being deemed untrustworthy.

Zhuge is also credited with having been a master of trickery. In one famous example he responded to his army's inadequate supply of arrows by floating ships filled with straw close to the enemy, waiting until the enemy archers unleashed volleys of arrows into them, then getting his men to drag the boats back into position in order to replenish his stocks. Books and poems celebrate his achievements and character. Most recently, Zhuge has been a video-game hero, wielding his trademark – a large white feather fan.

The Fall of the Han

The 'carving of the empire' was the division of China that followed the fall of the Han dynasty in 220. In the dynasty's last years, the country had suffered from weak rulers, factionalism and the rise of eunuch power at court, as well as natural disasters. Rebels in eastern China, known as 'the Yellow Turbans' for their headgear, assembled three hundred and fifty thousand followers, while other insurgents declared their independence in the west.

The death of the emperor Lingdi in 189 set off a succession struggle. A warlord took the capital of Luoyang, massacred two thousand eunuchs and put a new emperor – a boy of 8 – on the throne, but he soon fled from the competing warlords.

Zhuge was 19 at the time. He had been born in the eastern province of Shandong in 181, but his mother died when he was 9 and his father when he was 12. He and his siblings (two brothers and two sisters) were then raised by an uncle, but were forced to flee from Shandong when in 195 a northern warlord rampaged across their province. They moved to present-day Hubei in central China, and Zhuge wed the daughter of a well-known scholar – a vital connection as it turned out, since the scholar's wife was the sister-in-law of a local warlord, who was giving protection to a mercenary chieftain, Liu Bei.

The Three Kingdoms

Liu Bei's career had been rackety. He had been forced to flee the court of a northern kingdom, the Wei, after being implicated in a plot to assassinate its ruler, Cao Cao, the leading general of the time. Liu's safety came under threat after the warlord who was protecting him died, and his son allied with the Wei. That led to a battle in which Liu was defeated. At some point around this time, he heard about Zhuge, and went three times to the reed hut where he was living. On the third occasion, Zhuge agreed to receive him, making such an impression that Liu said he felt like a fish being put back into water. He had found his lieutenant – his *consiglière* – who would take care of matters for him.

The times were made for ambitious soldiers. While the Wei dominated northern China, the Yangtze Valley and regions to the south were controlled by the kingdom of Wu under Sun Quant. It was there that Liu now fled, allying himself with Sun, marrying the king's sister, and – with Zhuge – joining in his confrontation with the Wei.

In 207, Zhuge presented Liu with a programme to establish himself as a major player in China and to restore the house of Han at the head of a reunited empire. Known as the Longzhong Plan, this provided for Liu to set up a strong base in wild, fertile, mountainous Sichuan as a third kingdom, under the name of Shu. Administrative, economic and legal reforms would be implemented to create a strong state. Relations would be nurtured with tribal people to the south to counter their hostility to the Han Chinese.

From Sichuan, Zhuge's plan provided for a two-pronged attack on the Wei to the north, advancing on the major cities of Chang'an (the first imperial capital outside present-day Xian) and Luoyang in the Yellow River plain. The Wu would be neutralized by an alliance, though, once the northerners had been defeated, they would also be overcome as the Shu kingdom reunited China. It was quite a programme for a wandering military adventurer and his 26-year-old adviser.

The Battle of the Red Cliffs
The vital breakthrough came a year after Zhuge unveiled

his plan, when the Wei attacked the Wu kingdom along the Yangtze river, being resoundingly defeated in 208, at the Battle of the Red Cliffs by a combination of trickery and the superior skills of their adversaries at naval warfare. In one celebrated episode, a Wu general offered to surrender and hand over large supplies of food. Ten ships duly appeared, but they were filled with combustible materials. Set on fire, they were blown by the wind into the numerically superior Wei armada, while the Wu fleet attacked from the other side. Retreating by land, the Wei were harassed by ambushes and the king was said to have only one hundred members of his retinue left alive when he reached his northern capital.

According to the *Romance of the Three Kingdoms*, which undoubtedly exaggerates his role in the battle, Zhuge used his supernatural powers to conjure up the wind. A more prosaic version has him obtaining an accurate weather forecast and advising the Wu fleet accordingly. The grateful Wu king allowed Liu to establish himself in Sichuan to provide a base from which to seek to conquer all China.

In 220, Cao Cao died and the Han emperor abdicated. Cao's son promptly proclaimed himself emperor under the name of Wendi. In Sichuan, Liu went into mourning, but a Han ancestry was unearthed for him, and members of his entourage, including Zhuge, told him he had inherited the Mandate of Heaven, by which the gods designated emperors to govern on earth. So Liu duly declared himself the rightful ruler of China, at the head of the house of Shu Han, with its capital in the Sichuan city of Chengdu. (The Wu ruler joined the party by also declaring himself emperor.)

Liu soon ran into trouble. One of his generals alienated the Wu, who defeated him and sent his head to the Wei court. A counter-attack in 219 on the Wu from Sichuan was initially successful but then ran into difficulties as its different elements became disconnected from one another. Their supply lines were strained and, when the attackers moved out of the mountains into flat country, the Wu cavalry gained the upper hand. Zhuge did not take part in the campaign, staying in Chengdu to oversee the administration there.

Protecting the South

Having evaded direct battle with the Shu, the leading Wu general staged a night-time attack, setting fire to his adversary's positions in a dry forest, the Wu crossbow archers then cutting down the Sichuan soldiers as they ran to fetch water. After other elements in his army had been destroyed when rockslides devastated their camps, Liu took refuge in a fortified city where he was said to have died of grief at the age of 63. On his deathbed, he called for Zhuge, and named his son, Liu Shan, as his successor. If the young man proved incapable, he added, Zhuge should take the throne.

The young man did indeed fall short – Chinese historians call him 'degenerate'. But Zhuge refused to try to replace him, believing in the importance of maintaining the dynastic principle that underlay the Shu claim to the Mandate of Heaven. Still, as chancellor, he became the dominant figure in the kingdom, and set out to make it the dominant force in China, even though it was weaker in resources and men than the Wei or the Wu.

Zhuge saw the Wei as the prime adversary, so he formed an alliance with the Wu to protect the Shu's eastern front. To secure the rear, he launched expeditions to pacify rebel tribes in the mountains of Yunnan, to the south of Sichuan. His army defeated the much-respected main tribal leader, Meng Huo, seven times. On each occasion, Zhuge had him released as a sign of benevolence and to win his confidence. In the end, Meng submitted. 'You must be the valour of Heaven,' he told Zhuge. 'The south will not rebel again.'

Zhuge appointed Meng and other regional chiefs as administrators to win their loyalty while avoiding the expense and uncertainties of occupation. The Yunnan tribes paid the Shu tribute in gold and silver, horses and cattle, providing much-needed additional resources for the kingdom's army.

The March North

In 227, it was time to march north against the Wei in the next stage of Zhuge's Pingzhong Plan. The purpose, he told the ruler, Liu Shan, was to conquer the vast plain of northern China 'to exterminate the wicked, restore the house of Han and return to the old capital [Chang'an]'. Despite this ambition, the first northern expedition, like later Shu offensives, was marked by Zhuge's ultimate awareness of the relative weakness of the kingdom, the need to avoid putting his army at the mercy of larger northern forces, and supply-chain factors as the troops moved further and further from their home base.

The terrain that lay ahead was forbidding – notably the Qinling Mountains, with their deep valleys and sparse roads climbing through awesome passes. Rejecting a proposal for a frontal attack through the mountains, Zhuge opted for a typically deceptive move, sending two columns to act as diversions while his main force advanced along the upper valley of the Wei river on the way to Chang'an. The Wei ruler, Cao Rui, took personal charge of the defence. In addition to the garrisons in the area, a fifty-thousand-strong force of cavalry and infantry was sent in to oppose the attackers directly. A Shu general allowed himself to be isolated on a waterless mountain top, where he was defeated. Fearing encirclement by the Wei troops, Zhuge ordered his army to withdraw to Sichuan.

The following year, he was back on the offensive, seeking to take advantage of a conflict between Wu and Wei. A Shu army again marched to the Wei river basin, but, again, Zhuge ordered it to return home when grain supplies ran short. He did, however, score one signal victory when a leading Wei commander fell into an ambush set by Zhuge in the Qinling Mountains.

Back on the march again, Zhuge's troops occupied the western Qinling foothills in their third expedition in 209. They scored a significant success at the Battle of Wudu, but then ran into stiff defence from numerically superior Wei forces which led Zhuge to order a retreat, though the Shu held on to two commanderies across the mountains. By now, the Wei had had enough of the attacks from Sichuan and in the autumn of 230 invaded the Shu kingdom with an army said to total four hundred thousand men.

Zhuge sent agents to stir up anti-Wei sentiment among non-Han tribes on the route of the enemy's march, who sold weapons and horses to the Shu in return for silks. Heavy rain made the mountain tracks impassable. Shu forces operated behind the enemy lines. A Sichuan general defeated the main Wei army while Zhuge led in reinforcements on an arduous march. After a month, the Wei called off the attack and went home.

Supply Chain and Rain

Building on this success, at the beginning of 231 Zhuge swiftly launched another advance into Wei territory. Having drawn the main enemy force to defend the city of Qishan, he sent troops to seize other Wei positions. When the enemy left its defensive position to try to stage a pincer attack, Zhuge put them to flight.

He then halted the advance to harvest the spring wheat before marching south to confront the main Wei army. Its general held back from battle but, eventually, let criticism of his evading tactics get the better of him and launched a frontal assault that ended in disaster – the Shu were reported to have captured 5,000 swords, 3,100 crossbows and 3,000 suits of armour.

Despite this major victory, Zhuge did not advance further, worried as he was about the supply chain. Summer rain bogged down the roads, and his king ordered a withdrawal. There was, again, a final victory typical of Zhuge's skills at laying ambushes – the leading Wei commander and his men were mown down by Shu cross-bowmen as they followed the retreating army into a narrow valley.

The Shu chancellor launched his final expedition to

the north in the spring of 234, with an army of one hundred thousand men. However, it faced an enemy army twice as large which blocked its initial advance into the plain of the Wei river. Disease spread through the Sichuan ranks. Zhuge became increasingly depressed, foreseeing his own death as he issued orders about how the Shu realm was to be run after him. In the autumn of 234, at the age of 54, he died. The leading Wei general thought that he was really still alive and that the pretended death was a ruse to lure the northerners into a snare – stories were told of a double impersonating Zhuge or of a wooden statue dressed in his clothes being put on display to convince the Wei that he was still alive.

Zhuge thus failed to realize his plan to dominate China, but the manner in which he took the initiative on behalf of the weakest of the three kingdoms ensured his place as a major figure among Chinese commanders. The way in which he used diversion and sudden unexpected attacks to unsettle numerically superior forces was squarely in the tradition laid down by Sun Tzu in the *Art of War*.

Zhuge's overall strategy has been criticized for not clearly defining which was the principal line of advance and which were sideshows. But his main weakness lay in the relative poverty and isolation of Sichuan and the problems of long supply lines through forbidding terrain. On top of which, the political objective – the restoration of the Han in the shape of the Shu pretenders – was deeply flawed. The Wei had developed an effective system of government in their lands, and the third kingdom, the Wu, would never have accepted the rise of the Shu to primacy.

After Zhuge's death, his protégé, Jiang Wei, led further campaigns against the Wei, which ended in defeats and, in 263, the northerners conquered the southwestern kingdom. Jiang tried to continue resistance, but his troops refused to follow him, and he was killed in battle. In turn, the Wei were overcome in 264 by another dynasty, the Jin, while the Wu also went into decline. The end of the Three Kingdoms period then gave way to three centuries of disunion, before the empire was finally restored by the Sui dynasty in 581.

Zhuge's Tactics

Pits After capturing the rebel leader, Meng Huo, in the southern expedition, Zhuge took him on a tour of his camp before releasing him. When the rebels attacked, Zhuge ordered his men to withdraw. Meng thought he knew the camp so his army rushed in – only to fall into huge concealed pits dug to trap them.

Fire In another attack in the wars in Yunnan, the enemy used elephants and tigers to attack the Sichuan forces, but Zhuge set up fire-breathing machines which scared them away.

Mines For the final battle in the south, Meng allied with a king whose soldiers wore rattan armour that could withstand arrows and swords. Zhuge sent a force to lure then into a valley where mines were detonated beneath them, setting fire to their armour and burning them alive.

Wooden oxen Zhuge was the first commander to use primitive wheelbarrows to transport supplies over the mountains.

Ambushes Zhuge exploited the steep mountain country-side of Sichuan with its deep defiles to lure enemy forces into ambushes which became so celebrated that opposing generals altered their tactics even when they were not being set.

Empty fort On the first expedition to the north, as recounted in the *Romance of the Three Kingdoms*, Zhuge found himself isolated without any troops in a town which was being threatened by the enemy. He ordered all the gates to be opened, and told the citizens to sweep the streets as though nothing was amiss. He himself sat on a wall with two children, playing his zither. The enemy general had been caught in Zhuge's traps before and suspected that he was being lured into an ambush. So he marched his army away.

ALARIC I

c. 360/370–410

JOHN HAYWOOD

A HERO TO SOME, a villain to many, Alaric was the Gothic leader who exposed to the world the declining power of the Roman Empire when he captured and sacked Rome in AD 410. Alaric's career was dominated by his quest to find a secure home for his followers. Though this did not happen in his lifetime, his achievements made possible the foundation of the Visigothic kingdom in 417, the first autonomous barbarian kingdom within the frontiers of the Western Roman Empire.

Alaric was born near the mouth of the Danube at some time between AD 360 and 370. Later writers would invent a royal genealogy to match his heroic stature, but it is likely that he was a 'new man' who rose to prominence by his leadership ability. His formative years were a time of great upheaval and insecurity for his people. The Goths were divided into two main groups: the Tervingi, to whom Alaric belonged, and the Greuthungi, who were regarded as the most powerful of the German peoples and whose defeat by the Huns in around AD 374 spread panic among the rest.

As a result, the Tervingi decided to abandon their lands and seek refuge in the Roman Empire. Some Greuthungi who had fled rather than submit to the Huns decided to do likewise. The Romans had watched the mounting chaos in the Germanic world with ill-disguised glee, but the arrival of some two hundred thousand Gothic refugees on the north bank of the Danube in the late summer of 376 was an alarming development. The emperor Valens (r. 364–378) was fully committed to a war against Persia and did not have enough troops to stop the Goths. He therefore decided to allow the Tervingi to enter and use what troops he could spare to oppose the less numerous Greuthungi.

Roman emperors were no strangers to the manipulative interpretation of facts and Valens presented the admission of the Tervingi as a great opportunity for the empire. One of the most serious problems faced by the Romans in the fourth century was that of population decline. Agriculture was suffering from labour shortages, tax yields were falling and the army was forced to recruit Germanic mercenaries to fill the ranks. The Tervingi could be settled on vacant land in the Balkans, bring abandoned fields back into production, provide recruits for the army and pay taxes. What could be better? Many thousands of Germans had been settled successfully in the empire in the past but these had always been defeated, disarmed and leaderless prisoners of war. Admitting the Tervingi was far more dangerous. They had not been defeated in war, their leadership was intact, and Valens did not have the troops to control them if his plans went wrong, which they very quickly did.

The generals whom Valens had left to manage the resettlement were corrupt: they embezzled the funds allocated to buy supplies so that the Tervingi were soon reduced to selling their children into slavery in order to survive. In 377, the Tervingi rebelled and went on a plundering spree. Bands of Greuthungi took advantage of the disorder to cross the Danube illegally and joined them. In 378, Valens made peace with Persia, finally releasing troops to deal with the Goths. On 9 August he launched a badly planned attack on the Gothic camp near Adrianople (modern Edirne, Turkey) and was defeated and killed. For four years the Balkans were ravaged by war. The Romans harassed the Goths constantly, but were unable to inflict a decisive defeat on them or expel them from the empire. In a peace treaty agreed in October 382, the emperor Theodosius

(r. 379–395) allowed the Goths to settle in Thrace (roughly modern Bulgaria) as semi-autonomous *foederati* ('allies') under their own leaders. Theodosius' concession of federate status was intended to be withdrawn as soon as the opportunity arose, but because he had to spend most of the remainder of his reign suppressing two usurpers who had seized power in the west, Magnus Maximus (r. 383–388) and Eugenius (r. 392–394), it never was. Theodosius needed Gothic troops to fight these usurpers, so he could not afford to alienate them by attacking their hard-won autonomy.

The Battle of the Frigidus

Alaric first came to prominence in 391. The Balkans were in turmoil following an army mutiny and a popular uprising in Thessalonica, and the Goths had seized the opportunity to go plundering. Alaric made his name by ambushing Theodosius while he was sleeping off an alcoholic lunch during a lull in fighting, the befuddled emperor only managing to escape because some of his men still had their wits about them and fought a rearguard action. A few years later Alaric was fighting for Theodosius, as the commander of a unit of Goths in the emperor's war against Eugenius. In September 394, Theodosius led an army of regulars and Goths from the Balkan provinces across the Julian Alps into the valley of the River Frigidus (modern Vipava) on the borders of Italy. Eugenius was waiting in a well-chosen position, but two days of hard fighting saw Theodosius victorious. Eugenius was captured and executed. The Goths, whom Theodosius had deliberately placed in the first line, suffered very heavy casualties – ten thousand according to one source, around a quarter of their fighting strength. Theodosius did not enjoy his triumph for long. On 17 January 395 he died of heart disease at Milan, and the empire was divided between his two sons, the 17-year-old Arcadius becoming emperor of the east and 10-year-old Honorius becoming emperor of the west under the regency of the Vandal general Stilicho.

After Theodosius' death, Stilicho ordered most of the Gothic units to go home. Alaric, rightly suspecting that the Romans had been pleased to see the Goths weakened in the battle, was angered by this casual dismissal after the sacrifices the Goths had made at the Battle of the Frigidus. He felt that his personal contribution to the victory should have been recognized by promotion to a regular command. While travelling through the Balkans, Alaric rebelled and marched on Constantinople, the eastern capital, to demand the command he deserved. At first he was probably followed only by his own unit, but the discontented Goths rallied to him and he was accepted as king by both the Tervingi and the Greuthungi. Under

Alaric's leadership these two groups would be welded into a single people who became known as the Visigoths ('Western Goths').

Alaric found Constantinople too strongly fortified for an assault to succeed so he turned west, and spent the next two years pillaging along the Aegean coast as far south as the Peloponnese. In the spring of 395, Stilicho crossed the Alps to deal with Alaric but failed to bring him to battle. This may have been deliberate. Stilicho believed that Theodosius had intended him to be regent for Arcadius as well as Honorius, but the government of the east was dominated by the eunuch Eutropius. Stilicho may have left Alaric to pillage in the hope that it would discredit Eutropius. In 397, Stilicho intervened again, leading a naval expedition to Greece and forcing Alaric to move north into Epirus. Soon afterwards Eutropius negotiated a settlement with Alaric, more to remove Stilicho's pretext for intervention in the east than from a sincere commitment to peace with the Visigoths.

Alaric was given the generalship he craved and the Visigoths were permitted to settle on lands in the provinces of Thrace and Macedonia with tax revenues and a grain subsidy. Unfortunately, these concessions were regarded in Constantinople as appeasing the barbarians, and in 399 Eutropius was overthrown and executed by the general Gainas who, ironically, was also a Goth. The new government refused to honour Eutropius' commitments and Alaric lost his generalship and his subsidies, though the Visigoths could not be expelled from their lands. Soon after, Alaric was forcibly reminded of the precariousness of his position. Gainas was dismissed and executed and there followed in Constantinople a massacre of his Gothic followers.

Alaric's First Invasion of Italy

Having failed to extract concessions from the eastern government, Alaric invaded Italy to put pressure on Stilicho and the western government. His invasion was brilliantly timed. Taking the same route he had followed with Theodosius in 394, Alaric crossed the Julian Alps in November 401, just before snow closed the Alpine passes for the winter and cut Italy off from the heavily garrisoned northern frontiers. Alaric faced little opposition as he marched west up the Po river valley and laid siege to the imperial court at Milan.

It was not until February or March 402 that Stilicho was able to bring reinforcements into Italy. Learning that the emperor Honorius had escaped, Alaric lifted the siege of Milan and went in pursuit, but was intercepted by Stilicho at Asti. After an inconclusive battle, Alaric withdrew 25 miles to Pollentia (modern Bra) where, on 6 April, Easter Sunday, Stilicho brought him to battle again.

Alaric, brought up as a Christian, was apparently taken by surprise while attending a religious service. The Visigothic cavalry drove the Roman cavalry from the field but the Roman infantry captured Alaric's baggage train, along with his wife and children, and all his plunder. Alaric opened negotiations with Stilicho and agreed to leave Italy. However, he had reached only as far as Verona when he was accused of breaking the truce and was again forced into battle by Stilicho, probably in July or August. Once again Stilicho got the better of Alaric but the defeat was not serious enough to prevent the latter from withdrawing in good order back to the lands the Visigoths had held in 397. One of the consequences of Alaric's invasion of Italy was that Honorius moved the western capital to Ravenna, which was protected by marshlands and strong fortifications, and had good sea communications with Constantinople.

The failure of his invasion of Italy left Alaric in limbo until, late in 406, Stilicho offered him everything that Eutropius had previously offered him in 397 in return for an alliance against the eastern government. Stilicho's aim was to force the east to give him control of the Balkan province of Illyricum, which was one of the major recruiting grounds of the Roman army. The military situation in the western empire was deteriorating. In 405, Stilicho had defeated an invasion by a group of Goths under their king Radagaisus and it was clear that more trouble could be expected from that direction. Then in Britain, in 406, the field army mutinied and proclaimed as emperor its general, Constantine. To face these threats, Stilicho urgently needed to be able to recruit troops from the Balkans, since manpower shortages were more acute in the western than in the eastern empire. However, his plan backfired badly.

Alaric's Second Invasion of Italy

Alaric moved south into Epirus, where he waited to be joined by Stilicho and his regular Roman troops for a campaign against Constantinople in the summer of 407. Before that could happen, however, events began to spin out of Stilicho's control. On the last day of 406, a coalition of Vandals, Sueves and Alans crossed the frozen Rhine and invaded Gaul. Then early in 407, the usurper Constantine crossed the Channel to save Gaul from the barbarians. Stilicho had no choice but to abandon his plans and Alaric was again left in the lurch. In 408, Alaric led the Visigoths to occupy the Alpine province of Noricum, where he was well placed to invade Italy again, and threatened war if he did not receive a subsidy of 4,000 pounds of gold to maintain his people. Stilicho, who did not wish to add a third enemy to the two he already faced in Gaul, persuaded a reluctant Senate to pay up, but his reputation was fatally damaged. Now a grown man, Honorius was desperate to be rid of his overbearing general. In August 408, Stilicho was arrested on trumped-up treason charges and executed.

An anti-barbarian reaction flashed through Italy. German soldiers in the Roman army were massacred in their thousands, together with their families. The survivors fled and joined forces with Alaric. In the autumn of 408, Alaric invaded Italy for a second time and, plundering as he went, headed for Rome, where he set up camp outside its walls in November. Visigoth numbers were swelled by thousands of runaway slaves, many of them Goths who had been captured by Stilicho in 405. With these rein-forcements, Alaric had a fighting strength of perhaps forty thousand, a large force by the standards of the time. Alaric's men were also much better equipped than most barbarian armies. While in the Balkans, Alaric had taken over Roman arms factories and forced the craftsmen to make weapons and armour for his troops.

Over a year of fruitless negotiations followed. Alaric lifted his blockade when there appeared to be progress and imposed it again when talks broke down. Military confronta-tion was not an option for Honorius, as he needed to save his troops to combat Constantine in Gaul. Despite his strong position, Alaric was conciliatory, dropping his demands for a generalship and gold and asking only for the province of

Noricum and a grain subsidy. Even many Romans thought his demands were astonishingly moderate but Honorius would not give ground.

Alaric's on–off siege of Rome, which began in November 408, moved towards its climax in the summer of 410. Hoping to increase the pressure on Honorius, Alaric had lifted the siege of Rome late in 409 and persuaded the Senate to elect its own emperor, Attalus. Attalus proved less cooperative than Alaric had hoped, and he deposed him in July 410 and reopened negotiations with Honorius. Alaric went to meet Honorius outside Ravenna, but while he waited for the emperor he was ambushed by a small Roman force. Outraged, Alaric returned to Rome and renewed the siege. On the night of 24 August the Visigoths entered Rome through the Salarian Gate on the northeast side of the city. It is not known exactly how the city fell. One story is that Alaric had earlier given Gothic slave boys to several wealthy senators and it was this unsuspected fifth column who opened the gate. Another account implies that the Visigoths had to fight their way in.

The sack that followed was remarkably restrained considering the years of hardship and uncertainty suffered by the Visigoths. Alaric gave orders that churches were not to be damaged and advised his men to concentrate on pillaging movable wealth rather than on killing and destruction. The basilicas of St Peter and St Paul were nominated as places of sanctuary, and people who took refuge there were not disturbed. There were inevitably some who were killed or beaten to make them reveal where valuables were hidden, but the Visigoths seem generally to have heeded Alaric's advice. Refugees from the city would tell how some Visigoths had even escorted nuns to safety. Movable wealth, however, did include people – one of whom was the emperor's sister, Galla Placidia – and many were taken prisoner to be ransomed or sold as slaves. The Visigoths were mindful enough of their Christianity to leave the church most of its treasures, and only one important building, the Senate House, was seriously damaged. When the Visigoths withdrew after three days of plundering, Rome was a great deal poorer but still substantially intact and life quickly returned to normal.

Though no longer the capital, Rome remained a potent symbol of Roman history and power; news of its fall to an invader, for the first time since it was sacked by the Celts eight hundred years before, sent shock waves through the empire. Alaric had done his worst but, safe in Ravenna, Honorius still refused his demands.

Frustrated, Alaric led his troops into southern Italy. Recognizing its importance as the major exporter of grain to Italy, Alaric threatened to invade North Africa, but he died before the year was out. His successor, Athaulf, turned and took the Visigoths to Gaul. After helping the Romans defeat the Vandals in Spain, only seven years later they were finally given control of fertile lands in Aquitaine.

Alaric's Achievement

The surviving sources give few clues as to Alaric's true character, but it is clear that he was never bent on destruction for its own sake, nor was he a would-be empire builder. His restraint in the face of repeated Roman bad faith was outstanding but this reflects his real concern for the future of his people. Alaric was always prepared to trade a short-term military advantage for a long-term political settlement with the Romans. Though he is most famous for the sack of Rome, the significance of this act was largely symbolic. In itself it did not make the fall of the Western Roman Empire inevitable or even likely. Alaric was not the first barbarian to play an influential role in Roman politics. Many Germans – Stilicho, for example – had served in the Roman army, risen to high rank and played a dominating role in the empire's politics. Like them, Alaric became a Roman general but, unlike them, he never commanded a regular army unit or became absorbed into the Roman military hierarchy. Alaric was a king but he never had a kingdom or any secure territory to which he could retreat if things went wrong. Yet, despite this, he successfully resisted all military efforts to assimilate his people into the Roman system. The Visigoths lived in the empire but were not

Roman subjects, and their only connection to the empire was through Alaric and his relationship with the imperial government. By proving that it was possible for a barbarian king to maintain an independent power base within the empire, Alaric pointed the way to the establishment of the barbarian kingdoms and the eventual dismemberment of the Western Roman Empire.

AETIUS

c. 400–454

JOHN HAYWOOD

FLAVIUS AETIUS WAS THE LAST GREAT GENERAL of the Western Roman Empire. Supreme commander of the western Roman armies from 433 until his death in 454, he skilfully maintained Roman control of Gaul by playing one group of barbarians off against another. His death is often seen as marking the beginning of the end for the Western Roman Empire.

Born in around 400, Aetius was the son of Gaudentius, a common soldier from the Balkans who had joined the elite Praetorian Guard and risen to high command in the cavalry. His mother was an Italian heiress from a senatorial family. Aetius began his military career by following in his father's footsteps and joining the Praetorians while still in his teens. Because of his family's importance, Aetius spent part of his childhood as a hostage with the Visigothic king Alaric and he later spent several years also as a hostage among the Huns. Although their lives might be forfeit if diplomatic relations broke down, young hostages were normally treated more like foster children than prisoners. During his time with the Huns, Aetius learned horsemanship and archery and formed a friendship with one of their kings, Ruga (d. 434), and with his nephew Attila. Aetius married a Visigothic princess and one of their sons, Carpilio, was sent as a hostage to Ruga in 425. These relationships that the young Aetius forged with Visigothic and Hun royalty served him well in his subsequent career.

Rise to Power

When the western emperor Honorius died in 423 without a male heir, the eastern emperor Theodosius II (r. 408–450) appointed Honorius' 4-year-old nephew Valentinian III (r. 425–454) as his successor under the regency of his mother, princess Galla Placidia (d. 450). A child emperor was the last thing the embattled Western Empire needed. The army rebelled and raised an official called John to the throne instead. Refusing to accept the coup, Theodosius gave Galla Placidia an army to place Valentinian on the throne by force. To stop her, John sent Aetius to recruit troops of mercenaries from his friends the Huns. Aetius returned at the head of sixty thousand Huns to find that John had already been defeated and executed. Under different circumstances Aetius would have shared John's fate, but the Huns would have gone on the rampage in Italy if he had been killed. Expediently, Galla Placidia appointed Aetius master of horse with command of the field army in Gaul.

The situation that Aetius inherited in Gaul was a desperate one, with the Romans steadily losing ground to Germanic invaders. In 417 the Romans had been forced to allow the Visigoths to settle in Aquitaine as *foederati* ('allies'). The Visigoths, who had entered the empire as refugees from the Huns in 376 and who had sacked Rome in 410, were granted the tax revenues of the province in return for serving in the Roman armies. Though technically still subject to Rome, they gradually exploited its weakness to increase the territory under their control. In the north, the Romans faced a similar problem with the Franks, who were extending their control over the province of Belgica. Much of eastern Gaul was occupied by the Burgundians, while even those areas still nominally controlled by the Romans were insecure because of the activities of peasant brigands called *bagaudae*.

To deal with all these problems, Aetius had only around forty-five thousand regular troops, assuming that all his units were actually up to strength. Because of this he depended heavily on Hun mercenaries to supplement his forces and without them would have achieved little. Aetius' first success came in 425 or 426 when he defeated the Visigothic king Theodoric (r. 418–451), who was attempting to capture Arles. In 427 he defeated the Franks, who were trying to extend their territory to the River Somme. In 430 he defeated an invasion by the Alamanni. In the following year he suppressed a rebellion in the Alpine province of Noricum and again drove the Visigoths from Arles. In 432 Aetius inflicted another defeat on the Franks. This run of victories greatly increased his prestige and influence. In 429 Aetius was made second in command to Felix, the master general of the western armies. The following year he forced Galla Placidia to dismiss Felix and appoint him master general in his place. Felix ('Lucky') was then executed for treason and in 432 Aetius was appointed consul of Rome.

Civil War

Galla Placidia had never forgiven Aetius for supporting John and she had been merely waiting for an opportunity for revenge. In 432 she dismissed Aetius and appointed in his place Boniface, the commander of the army in Africa. Aetius refused to submit and met Boniface in battle near Rimini. Though Boniface won, he died of wounds soon after and was succeeded as master general by his son-in-law, Sebastian. Aetius fled to the Huns and with the support of Ruga was able to return to Italy and dictate terms to Galla Placidia in 433. Sebastian was exiled, Aetius was reinstated as master general and was made a patrician, the highest rank of the Roman aristocracy. Aetius' dominance of the Western Empire became complete in 437, when the regency of Galla Placidia came to an end with Valentinian's eighteenth birthday. Valentinian was a weak and ineffectual character and, with his mother politically sidelined, Aetius effectively became the ruler of the Western Empire. For all his ambition, Aetius never aspired to seize the throne for himself. To have tried would have invited the hostility of the east and Aetius had the political acumen to understand that he needed its support if the Western Empire was to survive: far better to be the power behind the throne.

The 430s saw the development of a new and serious threat to the Western Empire. In 429 the Vandal king Geiseric led his people on an invasion of North Africa from Spain, where they had been repeatedly attacked by the Visigoths. It is possible that Boniface, who was in rebellion against the western government at the time, may have encouraged Geiseric in the hope of using the Vandals to support his ambitions in much the same way that Aetius used the Huns. If so, it was a plan that quickly went badly wrong as Geiseric swept Boniface's forces aside and began to advance on Carthage, North Africa's richest and largest city. North Africa was the only region of the Western Empire still untouched by war. It was the main source of tax revenues for the western government and of grain for Italy. Fully engaged in Gaul, Aetius had few troops to spare for Africa, so to save Carthage he recognized Vandal control of Mauretania (roughly modern Algeria) in 435.

The Destruction of the Burgundians

To do anything about the Vandals, Aetius first had to stabilize the position in Gaul. In 436 he dealt a decisive blow to the Burgundians by unleashing an army of Huns against them. In a ferociously genocidal campaign it was said that twenty thousand Burgundians were slaughtered, including their king Gundahar. The cowed and demoralized survivors were settled by Aetius a few years later on lands south of Lake Geneva. The devastating defeat of the Burgundians passed into legend and forms the background to the German medieval epic, the *Niebelungenlied*. At the same time Aetius destroyed most of the bands of *bagaudae* that were plaguing the Gallic countryside, suppressed a rebellion in Armorica (Brittany) and, taking advantage of the departure of the Vandals for North Africa, restored Roman control to all of Spain other than mountainous Galicia, which remained under the control of the Suevi, former allies of the Vandals.

Two more years of difficult campaigning against the Visigoths culminated in a major victory at the Battle of Snake Mountain in 438.

With a lot of help from the Huns, Aetius had achieved much in a decade and more of constant campaigning. He had restored the Rhine frontier for the first time since it was overrun by the Vandals in 409. Most of the German tribes who had followed in their wake had been either expelled or thoroughly chastened and the Visigoths had been confined again to the lands granted to them by treaty back in 417. Peace and order were being restored in the countryside of Spain and Gaul, promising much-needed increases in tax revenue for the western government. Soon Aetius would have the resources he needed to deal with the Visigoths once and for all.

The treaty of 435 had left Geiseric dangerously close to Carthage, but the constant campaigning to restore order to Gaul left Aetius with little alternative other than to cut the city's garrison to the bone. By far the cleverest and most ruthless of the barbarian kings of his day, Geiseric was not a man to resist such temptation, and in 439 he seized Carthage and with it the richest provinces of North Africa. The loss of Carthage was by far the most serious setback yet suffered by the Western Empire in its struggle for survival. Without the tax revenues of North Africa, the western government was not fiscally viable: without its grain, the population of Rome would starve. Though Ravenna had been the administrative capital of the west since 402, Rome remained the symbolic heart of the empire. Aetius' authority would not survive a famine there. To keep the grain flowing, Aetius had no choice but to recognize Geiseric's possession of Carthage, but he almost immediately began planning a counter-attack. Realizing that his resources were insufficient for the task, Aetius successfully appealed to Theodosius for eastern support. Late in 440 a fleet of eleven hundred ships and a massive army from both halves of the empire began to gather in Sicily. If it succeeded, the expedition would transform the fortunes of the Western Empire at a stroke. With North Africa returned to Roman control, the re-conquest of the remaining barbarian enclaves in Gaul and Spain would surely soon follow. Flavius Aetius would be hailed as the saviour of Rome.

The great expedition never sailed. Attila's invasion of the Balkans in 441 forced Theodosius to withdraw his troops and the expedition was abandoned. From this moment on, the Western Empire was living on borrowed time. The failure did not diminish Aetius' personal prestige. Even the Britons, who had expelled the Roman administration in 410 and had been independent ever since, came to him in 446 asking for help against the barbarians who were attacking Britain. However, his hard-won successes of the 430s began slowly to unravel. Taking advantage of his preoccupation with North Africa, the Suevi emerged from Galicia and began to take over Spain. The limited forces Aetius could send to oppose the Suevi suffered a succession of defeats and by 443 almost everything south of the Ebro river was lost to them. At least Aetius' friendship with Attila protected the west from Hun raids. To keep Attila sweet, Aetius found a face-saving way to pay him a subsidy by making him an honorary master general, a post that brought with it a substantial salary.

Aetius Versus Attila

In 450 Aetius' friendship with Attila broke down and he was forced to prepare for a Hun invasion. Attila probably had ambitions to replace Aetius as the military strongman of the Western Empire and announced his intention to attack the Visigothic kingdom as an ally of the emperor. Attila received further encouragement from what he took to be a proposal of marriage from Valentinian's rebellious sister Honoria and the chance to intervene in a succession dispute among the Franks.

Aetius' last and most important victory, the Battle of the Catalaunian Plains, was as much a masterpiece of diplomacy as of generalship. Faced with an invasion of Gaul by his former ally Attila in 451, he built an unlikely coalition of his former German enemies in Gaul, including the Visigoths (under their veteran king Theodoric), Franks, Burgundians, Saxons and Alans (a former nomad people who had been driven off the steppes by the Huns). Most of Aetius' regular Roman troops were also Germans, so his army was Roman in name only. Attila's army also had a large German component drawn from his subject peoples, chief among them the Ostrogoths and the Gepids.

Attila advanced as far west as Orléans but was unable to take the city. Harassed by Aetius' forces, Attila withdrew to the more open country of the Catalaunian Plains (modern Champagne) where he could exploit his superiority in cavalry more effectively. On 20 June near the village of Châtres, between Châlons and Troyes, Attila laagered his wagons and prepared to make a stand against his pursuers. Attila formed his battle line with his Huns in the centre and his German allies on the flanks. Aetius placed the regulars on the left of his line and the Visigoths and the other Germans on the right. The Alans, whose reliability Aetius doubted, were placed in the centre, to stop them running away.

Fighting began around three o'clock in the afternoon with a struggle over possession of a low hill on the left of the battlefield. Aetius spotted the advantageous position slightly sooner than Attila, and Visigothic cavalry under Thorismund (Theodoric's son) managed to occupy the summit just ahead of the Huns. The fighting then became general. The Roman infantry formed an impenetrable formation behind interlocking shields so Attila concentrated his attack on the Germans, most of whom were also fighting on foot. In the mêlée, King Theodoric was thrown from his horse and trampled to death by his own men. Ferocious fighting was still continuing when darkness began to fall, some seven hours after it had begun. Attila began to withdraw into his wagon laager pursued by Thorismund. In the darkness and confusion Thorismund was wounded in the head and thrown to the ground, to be saved from his father's fate only by the quick action of one of his men. Aetius had had the better of the fighting and he called off the action rather than risk continuing in the dark. Casualties on both sides were heavy – sources speak improbably of one hundred and sixty-five thousand dead. Aetius did not order a pursuit when Attila began to withdraw the next day, probably because he wished to preserve the Huns to counterbalance Visigothic power in Gaul.

It was at this point that Aetius made the most serious miscalculation of his career. Assuming that Attila was chastened by his defeat and would be ready to restore friendly relations, Aetius neglected to garrison the Alpine passes. In 452 Attila, who had not given up his ambition to marry Honoria, was able to invade Italy almost unopposed and subject it to ravaging before supply problems forced him to withdraw. The following spring, Attila died unexpectedly and his empire immediately began to fall apart.

The fall of the Hun empire left Aetius militarily and politically bankrupt. Not only had he lost an irreplaceable source of ferociously effective troops, but also the delicate balance of power by which he maintained Roman authority in Gaul was shattered. With the Huns gone, there was no longer any good reason for the Germans to cooperate with him. Aetius' influence at the imperial court was also undermined. He alone had been able to manage the Huns: now he no longer seemed quite so indispensable.

Downfall and Death

Even before the death of Attila, Valentinian was growing increasingly resentful of Aetius' power. After the death of Theodosius in 450, Valentinian had conceived a harebrained plan to reunite the empire under his sole rule. Realizing that this would cause a civil war that the empire could ill afford, Aetius blocked the plan. Valentinian and Aetius soon disagreed again over a marriage alliance. Perhaps sensing that his position was weakening, Aetius proposed a marriage between his son Gaudentius and

Valentinian's daughter Placidia. Since Valentinian had no male children, this would not only have made Aetius' position unassailable, but it would also have made Gaudentius heir to the throne. This was too much for Valentinian. At a meeting to discuss tax revenues on 21 or 22 September 454, he suddenly drew his sword and murdered Aetius. A contemporary chronicler commented that Valentinian might as well have chopped off his own right hand. Valentinian lasted barely six months: on 16 March 455 he was cut down by two of Aetius' loyal Hun officers as he practised archery in the fields outside Rome. With no general of comparable ability to replace Aetius and no obvious successor to Valentinian, the Western Roman Empire entered its final decline. By the time its last feeble emperor was deposed by a barbarian general in 476, the Western Roman Empire consisted of Italy and little else.

The fall of the Western Empire did nothing to diminish Aetius' posthumous reputation, and in the sixth century the Byzantine historian Procopius described him simply as 'the last of the Romans'. Aetius' failure to save the Western Empire was largely the result of circumstances beyond his control. His military record speaks for itself – he lost only one battle in his career and was adored by his troops – and his political judgement was usually sound. His greatest weakness was his reliance on the Huns, which was forced on him by the chronic manpower shortage of the later Roman Empire. Aetius was rarely able to do more than contain one threat to the empire before he had to divert his limited resources to face a new one. What he did brilliantly was to use his military and political skills to buy time for the empire while he waited for a lucky break that never came.

ATTILA

c. 406–453

JOHN HAYWOOD

ATTILA THE HUN is quite probably the most notorious figure of what it is now unfashionable to call the 'Dark Ages'. King of the Huns from 434 to 453, Attila terrorized the declining Roman Empire and conquered an empire of his own that stretched from the Black Sea to the Rhine. Ultimately, however, he destroyed far more than he built and his achievements did not out-live him.

Of Attila's early life nothing much is known. His father Mundzuk, brother of Ruga, had become joint king of the Huns in the 420s. At this time, the Huns were a society in transition. A Turkic nomad people, they had migrated from central Asia to eastern Europe in the later fourth century and settled on the Hungarian plain. This was the most westerly area of steppe grassland suitable for pasturing the vast herds of horses on which the nomads depended for their military power. The area was also strategically well placed for raiding the Germanic peoples of central and northern Europe and both the western and eastern halves of the Roman Empire.

The Huns in the Fifth Century

At the time of their arrival in Europe, the Huns did not acknowledge a single ruler but had several power-sharing kings who operated within a ranking system, with one of their number recognized as senior king. To avoid over-grazing, the Huns needed to be dispersed over a wide area, and this led naturally to the formation of a devolved power structure. In the fifth century, the Huns began to abandon nomadic pastoralism and settle in villages. They became wealthy from raiding, collecting tribute from subject peoples and wages for mercenary service with the Roman armies. This made possible a process of political centralization that led to Ruga becoming sole king of the Huns in 432. Kings ruled with the support of a chosen elite called the *logades*, but the Huns still lacked formal institutions of government and their unity depended solely on their leaders' success in war. Loyalty had, in effect, to be paid for by distributing the spoils of war: a king who lacked the means to reward his followers would not last long.

Ruga died in 434 and was succeeded as king jointly by Attila and his brother Bleda. Their first act was to conclude a peace treaty that their uncle had been negotiating with the Eastern Roman Empire at the time of his death. Attila and Bleda declined to dismount for the peace conference, forcing the Roman ambassadors to conduct negotiations on horseback to maintain the impression that both parties were equals. In fact the Romans were desperate for peace – they needed to free troops to fight the Vandals who had invaded North Africa – and the brothers drove a hard bargain. Escaped Roman prisoners were to be returned or ransomed for eight golden solidi apiece and the annual tribute that the Romans would pay for peace was doubled from 350 to 700 pounds of gold a year. The Romans also had to hand over to certain death members of the Hun royal family who had unsuccessfully opposed Ruga and become refugees in the empire.

Invasion of the Balkans

For several years after the peace treaty, Attila and Bleda were fully occupied conquering what Roman writers vaguely called Scythia, meaning barbarian Europe. The exact bounds of their conquests are not known, but they certainly extended to the Baltic Sea in the north and to within a short distance of the Rhine in the west and the

Black Sea in the east. During this time the Romans failed to pay the Huns their annual subsidy. Then in 439 the Vandals captured Carthage and threatened to cut off Rome's corn supply. All of the Romans' military resources needed to be marshalled to recapture Carthage, presenting Attila and Bleda with an opportunity to exact vengeance. The Roman failure to abide by the terms of the treaty gave the Huns an unimpeachable reason for war and in 441 they crossed the Danube and invaded the Balkans. First Viminiacum (Kostolac, Serbia) fell and was razed to the ground, its population being marched off into slavery. Next to fall was Margum, then Singidunum (Belgrade), and with the fall of the great fortress city of Sirmium (Mitrovica) the defences of the Danube frontier collapsed. With a large swathe of Roman territory under his control, Attila agreed a truce with the eastern emperor Theodosius II (r. 408–450). Attila warned that any attempt at offensive action by the Romans would result in a renewal of war. Despite this, Theodosius used the respite to cancel the planned attack on the Vandals and transfer his troops to the Balkans.

As he had threatened, Attila went back to war. In 443 he captured the base of the Romans' Danube fleet at Ratiaria (Archar, Bulgaria). With his lines of communication now secured against Roman attacks, he marched south and sacked the major arms-manufacturing centre at Naissus (Nish, Bulgaria) before turning east and meting out the same treatment to Sardica (Sofia). He then moved quickly down the main road towards the eastern capital city of Constantinople. Up until then, he had met little opposition, but between Attila and Constantinople lay the main Roman field army under the master general Aspar. In a succession of battles Attila comprehensively outmanoeuvred Aspar, cut him off from the capital and scattered his remaining forces. Though Constantinople itself was so heavily fortified as to be impregnable, the Balkans were now completely defenceless and Theodosius sued for peace. Attila demanded payment of the arrears of tribute and in future an annual payment of 2,100 pounds of gold. The price of ransoming Roman prisoners was to rise from 8 to 12 solidi. The arrears were paid, peace was agreed in autumn 443 and the Huns withdrew from Roman territory.

Sole ruler of the Huns

In 444 or 445 Attila murdered his brother Bleda and became sole king of the Huns. It is not known why they fell out, but the brothers seem to have had very different characters. Bleda had a wantonly cruel and sadistic side to his character while Attila, though utterly ruthless, had a more pragmatic attitude to violence. Although his name has become a byword for tyranny, he was not regarded as a tyrant by his fellow Huns. His personal enemies might have suffered an agonizing death by impalement, but for the most part Attila relied not on terror but on personal charisma and successful war leadership to keep the Huns obedient to his rule. A Greek prisoner who had decided to remain with the Huns after being freed compared Attila's rule favourably with that of the Roman emperors with their high taxes and corrupt officials.

Little is known about Attila's movements until the spring of 447 when he again invaded the Eastern Roman Empire, on an even larger scale than in 441. This time Attila brought with him contingents drawn from his Germanic subjects. In January of that year Constantinople had suffered a series of severe earthquakes and a large section of the city walls, including fifty-seven towers, had collapsed. As the people of Constantinople laboured frantically to rebuild their walls, Attila approached, leaving the usual trail of smoking ruins behind him. This time, however, Roman resistance was stiffer. Near Marcianopolis, Attila met the Roman field army and, though he defeated it, he incurred heavy casualties. Learning that the walls of Constantinople had been restored, Attila turned aside and ravaged through the Balkans and into Greece. The price of peace for the Romans this time was to cede a strip of territory south of the Danube that was five days' travel wide (about 120 miles). The following year Attila left the Romans alone and campaigned in the east, conquering the Acatziri, a nomadic people who lived on the steppes between the Black Sea and the Caspian Sea. The attack was probably provoked by the emperor Theodosius' attempt to forge an anti-Hun alliance with them.

The Romans now resorted to desperate measures. In 449 Theodosius' government hatched a plot to assassinate Attila using a diplomatic embassy as cover. The plot was betrayed, however, and the ambassadors, who had not been told that their mission was just a diversion, counted themselves lucky not to be executed on the spot. Attila's show of mercy made it easier for him to exploit Roman embarrassment over this treacherous breach of diplomatic protocol to extract another huge payment of tribute. Satisfied that the Eastern Empire was now no threat to him, Attila turned his attention to the Western Roman Empire. Nominally ruled by the weak emperor Valentinian III (r. 425–455), real power in the west lay with the master general Aetius (d. 454). In his younger days, Aetius had been a hostage with the Huns and he had maintained close and friendly relations with them ever since, often employing them as mercenaries. Aetius had even made Attila an honorary master general in the western army.

Glittering Prizes Beckon

In early 450 Attila announced his intention to attack the Visigothic kingdom in Aquitaine as the ally of Valentinian. The Visigoths had been a problem for the Romans ever since they had entered the empire in 376 as refugees from the Huns, and the destruction of their kingdom would have served Roman interests. It is likely that Attila intended to make his honorific military rank into a real one, replace Aetius as commander of the western armies and so win effective control of the Western Roman Empire. Attila received further encouragement in the spring when a messenger arrived from Valentinian's sister Honoria with a plea to rescue her from an intolerable marriage. Attila demanded that Valentinian hand her over, together with a dowry of half the Western Empire. He refused. In the summer a succession dispute broke out among the Franks, one party appealing to Aetius for support, the other, a minority party, to Attila, giving him another reason to intervene in the west. Then Theodosius died in a riding accident and Marcian, the new eastern emperor, refused to pay any more tribute to Attila.

Attila continued with his planned campaign in the west – if successful he would easily be able to deal with Marcian. As in 447, he called on the services of his Germanic subjects crossed the Rhine near Coblenz with a massive army, and invaded Gaul. However, Attila had bungled the diplomatic preparations for the invasion. By threatening the interests of the Romans, Visigoths and Franks all at the same time, Attila drove them into an alliance. Attila got as far west as Orléans but, failing to take the city, he withdrew to the Catalaunian Plains (Champagne). There, somewhere between Châlons and Troyes, he was met in battle on 20 June 451 by Aetius, at the head of a mixed army of Romans, Visigoths, Franks and other Germans who had settled in Gaul. The two armies fought themselves to a standstill by nightfall, each suffering heavy casualties. During the night Attila briefly considered immolating himself on a pyre of saddles but thought better of it. In the morning Aetius watched as the Huns withdrew in good order. By September Attila was back in Hungary, and sending raiding parties into the Balkans to keep Marcian guessing about his plans.

Though he was still determined on marriage with Honoria, Attila learned from his mistakes; the next year he forced the Romans to face him alone by invading Italy, which the Visigoths and Franks had no interest in defending. Aetius, believing that Attila would be ready to negotiate peace after his defeat, had failed to guard the Alpine passes so the Huns faced no opposition until they reached Aquileia. Here Attila was held up for several weeks by the heroic resistance of the garrison, before his Huns scaled the walls and sacked the city so thoroughly that it never recovered. Attila swept west along the Po valley, sacking city after city, until at Milan he was met by a delegation led by Pope Leo I (r. 440–461) with offers of tribute in return for peace. It came none too soon. Italy was in the grip of famine and Attila would have been forced to retreat soon for lack of supplies. He returned home to discover that, in his absence, Marcian had sent troops to raid Hun territory.

The Collapse of Attila's Empire

Though the world still quailed at the mention of his name, Attila's position at the end of 452 was surprisingly weak. The Italian expedition had certainly been profitable in terms of plunder and tribute, but casualties had been heavy, and these came on top of the losses suffered in Gaul the previous year. He had not married Honoria and was no nearer controlling the Western Empire. The Huns' horses were tired and had returned home too late to benefit from summer grazing, so no campaign could be launched the following year until they had had a chance to fatten up again in the spring. The Balkans had been ravaged so often that there would be little profit in raiding them again and Attila knew, from previous experience, that Marcian was safe from his vengeance so long as he remained behind the walls of Constantinople. Yet Attila had an imperative need to maintain a constant supply of plunder to maintain his hold on power: it was impossible for him to do nothing.

In spring 453, while he was still contemplating what to do about Marcian's defiance, Attila decided to add a beautiful German girl called Ildico to his collection of wives. It has been speculated that she was a princess, handed over to Attila by a German king as a form of tribute. The wedding celebrations were long and Attila got as gloriously drunk as any self-respecting barbarian should do on such occasions. Retiring for the night with his new bride, Attila passed out on his bed. During the night, he suffered a severe nosebleed while lying unconscious on his back and quietly drowned in his own blood. The death of such a terrifying figure could not go unnoticed in heaven and, it was said, on the same night Marcian dreamed prophetically that the bow of Attila was broken. Deprived of his charismatic leadership, the Hun empire quickly disintegrated. As Attila's sons fought over the kingship, their German subjects rebelled, and at the Battle of Nedao in 455 they overthrew the Hun empire. Bands of surviving Huns scattered back to the steppes, within a century losing their identity as a people.

Attila's Legacy

Any objective assessment of Attila's career must conclude that he achieved nothing beyond perhaps hastening the decline of the Western Roman Empire by diverting forces that were needed elsewhere. True, Attila spread terror, destruction and death across much of Europe, and he relieved the Romans of a great deal of treasure, but he never even began to lay the foundations of a lasting state. He lacked the political imagination to make the transition from barbarian war leader to statesman. Despite this, Attila's reputation continued to grow after his death. By the eighth century the legend that he had called himself 'the Scourge of God' had gained wide currency and he was firmly ensconced in Germanic and Scandinavian legend, and in dozens of spurious tales of miraculous deliverances from Attila and of gory martyrdoms at his hands. Only among the Hungarians, or Magyars as they call themselves, is Attila regarded as a national hero. Even this is a legend, however; the Magyars, a Finno-Ugrian people originally from Siberia, are actually completely unrelated to the Turkic Huns. The Hungarians, despite appearances, did not get their name from the Huns – the term derives from a Slavic mispronunciation of On-Ogur ('Ten Arrows'), the name of the Magyar confederation that conquered the area in the late ninth century.

The Huns at War

Despite his many victories, there is no evidence that Attila was an innovative commander. The secret of Attila's success was mainly down to the Huns' style of fighting. Although by Attila's day the Huns were becoming increasingly sedentary, they continued the traditions of warfare that they had developed when they still lived on the Eurasian steppes. Like all the steppe nomads, they spent much of their lives on horseback, constantly moving with the seasons in search of fresh pasture for their flocks of sheep and herds of cattle and horses, and they made natural light cavalrymen. Blood feuds and fights with other nomad peoples over grazing rights were an everyday fact of steppe life. The favoured weapon of the Indo-Iranian nomads, such as the Sarmatians and Alans, who had dominated the western steppes before the arrival of the Huns, was the lance, and both rider and horse wore scale armour like the *cataphracti* of the Persian and Roman armies.

In contrast, the Huns were horse archers. They rarely wore armour and relied on speed and manoeuvrability for protection. Using their powerful composite recurved bows, the Huns could pour down a deadly and demoralizing hail of arrows on slower-moving armoured cavalry and infantry long before they could get close enough to retaliate. Made by gluing together layers of wood, horn and sinew, the composite bow's compactness made it ideal for use on horseback. The bows used by the Huns had the added refinement of a unique asymmetrical design that almost doubled its power, so that it could pierce armour at a range of up to 100 yards. This was comparable to packing the power of a medieval English longbow into a weapon half its size and weight. The importance of the bow to the Huns was such that it was a symbol of authority, and chieftains would be buried with gold-sheathed bows. When they arrived in Europe the Huns had no experience of siege warfare. By Attila's time they had learned to make siege weapons, probably from the Romans, which they carried with them on campaign in their wagons. They also carried rafts for crossing rivers.

The effectiveness of their cavalry was enhanced by their nightmarish appearance. The Huns practised deformation of the skull. Infants' skulls were tightly bound above the eyebrows so that as the skull grew it would be deformed into a long flat shape with a low forehead. The Huns also practised scarification of the face, which left them with little facial hair. Soldiers who had not encountered the Huns before must have found their appearance very unnerving, and stories that they were really the offspring of witches and wild beasts were widely believed.

FURTHER READING

THUTMOSE III

E. H. Cline and D. O'Connor (eds), *Thutmose III: A New Biography* (University of Michigan Press, Ann Arbor, 2006).

I. Shaw, *Egyptian Warfare and Weapons* (Shire Publications Limited, Princes Risborough, 1991).

M. Lichtheim, *Ancient Egyptian Literature: A Book of Readings. Volume II: The New Kingdom* (University of California Press, Berkley, Los Angeles, and London, 1976).

RAMESSES II

K. A. Kitchen, *Pharaoh Triumphant: the Life and Times of Ramesses II* (Aris and Phillips Limited, Warminster, 1982).

M. Lichtheim, *Ancient Egyptian Literature: A Book of Readings. Volume II: The New Kingdom* (University of California Press, Berkley, Los Angeles, and London, 1976).

I. Shaw, *Egyptian Warfare and Weapons* (Shire Publications Limited, Princes Risborough, 1991).

J. A. Tyldesley, *Ramesses: Egypt's Greatest Pharaoh* (Viking Penguin, London, 2000).

JOSHUA BIN NUN

The Bible, Book of Joshua.

R. S. Hess, 'Early Israel in Cana'an; A Survey of Recent Evidence and Interpretations', *Palestine Exploration Quarterly*, 125, 1993.

KING DAVID

The Bible, I Samuel 16–31, II Samuel 1–24, I Kings 1–2.

Jonathan Kirsch, *King David: The Real Life of the Man who Ruled Israel* (Ballantine, New York, NY, 2001).

TIGLATH-PILESER III

Mark Healy, *The Ancient Assyrians* (Osprey, London, 1991).

Doyne Dawson, *The First Armies* (Cassell, London, 2001), chapter 5.

SUN-TZU

Sun Tzu, *The Art of War*, translated and with introduction by Samuel B. Griffiths (Oxford University Press, Oxford, 1963).

C. P. Fitzgerald, *China, A Short Cultural History* (Cresset Press, London, 1950).

Marcel Granet, *Chinese Civilisation* (Barnes and Noble, London, 1957).

Mao Zedong, *Selected Works* (Lawrence and Wishart, London, 1955).

CYRUS THE GREAT

Pierre Briant, *From Cyrus to Alexander: A History of the Persian Empire*, translated by Peter T. Daniels (Eisenbraums, Winona Lake, Indiana, 2002).

Tom Holland, *Persian Fire: The First World Empire and the Battle for the West* (Little, Brown, London, 2005).

Josef Wiesehöfer, *Ancient Persia*, translated by Azizeh Azodi (I. B. Tauris, London, 2001).

LEONIDAS

Herodotus, *The Histories*, translated by Aubrey de Sélincourt (revised edition, Penguin Classics, Harmondsworth, 1996).

Paul Cartledge, *Thermopylae: The Battle that Changed the World* (Macmillan, London, 2006).

Tom Holland, *Persian Fire: The First World Empire and the Battle for the West* (Little, Brown, London, 2005).

THEMISTOCLES

Herodotus, *The Histories*, translated by Robin Waterfield (Oxford University Press, Oxford, 1998).

Robert Lenardon, *The Saga of Themistocles* (Thames & Hudson, London, 1978).

Barry Strauss, *The Battle of Salamis* (Simon and Schuster, New York, 2004).

N. G. L. Hammond, 'The Expedition of Xerxes', in John Boardman *et al.* (eds), *The Cambridge Ancient History, Volume 4* (second edition, Cambridge University Press, Cambridge 1988).

THUCYDIDES

Nigel Bagnall, *The Peloponnesian War* (Pimlico, London, 2004), which includes a good map of the Sicilian expedition.

Simon Hornblower, *Thucydides* (Duckworth, London, 1987).

Robin Lane Fox, *The Classical World* (Penguin, London, 2005).

Thucydides, *The Peloponnesian War* (New English Library, London, 1966).

ALCIBIADES

Thucydides, *The Peloponnesian War*, translated by Rex Warner, revised by Tim Rood (Penguin, London, 2008).

Xenophon, *A History of My Times*, translated by Rex Warner (Penguin, Harmondsworth, 1979).

David Gribble, *Alcibiades and Athens: A Study in Literary Presentation* (Oxford University Press, Oxford, 1999).

Walter Ellis, *Alcibiades* (Routledge, London, 1989).

XENOPHON

Xenophon, *The Expedition of Cyrus*, translated by Robin Waterfield (Oxford University Press, Oxford, 2005).

J. K. Anderson, *Xenophon* (Duckworth, London, 1974).

Robin Waterfield, *Xenophon's Retreat: Greece, Persia and the End of the Golden Age* (Faber & Faber, London, 2006).

PHILIP II OF MACEDON

M. Andronikos, *Vergina: The Royal Tombs and the Ancient City* (Ekdotike Athenon, Athens, 1984).

G. T. Griffith, 'Philip as a General and the Macedonian Army', in M. B. Hatzopoulos and L. Loukopoulou (eds), *Philip of Macedon* (Heinemann, London, 1981).

N. G. L. Hammond, G. T. Griffith, *A History of Macedonia II* (Clarendon Press, Oxford, 1979).

N. G. L. Hammond, *Philip of Macedon* (Duckworth, London, reprinted 2002).

N. Sekunda, *The Army of Alexander the Great* (Osprey, London, 1984).

ALEXANDER THE GREAT

J. F. C. Fuller, *The Generalship of Alexander the Great* (Eyre & Spottiswoode, London, 1958).

N. G. L. Hammond, *Alexander the Great: Commander and Statesman* (Chatto & Windus, London, 1981).

Robin Lane Fox, *Alexander the Great* (Allen Lane, London, 1973; reprinted Penguin, London, 2004).

N. Sekunda, *The Army of Alexander the Great* (Osprey, London, 1984).

HANNIBAL

Gregory Daly, *Cannae: The Experience of Battle in the Second Punic War* (Routledge, London, 2002).

Adrian Goldsworthy, *The Punic Wars* (Weidenfeld & Nicolson, London, 2000).

J. F. Lazenby, *Hannibal's War* (Aris and Philips, Warminster, 1978).

SCIPIO AFRICANUS

H. Scullard, *Scipio Africanus: Soldier and Politician* (Thames & Hudson, London, 1970).

Adrian Goldsworthy, *The Punic Wars* (Weidenfeld & Nicolson, London, 2000).

Adrian Goldsworthy, *The Fall of Carthage* (Cassell Military Paperbacks, London, 2003).

B. Liddell Hart, *Greater than Napoleon – Scipio Africanus* (William Blackwood & Sons, Edinburgh, 1930).

JUDAH MACCABEUS

I and II Maccabees, English translation, available at *http://st-takla.org/pub_ Deuterocanon/Deuterocanon-Apocrypha_ El-Asfar_El-Kanoneya_El-Tanya__8-First-of-Maccabees.html* and *http://st-takla.org/pub_Deuterocanon/ Deuterocanon-Apocrypha_ El-Asfar_El-Kanoneya_El-Tanya__9-Second-of-Maccabees.html* respectively.

B. Bar Kochva, *Judas Maccabaeus: The Jewish Struggle against the Seleucids* (Cambridge, Cambridge University Press, 1989).

POMPEY

P. Greenhalgh, *Pompey: The Roman Alexander* (Weidenfeld & Nicolson, London, 1980).

P. Greenhalgh, *Pompey: The Republican Prince* (Weidenfeld & Nicolson, London, 1981).

Adrian Goldsworthy, *In the Name of Rome* (Weidenfeld & Nicolson, London, 2003).

JULIUS CAESAR

Adrian Goldsworthy, *Caesar: The Life of a Colossus* (Weidenfeld & Nicolson, London, 2006).

J. F. C. Fuller, *Julius Caesar: Man, Soldier and Tyrant* (Eyre & Spottiswoode, London, 1965).

T. Rice Holmes, *Caesar's Conquest of Gaul* (Oxford at the Clarendon Press, Oxford, 1911).

ARMINIUS

Adrian Murdoch, *Rome's Greatest Defeat: Massacre in the Teutoburg Forest* (Sutton Publishing, 2006).

Tony Clunn, *The Quest for the Lost Roman Legions: Discovering the Varus Battlefield* (Spellmount, Stroud, 2005).

Dieter Timpe, *Arminius-Studien* (Winter, Heidelberg, 1970; untranslated).

Rainer Wiegels and Winfried Woesler (eds), *Arminius und die Varusschlacht: Geschichte, Mythos, Literatur* (Schöningh, Paderborn, 2003; untranslated).

TRAJAN

J. Bennett, *Trajan: Optimus Princeps* (second edition, Routledge, London, 2001).

S. S. Frere and F. Lepper, *Trajan's Column* (Sutton Publishing, Stroud, 1988).

I. Richmond, *Trajan's Army on Trajan's Column* (The British School at Rome, London, 1982).

ZHUGE LIANG

Luo Guangzhong, *The Romance of the Three Kingdoms*, translated by Moss Roberts in four volumes (Beijing, Foreign Languages Press, 2005).

Rafe de Crespigny, *The Three Kingdoms and the Western Jin in East Asian History* (Australian National University, Canberra, 1991).

ALARIC I

Peter Heather, *The Goths* (Blackwell, Oxford, 1996).

Peter Heather, *The Fall of the Roman Empire* (Macmillan, London, 2005).

AETIUS

There has never been a biography of Aetius in English (although there was one in French a hundred years ago).

J. B. Bury, *The History of the Later Roman Empire. Volume 1* (Macmillan, London, 1923; latest reprint Dover, New York, 2003).

Peter Heather, *The Fall of the Roman Empire* (Macmillan, London, 2005).

ATTILA

John Man, *Attila: The Barbarian King Who Challenged Rome* (Bantam Press, London, 2005).

Edward A. Thompson, *The Huns* (Blackwell, Oxford, 1999).

INDEX